Thomas O'

Liturgical Resources
for the Year of Luke

ORDINARY TIME, YEAR C OF THE LITURGICAL CYCLE

*To Kieran,
with best wishes*

Tom

20.10.06

the columba press

First published in 2006 by
the columba press
55A Spruce Avenue, Stillorgan Industrial Park,
Blackrock, Co Dublin

Cover by Bill Bolger
Origination by The Columba Press
Printed in Ireland by ColourBooks Ltd, Dublin

ISBN 1 85607 559 1

Acknowledgement
I would like to acknowledge the feedback I have had from so many
people – priests in parishes, musicians, liturgists, scripture scholars,
and most importantly many who 'sit in the pews' – to the materials
printed here during the time that I was putting together this collection
of resources. I would also like to thank Dr Francisca Rumsey of the Poor
Clare Monastery in Arkley for proofreading the manuscript.

Table of Contents

Preface

As I come to the end of the process of putting these resources together two very different thoughts are running through my head. The first is the thought of the number of church buildings I know which have been in continuous Catholic use – albeit with many re-modellings, re-buildings, and re-orderings – for over a millennium: and week-in, week-out, on each Sunday the Eucharist was celebrated there. These buildings have seen all the changes in the practice and theology of the Eucharist. They might have been built when the idea that a priest could celebrate without a deacon and other ministers would have been thought bizarre, it was still there when it became 'the priest's Mass' and was a virtually private affair which others 'heard' and at which they occasionally 'got Communion', and it is still there now with the restored liturgy and all its new demands on all who celebrate it whether they are priests, deacons, lectors, or without a special name for their ministry. But if the Eucharist is celebrated each week it makes demands on all to keep renewing themselves in their appreciation of their activity or else there is the danger of, what Augustine called, 'the revulsion at the monotonous.' These ideas in this book are offered in the hope that they will spark off other ideas so that there is a note of freshness in our weekly Sacred Meal.

The other thought that keeps running through my head is that the demands made on presidents of the Eucharist have never been so great. At every other gathering where communication is expected to take place today there are elaborate training events for all concerned and special care to group people into interest groups, attention levels, and in terms of their specific expectation. One has only to look at the care in training in communications given to those who sell cars in the major dealerships to see how ill-prepared the average minister is for Sunday morning! And this problem seems to be endemic: it is one thing to cel-

ebrate the Eucharist for a particular group – especially one
where the president is a committed member of this real group,
and quite another at an ordinary celebration on Sunday where
there is a wide span of involvement both in the particular community and in the liturgy – and where often the president is
there simply as he has to 'cover' several buildings widely scattered. Indeed, the priest is more often seen as an expert supplying a service collectively to those who want to avail of it in that
place, than as the leader of a community gathering to celebrate
its identity in Christ in his banquet.

These problems of communication and community produce
their own stresses for all involved in liturgy today; and if this
book provides some ideas that help with coping with those
stresses, it will have more than achieved its purpose.

T. O'L
Lampeter
Corpus Christi 2006

Psalm Numbers

In the *Lectionary* and *Missal* the numbers given to the Psalms follow that given in the Latin *Ordo Lectionum* which, being in Latin, naturally follows the Vulgate numeration. The Vulgate numeration followed that of the Old Greek translation ('The Septuagint') as this was seen as 'the Psalter of the Church.' However, most modern books, apart from Catholic liturgical books, follow the numeration of the Hebrew text of the Psalter.

Since this book's primary referents are the books of the Catholic liturgy, the Septuagint number is given first and the Hebrew numeration is then given in (brackets). The same convention as is used in the English translation of the Liturgy of the Hours. See *Breviary*, vol 1, pp 640*-641* for further information.

For example: The Psalm that begins 'My heart is ready' is cited as Ps 107(108).

For convenience here is a concordance of the two numeration systems:

Septuagint	Hebrew
1 – 8	1 - 8
9	9 - 10
10 -112	11 - 113
113	114 - 115
114 - 115	116
116 - 145	117 - 146
146 - 147	147
148 - 150	148 - 150

Sunday

The church celebrates the paschal mystery on the first day of the week, known as the Lord's Day or Sunday. This follows a tradition handed down from the apostles, which took its origin from the day of Christ's resurrection. Thus Sunday should be considered the original feast day.

General Norms for the Liturgical Year and Calendar, n 4

The Notion of Ordinary Time

Let there be lights in the dome of the sky to separate the day from the night; and let them be for signs and for seasons and for days and years (Gen 1:14).

The phrase 'Ordinary Time' came into existence with the translation of the 1969 Missal into English where it was chosen as a translation of the Latin name for the time outside Advent-Christmas and Lent-Easter which is *Tempus per annum* (literally: 'the time during the year'). However, the phrase 'ordinary time' is an excellent term to capture a most important aspect of ritual time: that there are differences in stress.

At the heart of any sense of time and ritual, time and religion, or time, calendars and memory is the alternation of stressed and unstressed time. Stressed time is the special occasion, that which is out of the ordinary, that which is marked aside for particular joyful celebration or special serious attention. In the modern secular year such stressed times would be the time for tax returns or the annual visit of the auditors or the 'Cup Final' or the week of a major sporting event. These are times that are not just any day, but known about, prepared for beforehand, and times when normal routine can be set aside. But if there are to be such special times, then there has to be unstressed time. When life becomes a perpetual holiday, you have no holidays!

The ordinary is, by contrast with the special times and notable events, the time when we just get on with the job. It is when there is 'nothing special happening' but also when we are acting 'normally'. So if we think of the two great festivals of the liturgy, Easter and Christmas, as the great events, then the time not connected with them is the ordinary time. It is this usage that gives rise to the phrase 'Sundays of Ordinary Time' and makes it such an appropriate designation.

We, as Christians, live in a complex calendar: over the course of the year there are stressed/unstressed times; but also over the course of the week there are stressed/unstressed times. In the annual cycles it is the difference between Lent-Easter and Advent-Christmas on the one hand, and all the rest of the time on the other. Within the week, it is the difference between Sunday on the one hand, and the rest of the time on the other. So we give these Sundays of Ordinary Time special attention as the key day for Christians during the seven days that make up the week; but these Sundays are lesser affairs than the special seasons.

One of the tasks of those responsible for celebrating the liturgy is to have a sense of the balance of these days of differing ritual quality.

For everything there is a season, and a time for every matter under heaven:
a time to be born, and a time to die;
a time to plant, and a time to pluck up what is planted;
a time to kill, and a time to heal;
a time to break down, and a time to build up;
a time to weep, and a time to laugh;
a time to mourn, and a time to dance;
a time to throw away stones, and a time to gather stones together;
a time to embrace, and a time to refrain from embracing;
a time to seek, and a time to lose;
a time to keep, and a time to throw away;
a time to tear, and a time to sew;
a time to keep silence, and a time to speak;
a time to love, and a time to hate;
a time for war, and a time for peace *(Qoh 3:1-8)*.

Lectionary Unit I

An Overarching Theme

The Year of Luke is envisaged by the Lectionary as comprising eight units ranging in length from one Sunday (units V and VIII) to eleven Sundays (Unit IV) (see *Lectionary*, vol I, pp lii-liii).

We can see Luke's agenda as broadly geographical and spread over his two works: the gospel and Acts.

Jesus travels from

NAZARETH TO JERUSALEM and death and resurrection and his return to the Father.

The church travels from

JERUSALEM TO THE EARTH'S ENDS through suffering and death to glory.

The Lectionary consciously adopts this theme, and Luke's travel narrative (chs 9-19) provides the readings for the core of Ordinary Time: Sundays 13-31. This journey is more chronological in structure than geographical, and so is well suited to being read sequentially in time, Sunday after Sunday.

This journey is also assumed to parallel the journey of the People of God, both collectively and as individuals for it is the journey through life's sufferings and joys. The Lectionary expects that each Sunday be seen in the light of the larger units (groups of Sundays) and the whole journey theme.

The First Unit

This consists of just two Sundays and focuses on the Figure of Jesus the Messiah.

The question, who is the Christ, is then explored with the story of Jesus's baptism (Sunday 1) and the manifestation of his glory at the wedding in Cana (Sunday 2).

The Baptism of our Lord
(First Sunday in Ordinary Time)

CELEBRANT'S GUIDE

Introduction to the Celebration

Today we celebrate the identity of Jesus our Lord: he whom we follow is the one who is the beloved Son of the Father and the one who is uniquely empowered by the Spirit. This is the great mystery of faith: Jesus is not just some teacher of wisdom or some guide to a happy or holy life, he is the one with whom the Father is well-pleased, and he brings us into the presence of the Father and sends his Spirit among us. We can gather here now for the Eucharist because the Spirit is giving us divine life, Jesus is in our midst, and so we stand and offer our thanks to the Father.

Rite of Penance (or consider Option A: the Asperges)

Lord Jesus, at your baptism John recognised you as the Christ. Lord have mercy.

Lord Jesus, at your baptism heaven opened and the Holy Spirit descended upon you in the shape of a dove. Christ have mercy.

Lord Jesus, at your baptism the Father's voice was heard: 'You are my Son, the Beloved, my favour rests on you.' Lord have mercy.

If you do opt for a Rite of Penance, then the third option for the opening prayer is most appropriate.

Headings for Readings
First Reading

The reading for Year A is more accessible for today; but if you use the option for Year C, then:

The prophet announces that when the Anointed of the Lord would come among his people a new time of peace would dawn. We believe this new era of peace between God and humankind began with Jesus the beloved Son of the Father.

Second Reading

One can use the option for Year C, but Acts 10:34-38 (the reading for Year A) is to be preferred because is the only passage in the New Testament outside the gospels that mentions today's feast. Moreover, since this year we are reading Luke's account in the gospel, it is most appropriate to have this reading from Luke also; in effect, we are getting two views of the same aspect of the kerygma.

However, if you use the Year C option:

God's love was shown by sending us Jesus who has freed us from our sins and renewed us with the gift of the Holy Spirit.

Gospel

When we look on Jesus we see the beloved Son of the Father and the one who sends us the Holy Spirit.

Prayer of the Faithful

President

Today we celebrate the mystery of Christ with whom the Father is well pleased and upon whom the Spirit rests. Now may the Spirit give voice to our prayers as, gathered in Christ, we make our needs known to the Father.

Reader (s)

1. That the whole church of God may offer praise to the Father. Lord in your mercy, hear our prayer.

2. That this church gathered here may bear witness to the Christ. Lord in your mercy, hear our prayer.

3. That every Christian will be attentive to the promptings of the Spirit. Lord in your mercy, hear our prayer.

4. That we may respect and care for the creation as the gift of the Father. Lord in your mercy, hear our prayer.

5. That we may minister to all who are oppressed, all who are sick, all who are suffering injustice, and to all who are poor or hungry, following the example of the Christ. Lord in your mercy, hear our prayer.

6. That we may have the courage to profess our faith and to follow the road of discipleship empowered by the Spirit. Lord in
your mercy, hear our prayer.

President
Father, you listened to the prayers of your Son our Lord, listen
now to these prayers from us his disciples for we make them in
the power of the Holy Spirit through that same Christ, our Lord.
Amen.

Eucharistic Prayer
Preface of the Baptism of the Lord (P7), (Missal, p 410).

Invitation to the Our Father
The Father's voice was heard declaring Jesus his Son, the
Beloved; now in the voice of Jesus let us pray to the Father:

Sign of Peace
The work of the Messiah whose beginnings we are recalling was
to bring peace and reconciliation on earth, let us embark on a
year of peacemaking.

Invitation to Communion
This is the Son of God, the Beloved of the Father, happy are we
who are called to share his table.

Communion Reflection
The hymn given in the Breviary, 'When Jesus comes to be bap-
tized' (vol I, p 371), for Evening Prayer I of this feast is appropriate as a reflection today.

Conclusion
Solemn Blessing 3 for the Beginning of the New Year (Missal, p
368) is appropriate as for most people what is most obvious
about this time is that it is the beginning of the new year – and
we should within our Eucharistic assembly formally ask God's
blessings on the coming year.

Notes

It seems strange at first sight that this feast is included in a book dedicated to Ordinary Time as it is presented in the Missal and Lectionary as the last moment of the Advent-Christmas cycle. However, it is this feast that really marks the beginning of the public ministry of Jesus in the gospels and, therefore, of the sequence of Ordinary Time. Ordinary Time is, in effect, the set of Sundays that begin with the feast of the Baptism of Jesus and end with the celebration of Jesus Christ, the Universal King. For a simple justification on its inclusion here, note that its readings are given twice in the Lectionary: the first time is on pp 179-188 at the end of the Christmastide section; and again on pp 639-641 (Year A), pp 735-740 (Year B), and pp 833-838 (Year C) as the readings for the feast that falls on the First Sunday in Ordinary Time.

This feast's history really begins in 1970 when it was chosen as the last moment of the Christmas cycle. It has no conceptual link with Christmas; except it could be argued that in the eastern rites it is part of Epiphany and so could be seen as an extension of Epiphany (and it is so linked in the current western Liturgy of the Hours). However, that is not how it is presented in the eucharistic liturgy where it is celebrated as a distinct 'event' in the life of Jesus. So how should we approach this feast?

First, it is now approaching mid-January and for everyone in the congregation, the president included, Christmas is long in the past, people have been back at work for weeks, schools have re-opened, people are already thinking of a 'Spring Break', and even chatter about the New Year seems a little dated. So looking back to Christmas or referring to this as the close of Christmas is just adding noise to the communication.

Second, this is about the baptism of the Christ by John, it is not a celebration of baptism as a sacrament or even the concept of baptism within the Paschal Mystery. Such thoughts belong to Easter, and the Easter Vigil in particular, not to this day. So this is not a day for having a baptism during the Eucharist. Such a

celebration just confuses the understanding of what is being recalled and fills the understanding with muddle. Indeed, if it is
the community's practice to celebrate the baptism of new members of the gathering during the Eucharist, then this is one of
those Sundays which should not be used for baptisms.

Third, when we look at the position of the baptism of Jesus
within the gospel kerygma we note that it is the public an-
nouncement of the beginning of the work of the Messiah. It
marks a beginning of a period, not a conclusion. The basic structure can be seen in Mark: after the opening of the gospel comes
the work of John which comes to its conclusion in his baptism of
Jesus and the glorious theophany of approbation, 'Thou art my
beloved Son: with thee I am well pleased' (Mk 1:1-11). The other
synoptics maintain this structure except that they add the pre-
lude of the Infancy Narratives; while in Jn 1:29-34 the testimony
of John the Baptist concluded by his reference to the theophany
of the Spirit descending on Jesus like a dove. In all the gospels,
this 'event' is then followed by the messianic ministry (what we
often refer to as the 'public life'). So the baptism of the Lord by
John had a distinct place in the preaching of the church, it
marked the 'visible' anointing by the Father in the Spirit for his
work. It is the great beginning.

Fourth, the baptism of Jesus now has a definite place in the
liturgy of the church; it is now a moment in our common memory
and celebration of the Lord. So it would be appropriate to look
on it as the beginning of Ordinary Time and, in particular, a celebration of Jesus as 'the messiah,' 'the anointed one,' 'the christ'.
So the tone of these notes is that of beginnings, not of conclusions.

COMMENTARY

First Reading: Isa 40:1-5, 9-11
This passage describes the hope of Israel that after the exile they
will find a wilderness turned into that joy of a society living in
close contact with food-production: a pasture. The perfect time
will be when a land familiar with warfare will encounter the

God of peace, and human death will encounter divine life. The use of this reading today provides a context in which to hear today's gospel.

Second Reading: Tit 2:11-14, 3:4-7

The use of Year A (Acts 10:34-38) is preferable. However, if you do decide to use the optional reading for Year C bear in mind that the two passages that go to make up this reading do not fit well together. Indeed, it is really only the latter passage (3:4-7) that has any connection with today's celebration. It was selected because of its reference to 'the water of rebirth' and the renewal of each Christian by the Spirit, but it relates to the sacrament we receive rather than to the event of the Baptism of Christ (where it would be inappropriate).

Given how unconnected, and unsuitable, both the first and second readings are to the day being celebrated, one suspects that the choice indicates either haste in selection or desperation to find some reading that was even remotely connected with the feast – and in these two readings the connection is truly remote!

First Reading > Gospel Links

The link between Isa 40 and the gospel is one of prophecy and fulfillment. The passage in Isaiah is read as text from the past pointing to a particular moment in the future (time of service ended, the work of the one who prepares) which has now come with John the Baptist and Jesus, and indeed that moment is now the past and the background of the church. This use of this Old Testament passage is wholly in line with the way that Luke himself used Isaiah.

Gospel: Lk 3:15-16, 21-22

As edited for today's reading, Luke's account of the Baptism of Jesus is almost identical to that of Mark. Hence while we announce the name of a different gospel writer each year over the three years of the liturgical cycle, we read only one account of this 'event'. The three have been made to fit a single image of the

day that we celebrate. This means, in effect, reducing Mt and Lk
to what is found in Mk: John meets Jesus, announces one greater
than him who comes after him, then follows the theophany.

The key to the scene is not in its details of how one evangelist
presents it in contrast to another, but in its overall impact: the
human and divine worlds, heaven and earth, the history of
Israel and the eternity of God's inner life all come together in an
unforgettable image. This is a mighty event that is fitting to act
as the marker of the commencement of the work of the Christ.
And so, it is one of the most explicitly theological scenes in the
gospel narrative: the Father identifies Jesus as his Son and the
Spirit is seen. Here lies the whole of later christology presented
not as propositions but as something that the imagination can
work with, while still not giving the false notions of 'seeing'
God. We see the Christ, the Son acclaimed as such by the voice
from heaven which is heard and not seen, while the Spirit is seen
'descending like (*hosei*) a dove.'

Scenes such as this have become victims of two types of exegetical confusion during the twentieth century. The first was
the product of a materialist notion of truth. It began with the
materialist question 'If I were there that day what would my TV
camera have recorded?' Then when the exegete said 'nothing', it
seemed as if the scene was false and so the whole thing was a
concoction to be avoided. We have to realise that this scene is
sacramental and placed within a narrative precisely so our
human imaginations can handle the mystery: to ask the 'TV
camera' question is not to get at the truth but to commit the
blasphemy of Wisdom 15 and imply 'god' as referring to another
object, a thing, in our universe. The second confusion is that of
assuming that 'theology' is an obscurity overlaid on the 'simple
message of Jesus'. The confusion runs like this: Jesus was a loving guy who spoke about God and captured hearts; then came
the boffins and made everything complicated with notions of
the incarnation, the trinity, and what not, but you can by-pass
this and get to the 'heart of the matter'. It's a lovely picture and
one that still wins adherents, but there is no evidence for such a

'simple time.' By the time that Mark began preaching his gospel – in the sixties – we see in the baptism-event a fully developed Christian doctrine of God, and it is this that we read again today in the liturgy.

HOMILY NOTES

1. Between today and the end of next November, except for some special days around Easter, we will be reading passages from St Luke's gospel each Sunday at the Eucharist. This year is known in the order of our readings as 'the year of Luke'.

2. We can divide his gospel into three parts: the first deals with the events before and around the birth of Jesus (and we have just read this portion over Christmas); the third part deals with the last week of Jesus's life in Jerusalem, his passion, death, and resurrection (and we will read this at Easter); and in between we have all the preaching and miracles of Jesus during his public ministry which St Luke sets out as taking place as Jesus moves along the road from Nazareth to Jerusalem.

3. This central part of the gospel – the teaching and preaching with recollections of healings and meals – all belong to what we traditionally call the public ministry of Jesus, his adult life, his activity among the people of Israel. It is this central part of the gospel that provides the passages for the ordinary Sundays during the coming year. This central part opens with the great scene of the baptism in the Jordan we have just read when Jesus takes over from John the Baptist. The work of the time of preparation is over; the time of the work of the Christ has begun.

4. Luke places this wondrous scene – the two great prophets meeting, and then the Father's voice being heard and the Spirit appearing in the form of a dove – at the beginning of the public ministry to show us that this is the mysterious inauguration of the new age of the Christ. He also does it so that when we hear what follows – Jesus doing this or that,

saying this or that, meeting this person and then that person – we will keep in mind the full identity of the One we call 'Lord'.

5. Luke presents us with a highly visual mysterious scene – picture it in your minds – of Jesus and John in the river, crowds of followers around and then from above the heavenly voice and the dove: this is the true identity of Jesus. Jesus is a human being like us, the final prophet, the uniquely beloved Son of God, the one empowered by the Spirit, the revelation of the Father, Emmanuel: God with us, the glory of God made manifest to us.

5. We have to keep this wondrous image of Jesus in the Jordan, the revelation of his true identity, in our minds as we move onwards in our recollection of his words and deeds in the weeks and months ahead.

Second Sunday of Ordinary Time

Introduction to the Celebration

This is the time of year when we start new endeavours. Therefore, today, we recall the beginning of the public preaching and ministry of Jesus. The wedding feast at Cana was like his 'coming out': 'He let his glory be seen and his disciples believed in him' is how St John describes it. We are his disciples now, but we often fall short in the way we follow him and we often fail to reflect his glory to those around us. So let us examine ourselves to see what sort of disciples we are.

Rite of Penance

Lord Jesus, at Cana in Galilee you showed your care so that your friends might not be in need. Lord have mercy.

Lord Jesus, at Cana in Galilee you showed your generosity so that your followers might rejoice. Christ have mercy.

Lord Jesus, at Cana in Galilee you showed your glory that your disciples might believe. Lord have mercy.

Headings for Readings

First Reading

The joy of the coming of Lord's anointed is likened to the joy of a wedding and the joy of being married; so we think how fitting it was that the first public manifestation of Jesus showing that he was among his people was at the wedding in Cana in Galilee.

Second Reading

Everyone gathered here for this Eucharist is different. But each one of us has been given a special gift by the Holy Spirit to use for others and ourselves as part of the church. The task is, first, for everyone to recognise her or his particular gift and, second, to start using it to build up God's house.

Gospel

When Jesus showed his care for the needs of the wedding party at Cana, he let his glory be seen and his disciples believed in him.

Prayer of the Faithful

President

We, sisters and brothers, have assembled here because the Spirit has spoken in our hearts and has given us the gifts we need to form ourselves as Christ's holy Body, the church. Let us pray to the Father now that we will appreciate and use the gifts his Spirit has given us.

Reader (s)

1. That all of us will recognise in each other the variety of gifts working in all sorts of different ways in different people. Lord hear us.

2. That any of us who have the gift of preaching with wisdom will use that gift to proclaim the good news of Jesus. Lord hear us.

3. That any of us who are teachers, with the gift of preaching in-struction, may bring light and hope into our community and world. Lord hear us.

4. That any of us who have the gift of faith may help those who doubt, are anxious, or in fear. Lord hear us.

5. That any of us who have the gift of healing may help the sick in our community and promote harmony amongst us. Lord hear us.

6. That any of us who have the gift of prophecy may bear wit-ness to Christ before our world. Lord hear us.

7. That any of us who have the gift of tongues may sing the praises of God for us all. Lord hear us.

8. That we may all recognise the Spirit's presence in us through our gifts, and so become more fully the body of Christ to the glory of the Father. Lord hear us.

President

Father, it is the presence of your Spirit among us that enables us to make our needs known to you. Hear us, we pray, that we may grow to the full stature of Christ, your Son, our Lord. Amen.

Eucharistic Prayer
The theme of the Spirit creating the church and empowering it with gifts is better expressed in the Preface of Christian Unity [P76] (p 479) than anywhere else among the prefaces. Its themes can then be picked up again by using Eucharistic Prayer II.

Invitation to the Our Father
The Spirit has gathered us here as the church; now empowered by the Spirit to cry out 'Abba, Father', let us pray together:

Sign of Peace
The Spirit gives each of us a different gift to use for the common good and unites us as the body of the Christ, so now let us express our unity in the Spirit to one another.

Invitation to Communion
Those gathered at the table in Cana beheld his glory. Now we too gather at his table and behold him who died and rose for us.

Communion Reflection
Jesus was in Cana at the banquet with his disciples.
He provided for their needs with an abundance of wine.
He enabled them to rejoice in the goodness of the creation.
He surprised them with the wonder of the Father's love.
It was the first great sign that the kingdom was at hand.
He let his glory be seen; those with him placed their faith in him.

Jesus is here at our banquet with his disciples.
He has provided for our needs with an abundance of wine.
He has enabled us to rejoice in the goodness of the creation.
He has surprised us with the wonder of the Father's love.
He is the great sign that the kingdom is at hand.
He lets his glory be seen; we too place our faith in him.

Conclusion
Use the Solemn Blessing from Wedding Mass C (Missal, p 775) which is based on the Cana scene but is suitable for any celebration at which today's gospel is read and not just weddings.

Notes

One of the great symbols of the coming of the kingdom was that
there would be an abundance of wine bringing joy to the hearts
of God's people (e.g. 2 Kgs 18:32; 1 Chron 12:40; 2 Chron 2:15;
Ezra 7:22; Ps 4:7; Isa 36:17; Zech 10:7) and this would be the gift
of God showing his generosity (e.g. Isa 55:1). Jesus at Cana has
to be seen within that symbolic tradition: the jars of water become wine are indicative of the goodness of God's kingdom. It is
this same symbolism that stands at the heart of the use of wine at
the Eucharist: the wonderful gift indicative of the presence of
the Lord becomes the sacramental gift of the Lord's presence.
But all this is lost – reduced to mere abstract sounds – if everyone at the celebration cannot share in the cup. If you are in a
community that is not ready or willing for the sharing of the cup
at every Eucharist, this is a day when one really should strive to
celebrate the Lord's gift fully.

COMMENTARY

First Reading: Is 62: 1-5

This is part of the Hymn of the Glory of the New Zion (62:1-9)
from Third-Isaiah. This future time has been read by the church
as the time of the Christ (as in today's liturgy) and as the
Eschaton. In the section we are reading the Lord breaks out in a
declaration of the joy that Israel – which has been at times unfaithful – will have in the time which is promised. Here the imagery of the perfect future time is linked to the notion of a wedding (hence its use with today's gospel) and the imagery of marriage as the perfect life and indeed the basis for the Eschaton
being a marriage banquet. Not surprisingly this use of marriage
imagery has meant that this passage has not been used much in
the history of the church in comparison with other passages
from Isaiah; its imagery jarred too much with the monastic and
celibate images of complete consecration to God.

Psalm: 95: 1-3, 7-10

The choice of this psalm is due to the verse that the people have seen the Lord's wonders and so should give him glory.

Second Reading: 1 Cor 12:4-11

Paul envisages each church as empowered with all the gifts/skills it needs to be a complete body of Christ. See homily notes.

First Reading > Gospel Links

The link is that the symbol for the coming of the Anointed One is a wedding celebration and therefore it sets the backdrop to the wedding in Cana as the place for the manifestation of the Lord's glory. This is a very good combination of texts because the imagery of the wedding day as a prophetic image is in the mind of John in placing the Cana story at the opening of his gospel.

Gospel: Jn 2:1-11

This is one of those texts that we tend to know too well to be able to hear it afresh: we use it at weddings (simply because of a similarity of scene) and we use it in a marian context (simply because it is one of the few occasions outside the infancy narrative when we have words put in Mary's mouth). However, it stands in John as a unit because it is the story of the first 'sign'. In John a 'sign' is a miracle that can be said to be a glimpse that the kingdom promised has come in Jesus (see, for example, Jn 4:54: 'the second sign'; 6:14: 'When the people saw the sign which he had done, they said, "This is indeed the prophet who is to come into the world!"'; 12:18: 'the crowd … heard he had done this sign'; or 20:30: 'Now Jesus did many other signs in the presence of the disciples, which are not written in this book'). These 'signs' announce who Jesus is and in the disciples they produce the commitment of faith in him. In all likelihood there was an early Christian text, which we call 'the Book of Signs', which gathered up these stories about Jesus into one place and then this was taken up by John who interweaved its contents into his gospel.

We can see this earlier text beneath today's reading in the way that we hear explanatory comments that have been dropped into the story (e.g. 'there were six stone jar standing there each holding twenty or thirty gallons' but the evangelist knowing that his audience might wonder at the presence of such jars dropped 'needed because of the rites of purification found among the Jews' into the story).

So what glimpse of the kingdom are we to see here in this first sign? The promise of the abundance of joy and wine has been fulfilled, and God who has been generous to his people in the past has kept the good wine until now: it is only 'now' (i.e. at that moment that the chef at the feast tastes the water become wine) that the greatest gift has been given to Israel. The moment of the best wine at the wedding is also the moment of the Christ; it is the moment when his glory is revealed to Israel; and the moment of that 'now' continues to include the 'now' of each person who hears the gospel.

HOMILY NOTES

1. The liturgy presents us with an embarrassment of riches today for preaching. First, there is the Cana incident, which is the dramatic, and memorable, opening of the ministry of Jesus in John's gospel. Second, there is the passage from Paul on the gifts given to each church by the Spirit, which is one of the very few occasions in Ordinary Time when the second reading is such a sufficiently contained unit, and is also accessible to the gathering from just listening to the passage, that it could be the basis of a homily. However, since there is no intrinsic nor intentional link between the second and the gospel, one must choose to preach on either one or other readings. In either case, the content of the homily can be approach fairly directly.

   If you opt for the Cana story, then use notes 2 and 3; if Paul, then notes 4 to 6.

2. We think we know the Cana story – we all have heard it umpteen times, and it is so well told by John with its powerful

image of gallons of the best wine in giant jars that it is firmly planted in our memory. But do we see it as a 'sign'?

3. The key message of John's first 'sign', and one of the very foundations of our believing, can be summed up in ten words: The Divine One is with us and knows our needs. That which was promised to Israel is now among his people. Israel thought of God as good and loving and caring – and a key image of that relationship was that God not only provided food – basic needs – but wine, wine in abundance and freely available – symbolising all that is pleasant and joyful in the world. Wine, in ancient culture as in our own, was associated with having a party – we still bring a bottle when going to a dinner or a party – and wine in abundance was the symbol of generosity – we still do not want to be stingy with wine and then as now people thought of ways of not appearing stingy as we see in the chef's comments that people serve the good wine first. The abundance of the best wine shows that God is not only infinitely generous, but that his greatest gift was what was only made known in that moment: the Son of God has come among us. Like the best wine which only came at the end of a long period of waiting, so came Jesus in the history of Israel. God is generous and loving and wine is a fitting image of his care, but his greatest generosity is sending his own Son among us. It is this gift of the Christ that we thank the Father for every time we gather for the Eucharist and we celebrate his gift in our banquet of bread and wine.

4. Paul looks at how the various members of the church to whom he is writing have received a variety of gifts. We Christians see the diversity of people with all the various talents as an indication of the goodness and wisdom of God: it is all this variety working with co-ordination that makes the church and builds the kingdom.

5. However, while we know that there is a variety of gifts and the one Spirit, we are often slow to act on it. Until a generation ago, for example, it was often said that only priests and nuns had vocations. Until just before 1970 everything at

Mass, except bringing the cruets to the altar, was done by the priest, and all the people were just 'at Mass' or were 'getting Mass' or simply 'hearing Mass'. All their gifts were simply ignored and the clergy acted as if they not only had all the gifts but that only they had the gifts of the Spirit. Moreover, many people liked it that way: the priests and nuns could do all the religious tasks and they could be left to get on with them, while other people could be Christians with minimal involvement.

6. So this reading prompts a series of questionings: first, each of us must ask what gifts have I for use within this community; second, as a community are we using all these gifts from the variety of all the members of the church for the good of the whole (or are ministries just in the hands of the priest and a little clique that do all the tasks in the community?); and third, to what extent are we still in the old two-class church where vocation and ministry could be dodged by leaving it to 'the professionals' (i.e. priests and nuns)? These are hard questions, for both priest and communities have to have the courage to be able to change their minds.

Lectionary Unit II

Luke's Progamme

The second unit is made up of two Sundays with a common theme – indeed they share a single narrative section of the gospel – which is Luke's programme for the ministry of Jesus.

It consists of Sundays 3 and 4 both of which focus on Jesus's visit to the synagogue in Nazareth. These two Sundays (with the prologue and Jesus's identification of himself as the one fulfilling the prophecy of Isaiah) set the tone for the year: the Jubilee Year has come and with it a new relationship of righteousness between God and his people and so a new relationship of justice among God's people is called for.

Third Sunday of Ordinary Time

Introduction to the Celebration

We are gathered here in the name of Jesus the Lord; he is present among us in the midst of our gathering. We are his people, his body in this world, and we have heard his gospel: good news for the poor, sight for the blind, liberty for all who are enslaved. Let us recall why we follow him and ask pardon for those times when we have not brought joy or enlightenment or peace to our world.

Rite of Penance

Lord Jesus, in the power of the Spirit you brought good news to the poor. Lord have mercy.

Lord Jesus, you proclaim liberty to captives and give the blind new sight. Christ have mercy.

Lord Jesus, you set the downtrodden free and proclaim the Father's care for us. Lord have mercy.

Headings for Readings

First Reading

Ezra read out the law and interpreted it for the people, the law was the presence of God among his people and so the people could rejoice.

Second Reading

Who are we who are gathered here? Are we just a collection of individuals? St Paul says we are all as intimately related as my arm is to my leg: parts of single body, and that body is the presence of the risen Christ in the world.

Gospel

The gospel announces who Jesus is: he is the Anointed One, the Christ, he fulfils the promises God has made to his people, and he proclaims the new relationship with God.

Prayer of the Faithful

President

We have gathered, listened to the Word of the Lord, and reflected on it implications for us as a body; now standing before the Father as that body of Christ, let us put our needs before him.

Reader (s)

1. For ourselves gathered here, that we might appreciate that we are not just a bunch of separate individuals, but also a community of sisters and brothers united to one another. Lord hear us.

2. For all who claim the name of the Christ, that we all will grow closer to one another in unity. Lord hear us.

3. For all people of good will, that peace and justice may reign in the creation. Lord hear us.

4. For the poor and down-trodden, that the new society Jesus calls on us to build will bring them hope and liberation. Lord hear us.

5. *Specific local needs and topics of the day.*

President

Father, your Son's coming brought about the year of your favour when the poor are given justice and all are called to work for peace; hear now our prayers which we make in his name, and help us manifest your generosity in the world. Amen.

Eucharistic Prayer

While Eucharistic Prayer IV was not envisaged for use on Sundays, its use of the theme 'To the poor he proclaimed the good news of salvation' means that it is well suited to be used in conjunction with today's gospel.

Invitation to the Our Father

Each of us here is a different part of Christ's body, each of us has a different role and task in the mission of the church, but we are one in Christ when we call on the Father together:

Sign of Peace

St Paul reminded us that all the various parts of the body have to work harmoniously together. We are a body and there must be peace and harmony between every one of us if we are to encounter Christ, so let us begin by seeking reconciliation and peace with our sisters and brothers at this table.

Invitation to Communion

We though many are one body for we all are called to share the one loaf; behold the Lamb of God who takes away the sins of the world: happy are we who are called now to his table.

Communion Reflection

The rarely heard Preface of Christian Unity [P76] (p 479) can provide a very suitable reflection with a little adaptation. Begin: 'Father, through Christ you bring us to the knowledge of the truth'; continue to 'guiding it by your wisdom!', and add 'Amen'.

Conclusion

Solemn Blessing for Ordinary Time IV (p 373) is suitable.

Notes

1. Reading the Gospel today

Although we refer to Year C as 'the Year of Luke,' this is the first day on which we read from his gospel. Then, because we have read the infancy narrative and connected passages such as the genealogy during Advent and Christmas, the baptism two weeks ago on that feast, and the temptation will be read on the First Sunday of Lent, we now begin with the opening lines and then jump more than three chapters – 181 verses in all – to the scene at Nazareth which marks the beginning of the public ministry of Jesus in Luke. So this is an artificial reading in its shape within the gospel text, but a well formed reading for the liturgy to begin our continuous reading of the gospel. Viewed within this liturgical framework one should treat this gospel reading as the beginning of the gospel and announce it as such: 'The Beginning of the Holy Gospel according to Luke'. This fact alone makes this day's gospel reading special, but the content shows that Jesus participated in the ritual of publicly reading the scriptures: he took the scroll, then unrolled it, found the place, read, re-rolled it, and gave it back to the server (*hupéretés*), sat down, and then spoke. Very often the reading of the gospel is done from a missalette as if it were simply a snippet from a newspaper. Today is an opportunity to review your community's practice, and at least for today to draw more attention to the fact that reading the story of the good news in common is part of our identity as church. So the Book of the Gospels could come in to the assembly in procession, then be taken to the ambo solemnly, then incensed, and flanked by lights.

2. The Second Reading

The second reading is very long, hence the shortened form provided. However, while we frequently use 'body' language ('we are the body of Christ,' the church is the 'mystical body', 'The body of Christ') that Pauline language loses a lot of its force without Paul's elaborate explanation that is given here but which is rarely heard in the liturgy. So, given the frequency of 'body' language, this reading is important catechetically and should be read in its longer form.

COMMENTARY

First Reading: Neh 8:2-10

This is a great set-piece of historical writing. The people have returned from Babylon and now they must begin to learn the law again – and, consequently, be happy. The set piece was written by a professional teacher – it is very much in the mode of the P-author in Genesis – and so the whole of life is viewed like a big classroom exercise: the teacher teaches, there are tutorial assistants, and attentive students. This is every teacher's dream; and no doubt the author hoped that the people who would hear his history would seek to imitate the lovely scene he has put before them for their edification. However, if this is a set-piece setting forth a priest's ideal vision of an obedient and well-ordered people, we should not forget that the image of Ezra, built up from this and similar passages, not only inspired ancient rabbis, but Christian teachers down the centuries – indeed, the origins of the notion of *magisterium*, that which relates to the teaching of a *magister*, are to be found in this passage.

Psalm: 18

This is *the* psalm in praise of the Law as God's gift. The word 'law' has been used to translate *torah* since long before the time of Jesus when it was rendered *nomos* in the Septuagint. However, a glimpse at this psalm shows that, given our attitudes to the word 'law,' it is not an adequate translation. Moreover, because of this there is a pernicious history of using 'law' – with our range of meanings – to describe the older relationship/covenant/testament (as when one hears 'The Old Testament God is a God of law, but the New Testament God is a God of love.') Such rubbish ignores the fact that one can only understand Jesus in terms of the scriptures that he and his followers held to be the authentic voice of God, and it is basic to Christian faith that it is a continuum of revelation. This psalm corrects the notion of 'law' by showing that it is more like 'the programme God built into the creation and revealed to creatures that they might be holy'.

Second Reading: 1 Cor 12:12-30

The body image as a metaphor for understanding organisations is an obvious one: he is the voice of the organisation, they are the heart of the group, they are the brains behind it, he is the head of the company, they are the hands-on managers, they are the lifeblood of the organisation, and on and on. We are bodily creatures, nothing is so close to our imagination, so we describe groups as bodies, and explain those bodies by parallels, analogies, similes, and metaphors from the parts of our own body. The practice was as widespread in the ancient world – for instance among the Stoics – as it is today. And, of course, following from this very passage, there is a long tradition of describing the church in terms of the body.

However, because the body metaphor is so close to us we tend to focus on it here as simply a way of describing an organisation and reminding us that to be a Christian is not to be an individual who happens to share religious ideas with others, but to be a member – another body image in its primary sense – of a collective unity which is Jesus. But Paul wants to go beyond this to point out that the internal variation is as important as the unity. Each distinct member is part of the providence of God and ordered to working with others, where each does something distinct so that the whole will achieve its purpose.

Organisations are good at promoting unity, but the Christian grouping must equally be good at valuing diversity for, argues Paul, it is as much God's will as the unity of being one body: that of the Christ.

First Reading > Gospel Links
This is one of parallel situations and actions. Ezra took the book of the law, read it in public ritual situation, and then interpreted it. Jesus likewise took up a copy of the written law, read it in the liturgy, and then gave an interpretation. There is also the theme of the continuity of the written law as a basis for expounding the mind of God, and so the similarity of pattern between the testaments. Although there is no hint in Luke that he had this passage from Nehemiah in mind, there is a very close fit between the two readings today.

Gospel: Lk 1:1-4; 4:14-21
1. Lk 1:1-4
This opening reminds us that there were many attempts to tell the story of Jesus in the early church and that those which eventually made it into general use were not the only ones heard. Thus the text reminds us of two crucial points. First, the 'tradition' is not something distinct from 'scripture', but rather the tradition is the context, mechanism, and content of the scriptures which, in turn, are among the earliest accessible elements of the content of the tradition. Second, the scriptures came into

existence within the life of the church to fulfill its needs, and it was through its use of those documents that they gained their status within the communities. It is in the church that the gospels were written, and it was within the church's life that they were handed on and valued – indeed it was there that they so grew in stature that in Latin Christianity they have been even given, on occasion, a status as if they were anterior to, independent of, and more important than the tradition of Christian life and liturgy in the church.

2. Lk 4:14-21

This passage brings before us the whole complicated issue that is the relationship of Christians to the writings that are seen as the scriptures of the earlier covenant. The problem can be illustrated with this simple question: Should you print Lk 4:18 as 'The Spirit of the Lord is upon me' (as in some translations) or 'The spirit of the Lord is upon me' (as in the current Lectionary) and note few would disagree that you should print Lk 4:14 as 'in the power of Spirit'? If you use the upper-case initial then the prophet is speaking about the Holy Spirit, the person of the Trinity; but if you use the lower-case initial then you are being true to the text of Isaiah as it would have been found in an ancient pre-Christian scroll where 'the spirit' is a circumlocution for the presence and work of God. In fact, one has to read Lk 4:18 in both ways.

On the one hand we have to read it as it tells us how Jesus spread his message in terms of the scriptures and their fulfillment in his moment: the acceptable year of the Lord having come. On the other hand, we have to read them with the community who heard, and then read, Luke's telling of the gospel: they now read those scriptures from the new vantage point that they all spoke about and become clear in relation to Jesus the Son of the Father who worked in the power of the [Holy] Spirit. Of all the evangelists, none made this new perspective more clear than Luke: 'And beginning with Moses and all the prophets, he interpreted to them in all the scriptures the things concerning himself' (Lk 24:27). This tension in reading is an essential part of the Christian understanding of the texts belonging to the time of the Older Covenant. This tension is something we have to live with, and that means eschewing some of the simplistic strategies which are popularly in use such as describing these texts as 'the Hebrew Bible' rather than the Older Testament: they can only be described as 'The Hebrew Bible' if they are being studied as ancient texts as such (independent of any present religious significance) or in terms of the Jewish interpretation of their religious meaning. If they are being read, as in our liturgy, as scriptures that the Christians today hold as their 'scriptures', then they must be heard with several voices in creative tension.

What we have as today's gospel is half of a section where Jesus announces his mission in the synagogue in Nazareth and then is rejected, but the core of today's gospel (vv 17-21) is found only in Luke. For Luke this is the beginning of the new covenant/social contract/situation in the creation that has begun with Jesus. Behind the speech of Jesus is the practice of the Jubilee Year when justice was to be restored to the community of Israel. At that moment there was to be a re-creation of just society, based on the gift of God to each member of the community that he/she could live secure from hunger and want in the land. The advent of Jesus is both the beginning of the new kingdom of God's generosity, and it is the beginning of the new set of community relationships which are based on acting with justice rather than the rich living at the expense of the poor – a theme already announced by Luke in 1:53: God 'has filled the hungry with good things, and the rich he has sent empty away'. So the new covenant between God and the people is come, but then the people must adopt a new covenant with one another.

HOMILY NOTES

1. The sermon/homily/address is very often the least popular part of the liturgy. There are many reasons for this especially when preaching takes place in the context of the Eucharist where time is limited and one does not have a pre-selected

audience with a particular interest in what might be said on the occasion. However, it is also the case that many people have never even thought about why there is a sermon at all. So why do we preach? The answer requires some preaching about preaching.

2. The starting point is to look at both the principal readings today: in each of them an earlier text is read, and then it is converted into a message that makes it something living for all who are there listening. The act of preaching is this act of converting, of translating, of making sense of text in our immediate situation as believers.

3. So we have to ask by what criteria do our audience judge our performance of this task that was once carried out by the prophet Ezra, then by Jesus in Nazareth, and now by ministers across the world? Is it that the sermon is easy to understand? Is it that it is amusing? Is it that it is challenging? Is it that it addressed 'questions of the day'? Is it that it is persuasive? Or is it simply that it is short and not too boring? All of these are used, but they are all limited.

4. Some people can explain difficult matters simply, but the issues of faith are not simple because life is not simple. Simple messages, easily appropriated are usually the work of those who want to bluff us. Propaganda is always simple. An ability to amuse is a gift, but reflection on the meaning of faith in our moment in history is not usually the stuff of entertainment. The sermon itself is not where any challenge to someone should appear: the gospel challenges the sin of the world of sin and the homily is there to help the individual to see any challenge that it might pose to them as individuals or as members of groups. The sermon is exposition rather than a tongue-lashing. There are always questions of the day and urgent issues towards which Christians should be directing attention, but at the Sunday Eucharist the normal course of events is that we hear the gospels in sequences and then see what each passage has to say to us. Lastly, persuasion may be the result of the preacher's work – some people have the gift

of being persuasive without looking like salesmen – but if someone is persuaded it is because they have been helped to see what is the Word of God by the preacher, then her or his faith has given them the acceptance of that truth, and God's help has enabled them to bring it to fruitfulness in their lives.

5. Here is an example: Jesus says that the acceptable year of the Lord has now come. What does this mean? It means that Jesus says that the time for the renewal of the creation is at hand as in one of the special Jubilee Years that were held every fifty years. On those occasions there was to be a rebalancing of wealth and resources between the rich and the poor, and a re-creation of a just society. This is the gospel message: the Father is not happy with any situation where his gifts given to all are so tied up with one group in his creation that others are suffering and downtrodden. Whether you see this as the truth or not is now a matter for faith: down the centuries there have been Christians who have worked with the poor and who have sought the just distribution of wealth. Others have rejected this and seen it as Christianity nosing into politics. However, it is a matter of whether one believes Jesus is the Son of God or not. And, if one does, then his message is the Word of Life, and one has to ask for the strength to do something about it. However, it is not the sermon that persuades: the sermon has done its job when it points out the significance of the gospel and notes that the situation is still the same: if Jesus enters our community, then it includes interest in poverty, injustice, and hunger for these do not come from the Father, but from us.

Fourth Sunday of Ordinary Time

Introduction to the Celebration

Jesus announced the new covenant in a gathering of the People of God assembled to praise God and to reflect on God's message for their lives. But when Jesus pointed out to them their short-comings they raged at him and wanted to push him away from them. We have all done this in one way or another in our lives: we have heard the call to change our lives or to begin changing our world and have wished the call to go away or declared it silly or irrelevant. Let us now spend some moments remembering that we are here because we have heard Jesus's call to be the people who bring God's justice to the world and ask pardon for the times we have failed in this vocation.

Rite of Penance

For the times we have not listened to the voice of the Lord. Lord have mercy.

For the times we have been angered by what the Lord asks us to do. Christ have mercy.

For the times we have sought to hustle the Lord out of our lives. Lord have mercy.

Headings for Readings
First Reading

In this reading we hear that the prophet was not only to bring the word of the Lord to his own people, but it was good news for all the nations: God's care knows no limits

Second Reading

In every gathering there are from time to time factions and disagreements; there are arguments about how the parish should be run, there are arguments about liturgy and about the hymns we sing or don't sing, the way this is done or not done. Paul had to chastise the Corinthians over some of their behaviour at the Eucharist, and then he said this to them to show how we must behave towards one another in this holy assembly.

Gospel
Jesus preaches in his own home town of Nazareth but while they marvel at the local boy made good, they do not welcome his message that God finds holy people even among a foreign group whom they despise.

Prayer of the Faithful
President
Each week we gather to share the Lord's supper, and with him we thank the Father for his generosity; let us ask in the name of Jesus the Lord for all that we need.
Reader (s)
1. For the church of God, that we be given strength and wisdom to promote understanding between people and cultures in the world. Lord hear us.
2. For the church that is our community, that we will be enlightened by God to see our prejudices and to become a more welcoming community. Lord hear us.
3. For all who are strangers, that the Lord will comfort them in the face of rejection. Lord hear us.
4. For all who are discriminated against, that the heart of those who do the discriminating will be softened and changed by God's grace and our example. Lord hear us.
5. For the homeless, for refugees, that God will give them help and help those with wealth to know their obligations. Lord hear us.
6. *Specific local needs and topics of the day.*
President
Father, your Son is our great prophet. Grant that we will welcome him into our hearts by becoming a people who work for justice and peace for we know that he has proclaimed that 'the Acceptable Year of the Lord' has come. We ask this through Jesus our Lord. Amen.

Eucharistic Prayer

There is no Preface or Eucharistic Prayer that is especially suited to today's readings if you pick up the theme that God's mercy is unlimited by any human boundary. However, if you develop the theme of God's mercy as seen in the theme of the rejected prophet, the Eucharistic Prayer IV – although the rubrics do not envisage its use on Sundays – suggests itself because this prayer employs that very theme in its history of salvation section: 'Again and again you offered a covenant to the human family and through the prophets taught us to hope for salvation.'

Invitation to the Our Father

Jesus came among his people in Nazareth to tell them of the Father's love; now he is among us here, and with him we pray:

Sign of Peace

To be the people of Jesus is to be the community of peace and justice: so let us show welcome and peace to one another.

Invitation to Communion

At the Lord's table there are no strangers or foreigners. We, a people forgiven, are made welcome and offered his love in abundance. Lord I am not worthy …

Communion Reflection

We have just received the Lord's generosity by being guests at his table, this should establish a pattern in our lives: God is generous with us in our need; we, therefore, act with generosity to others in need. (This is the principle: 'Forgive us our trespasses as we forgive those who trespass against us.') So when can we begin? A practical start is to have a collection of money at this point which is clearly to be set aside to help those who are 'foreign' to us either in a disaster that is happening now or which will be held for the next disaster we hear of in some far off place. To imagine that one could not have a reflection involving concrete material action (remember that most people spend more time worrying and reflecting on money than on the things of the spirit), would be to reduce the religion of the Incarnation to a Gnostic cult. So as the reflection have collectors organised and then explain why we are doing this and what the money will be used for or held for.

Conclusion

Prayer over the people 20 (Missal, p 383) is suitable. Change the last word 'men' to 'people'.

Notes

The shorter form of the second reading is preferable as it is a more focused text. The longer form (1 Cor 12:31-13:13) gives the context but unless one knows what has gone before, the transition from desiring the higher gifts to the description of love is abrupt and lacking in clarity.

COMMENTARY

First Reading: Jer 1:4-5, 17-19

The book of Jeremiah as we have it is the result of much editing, the equivalent of our cutting and pasting, over a long period before anything like our present text came into being. Thus we have close to the beginning of the book the call of the prophet but this is made up of two separated snippets of text: 1:4-10 and then 1:17-19. It is the latter of these snippets that forms the core of the reading today, with two verses from the first snippet simply used as a scene setting device. However, reading just the second part does not allow us to appreciate its original setting adequately – perhaps in some future revision the Lectionary will read vv 4-10 and then 17-19!

So today we have to read this text as supplying a parallel situation to that of the gospel (see below), and here we should notice the commitment that God makes to be with his prophet in his difficulties: 'I, for my part, today will make you.' To be called by God to take part in his plan of salvation is not to be dragooned into service: it is a covenant, and a sharing of tasks and responsibilities.

Second Reading: 1 Cor 13:4-13

This passage about love, one of the most lyrical in the whole of
early Christian literature, is so often commented upon theologically that we forget its setting: Paul writes this to the Corinthians
in the context of the problems at the assemblies for the
Eucharist. This is directed at those who are causing splits in the
community and promoting factions at the Eucharist. Given what
John Wesley once said about the devil entering a community
through the organist, and all the factions that have arisen within
Catholicism due to the need to reform the liturgy, one can see
that nothing can provoke community internecine strife like community rituals. This is a phenomenon that anthropologists of
human rituals say is virtually endemic in the nature of ritual as it
is found in all societies and religions and ages for which we have
evidence.

However, for Christians, such dissention at the Eucharist –
given what we believe this meal means to us and shows us
about love, forgiveness, and welcome – seems particularly
painful and inappropriate. It is in the light of that unity that
should be among us, which we have through the Eucharist (1
Cor 10 and 11), that Paul wrote this passage, and in which we
should read it.

First Reading > Gospel Links

The link here looks as like one of prophesy – fulfillment: a statement is made about the prophet being known before he was
born and bringing his message to the nations; then this is perfectly fulfilled in Jesus's coming. However, there is a far more
subtle link between these readings – and one which is far more
characteristic of the way these lectionary couplets were chosen:
similarity and continuity in the manner of God's working. Both
readings show a prophet setting out on his God-given ministry.
In both cases there is a providence: both are known before they
are formed in the womb, both are specifically appointed for
their task, and in both cases the message of God that they convey
is not limited to one people, but for all. In the case of Jeremiah he

is told that he will have to bear witness before the nations; in the case of Jesus he bears witness in Nazareth that God brings the nations within his plans. In the case of neither prophet is there a national boundary on God's message.

Gospel: Lk 4:21-30
This is the second part of the visit to the synagogue in Nazareth which we began to read last Sunday, and whose details are found only in Luke. Jesus takes possession of his duty as a prophet by interpreting in his own moment the Law and then pointing out to the people their shortcomings.

This passage also shows us an important theme in Luke which he saw as in continuity with the [Old Testament] scriptures: the rejected prophet. The real significance of the rejected prophet is that no matter how rebellious the people, God's covenant love is enduring and unconditional. God continued to send prophets to an unfaithful people. Now he has sent his Son, and he envisages new life for all nations and, as the examples Jesus gives make clear, he sees this new life applying equally to women (the widow at Zarephath) and men (Naaman).

At the end of the incident there is the miraculous escape of Jesus from their enraged hands: for Luke it is not yet the time or the place for Jesus to suffer for carrying out his mission.

HOMILY NOTES

1. It is amazing how quickly people can turn from praising someone or something to reviling them or rejecting their ideas. One little word that touches something that is close to us in our selfishness is all it takes. We might talk about the environment and ecology for years, but one little curtailment of our enjoyment – a few extra pennies of tax – and suddenly all the talk about climate change gets forgotten and is dismissed as just more 'theory'. We see this phenomenon in the gospel: at the start they are all amazed and filled with wonder and praise for a great prophet has arisen and he is one of their own, they even know the family! Then, in a moment, all

changes: they are enraged by him, they reject him, and they even want to kill him. But what can get people so annoyed?

2. It is deep within us that our group is the gathering of nice people. We represent civilisation, modernity, and all that is best in the world. We might not be smug as individuals, but group smugness is rarely far away. It is confirmed by the fact that people want to be like us or emigrate to be with us. They recognise that our way of life, our school system, our hospitals, our ways of enjoying ourselves all represent a peak of human achievement.

3. However, there are others in this world. Indeed, when we compare them with ourselves we are shocked at the contrast: we are even brighter and more enlightened than we thought we were, and they are darker, dimmer, and more dangerous. Indeed, the very fact that they are different shows that they are bad and a threat to us and our values. And, if they were to oppose us they are opposing civilisation itself.

4. This sort of reasoning is close to nearly every war that is fought and people who wish to lead by fear rather than by vision always need the wicked other. Once war has broken out, then we are usually fighting for nothing less than civilisation itself! What a burden is laid on us amidst such dangers!

5. We even get smug about religion: if one is in the right camp, then one is OK. And, being in the right camp becomes more important than seeking the truth, working for justice, and acting with integrity and mercy. Religious slogans replace wisdom.

6. This is the blind spot that Jesus irritates in this gospel. He has told them the time of God's justice has come, but they are more interested in seeing will he perform miracles. God's servants are not confined to any pre-packaged group. Sidonians and Syrians – foreigners – maybe as much in God's plan as we are. This is not a nice message. It is not a message that comforts us, but one that asks us to examine some of the dangerous ideas of exclusion we harbour. It is a message that asks us to begin building the kingdom of justice, peace and love, rather than simply thinking that we belong to it because of a label we sometimes wear.

Lectionary Unit III

Galilee

This unit is devoted to Jesus's ministry in Galilee. It runs from Sunday 5 to Sunday 12, and contains seven or eight Sundays depending on whether a particular year has thirty-three or thirty-four Sundays in total. This is probably the least useful unit from the standpoint of preaching or teaching as it is always broken up by the period of Lent-Eastertide-Trinity (and in some places Corpus Christi).

Its sections / themes are:

Sunday 5	*The call of the first apostles*
Sunday 6	The sermon on the plain (1)
Sunday 7	The sermon on the plain (2)
Sunday 8	The sermon on the plain (3)
Sunday 9	Curing the centurion's servant
Sunday 10	*The widow at Naim/Nain*
Sunday 11	*The woman anoints Jesus's feet*
Sunday 12	Peter's confession of faith

The sections of the gospel referred to in italics in this chart are incidents that are only found in Luke's gospel and so are texts that are only preached upon on these Sundays in the Three-Year Cycle, whereas the Lukan texts on the other Sundays may be verbally very similar to texts met elsewhere in the gospels and consequently read on other Sundays over the three years.

Fifth Sunday of Ordinary Time

Introduction to the Celebration

In the gospel we hear that when Peter and James and John were called by Jesus to follow him, they left everything they were doing and followed him. That call somehow touched each of them so profoundly that they recognised it as an encounter with the all-holy God: Peter's first reaction was to say: 'Go away from me Lord because I am a sinful man.' Yet the Lord still wanted him to be one of his intimate group, and Peter followed. Now we have been called to the intimacy of the Lord's table at this gathering. In the presence of the Lord here with us we acknowledge our sinfulness, but also recognise that God's love bids us welcome and wishes us to be the followers of Jesus today.

Rite of Penance

Lord Jesus, you have called us to be your disciples. Lord have mercy.

Lord Jesus, you have called us to be your witnesses. Christ have mercy.

Lord Jesus, you have called us to be your people. Lord have mercy.

Headings for Readings
First Reading

In this reading we hear about the call of God's prophet, Isaiah. In a specific situation he was called to a very specific service of the People of God.

Second Reading

Paul tells the church in Corinth that the core of our faith is that the Christ has died for our sins, in accordance with the scriptures, was buried, and was raised to life in accordance with the scriptures, and that the people of God can encounter the risen One as we encounter him today in this Eucharist.

Gospel

Jesus called all those who heard him to follow him in living a new life, and some he called to follow him as his closest disciples: they left their fishing nets to become fishers of men.

Prayer of the Faithful

President

We are here because we have heard the call of Jesus to become his followers, and through him have been transformed into being his sisters and brothers, his community on earth, his priestly people. Because of whom we have been called to become, we can now stand before the Father and intercede for ourselves, the whole church, and all humanity.

Reader (s)

1. For the whole church, that it may be faithful in following the Lord. Lord hear us.

2. For this church, that each of us may hear the Lord's call in our lives. Lord hear us.

3. For all our sisters and brothers, that every human heart may hear the stirrings of the Spirit. Lord hear us.

4. For everyone who is finding the following of their vocation a trial, that each may be strengthened. Lord hear us.

5. *Specific local needs and topics of the day.*

6. For all who have died, that they may hear the Lord's words: 'Well done good and faithful servant.' Lord hear us.

President

Father in heaven, we walk onwards on our pilgrimage of faith seeking to follow your Son. Hear us now as we place our needs before you for we make these prayers as your priestly people in Christ Jesus our Lord. Amen.

Eucharistic Prayer

Preface of Sundays in Ordinary Time I (P29) which expresses the notion that we are a people who have been called to be the people of Christ. Eucharistic Prayer I, which lists the names of the apostles given in today's gospel, is appropriate provided you use the full form of the *Communicantes*: i.e. 'Peter and Paul, Andrew, James, John, Thomas …'

Invitation to the Our Father
You taught those you called to follow you how to pray when they asked you to teach them; so we now pray using the words those first followers handed on to us:

Sign of Peace
The company of the followers of Jesus is called to be the new community of peace; let us now express that peace to one another.

Invitation to Communion
Jesus called his first followers to share his table with him and so establish the new People of God, now he calls us to this table to share one loaf and one cup and so become the one Body of Christ; happy are we who are called to this supper.

Communion Reflection
Lord Jesus, you sat down and taught the crowds by the lake of Gennesaret.
Lord Jesus, you have sat with us today as we listened to your word at the Eucharist.
Lord Jesus, you asked Simon Peter long ago to cast his nets despite his hesitations.
Lord Jesus, you call us to obey your word even when it flies in the face of our expectations.
Lord Jesus, you called Simon and James and John to follow you and to be your witnesses.
Lord Jesus, you have called each of us to witness to your new life in some particular way.
Lord Jesus, you united the first apostles to you in the bonds of sharing your table.
Lord Jesus, you have united us to one another and to you around this table today.
Lord Jesus, you bid the apostles to follow you to the end.
Lord Jesus, gather us to yourself at our end. Amen.

Conclusion

Since the gospel presents us with the call of some of The Twelve/ 'the apostles', Solemn Blessing 17 (Missal, p 375) is suitable. However, the second line of the first petition has to be changed from 'bless you through the prayer of Saint N. and Saint N.' to 'bless you through their prayers'.

Notes

The Second Reading

The shorter form is only shorter by four verses but it is far more focused; and in the liturgical context, where we are reading only snippets, this makes it preferable.

COMMENTARY

First Reading: Isa 6:1-2, 3-8

Although it is not now located at the beginning of the book of [first] Isaiah, this call story is the real beginning of the work, which was intended to open with memoirs of the prophet (6:1-8:18). In that context the call story presents Isaiah's credentials as a prophet, and therefore someone whose words deserve attention no matter how unpalatable they may be.

As a call story – and it is as such that we are expected to read it today in parallel with the gospel – it follows a recognisable pattern. First, the narrative is located in the 'ordinary' world of space and time: 'In the year of King Uzziah's death'; and then that space and time are transcended: what is seen and heard belongs to another realm: the Lord on his throne in his heavenly sanctuary – what is seen is not part of worldly material space nor the ageing time of humanity. However, what is central to the call narrative as distinct from apocalyptic visions, the visionary remains in this universe while being granted a sight into the world of the throne of God. That vision is then elaborated with a scene that is furnished with metaphors from the royal courts of Mesopotamia (the great garment whose hem alone fills the whole scene [the JB translation of 'train' is to my mind foolish as when I hear that word I do not think of the train of a dress or of the old *cappa magna* of bishops, but of trains in a station]; and the six-winged seraphim) but which has been sacralised by being described as a 'sanctuary.' The effect of this theophany is that the whole created universe is seen to be unstable both at the level of matter and of the human seer: 'I am lost because I am a man of unclean lips.' Then follows the visitation of the angel who commissions the prophet, and the acceptance of the commission by the prophet.

This passage has a long history within Christianity as creating the paradigm for the commissioning of a disciple to be a messenger of the Word of God, and so it highlights the call of those mentioned in today's gospel as preachers of the Christ. The influence of this lection from Isaiah can be gauged recalling that this was the incident that was invoked in the private prayer of the gospel-reader in the pre-1969 liturgy: 'Cleanse my heart and my lips, O almighty God in that manner in which you did cleanse the prophet Isaiah's lips with a burning coal …'

While the *Lectionary*, p 849, states that this lection is 6:1-8, this is not actually the case as part of verse 2 ('two of the seraphs' wings covered their faces, two their feet, and with two other they flew') has been omitted. The purpose of this editing is obtuse: does it make the text any less 'otherworldly' to omit this detail? Surely, if one mentions angelic beings at all, one is already using non-empirical language. And, since the whole purpose of the passage is to stress the wondrous transcendence of God, this detail should have been left in place.

Second Reading: 1 Cor 15:1-11

This is part of the final section of the letter in which Paul wants to stress the importance of the line of tradition in which he, and the church in Corinth, stand. The authentication of this line of tradition is that he belongs to the community that has the task of being the primary witnesses to Jesus's risen life. The significant detail to note is the order of those to whom Paul believes Jesus appeared: first, Peter who was already taking a leadership role over many churches; then, the twelve – they are still a significant group in the memory of the church (note they are still clearly distinct from the category of 'apostles') which is a position they would not occupy in the memory of the church in the next generation when the gospels of Matthew and Luke were being preached; then there are other specific group; and lastly Paul.

First Reading > Gospel Links
The relationship here is one of parallel narratives. In the first reading, Isaiah is called, he becomes aware of his unworthiness in the divine presence, yet has the courage to set off to carry out the specific task he has been given. In the gospel, Peter is called, he becomes aware of his unworthiness in the divine presence, yet has the courage to set off to carry out the specific task he has been given. It is the similarity between Isaiah and Peter that forms the link, everything else in today's gospel is peripheral. This is a very good example of how the first reading narrows and specifies the focus on what we are looking at in a particular gospel.

Gospel: Lk 5:1-11
When Luke wrote this passage of his gospel about the call of some of the first disciples he took the story of a scene that was often told in the churches (see Mk 1:16-20 and Mt 4:18-22 which contain parallels) in its most developed form (see Jn 21:1-11 and 15-19) and give it a completely new meaning. To appreciate today's gospel is to appreciate this transformation.

In Mark and Matthew we have Jesus just happening upon two sets of brothers (Simon Peter and Andrew, James and John who are the sons of Zebedee) and the focus is brought to a fine point: when Jesus called, they left everything immediately and followed him. This has become the paradigm for a vocation story for many Christians. Jesus calls, and the one called moves quickly and absolutely: everything is abandoned and there is no hesitation.

When we move to John we find a resurrection story – and one which belongs to the appendix of that gospel which may indicate that it circulated within the church for longer than stories in the main body of John's gospel – where Jesus manifests his presence by asking the disciples to cast their nets and then they encounter the wonderful haul of 153 fish. Here the focus is upon the recognition of the risen Jesus present with his followers, who are listening to him and are made aware that they are in the very presence of the living God – hence the gesture of Peter jumping into the water because, in perfect continuity with the religious insight of Isaiah, once he knows he is in the wondrous presence – albeit on the shore of a lake while he works his trade – of the All-Holy One, he knows that he is a sinful creature. In the story found in John, there is no focus upon vocation, but solely on the wonder of sacramentality: in the midst of ordinary life, to those who listen for his voice the Risen Jesus stands among us, and in encountering him we encounter God whom Isaiah could only describe in the hieratic court imagery of a sacral 'other' world. So while this story belongs to the appendix to the gospel, it has been thoroughly transformed to the joannine agenda: at the beginning of the gospel we are told that the *Logos* has 'pitched his tent' among us; in this story it is made clear that the Risen Lord, now in the glorious presence of the Father (17:5), still has his tent pitched among his people.

Luke employed the wondrous haul of fish scene, without any explicit reference to the resurrection, and combined it with the calling scene by using the simple narrative device that both scenes are located beside the Sea of Galilee. The effect of this combination is to present the call of the first disciples as being the equivalent to an encounter for his hearers with the Risen Jesus, and an encounter which is equivalent to the call of Isaiah. This is a profoundly different theology of vocation in Luke to what we have in Matthew or Mark: to encounter the Risen Jesus is to be called to follow him, and the experience of vocation is not a voice to be obeyed because it is a voice of power but because it is heard in the midst of the wonder of encountering sacramentally – for Peter does not have an otherworldly experience in the manner of Isaiah – the Risen Lord.

HOMILY NOTES

1. The theme of vocation is one that we tend to hear about once a year after Easter on 'Vocations' Sunday' when we do not usually preach on vocation, as such, but on 'vocations' understood as the need for priests (and sometimes nuns and brothers). The priest then becomes the paradigm for all ministries (there are ministries and lesser ministries and lay ministries); and ministry becomes the paradigm for 'vocations'; and seeking such 'vocations' – which then often has the epithet 'vocations to the priesthood and religious life' – dulls our understanding of vocation. So it is worth clearing up the difference between vocation and ministry. Within the tradition, it should be remembered, this confusion of vocation with priesthood and/or religious life is a phenomenon that only becomes obvious in the post-Tridentine period.

2. The notion of 'a vocation' is itself one that gives many people the shivers; and meeting someone who is very clear about his or her vocation can be a rather trying experience. Most of us only discover our vocation day by day, and bit by bit, and it is often a very humdrum business, but without people following their many vocations day-in and day-out, without spectacular gestures or events, then the presence of God would disappear from our world. However, for many people the notion of a religious vocation is so tied up with a particular public and ministerial task – in the case of Catholics it is often just priests, nuns, and monks who are thought of as having a 'vocation' – that people are often poorly equipped to see their own life situation and work in explicitly vocational terms. Indeed, this is exacerbated by the fact that dioceses have 'Vocations' Directors' whose primary task is not helping the people who make up that church to discover their individual vocations, but to encourage 'vocations' in the sense of getting men to consider entering a seminary. Thus 'Vocations' Director' is simply a pious euphemism for the personnel-recruitment function of an organisation. However, as we read through the gospels we see Jesus again and again

helping people discover their vocation; and so this is part of the task of leadership within the churches. So can we sketch out some of the characteristics of vocation in a homily?

3. Vocation is individual, personal, and inter-personal.

The unique task that each is called to carry out to build the kingdom depends on our situation, the people we meet, our gifts, our limitations. Each of us lives in a unique set of relationships, and each is the only person in that situation, so each of us can bring that little bit of the creation to its fulfilment in Jesus Christ. This calling is personal and is related to persons. The analogy is a family group: each must play a different role in keeping the group happy; and if one person fails in that work, the whole group suffers. So it is in our other relationships: if the kingdom brings peace and forgiveness, I may be the only person in a situation that can promote this here today. And on a larger scale, each has a unique set of gifts which can help those around them – if she/he chooses to use them – and these build up the Body of Christ.

However, we do not discover our different vocations as lone individuals. We discover our personal and unique contribution to the building of the kingdom in relationship with other people: those people around us with whom we live in a series of relationships. I discover my vocation within a set of interpersonal relationships of needs and gifts. Discovering my vocation makes me more truly human, and helps me to grow in true awareness of the humanity of others.

4. Vocation is developing and unfolding.

Vocation is not taking a job with a fixed job specification: it changes as our lives change, as we change through growing older, and as the needs of the society within which we live change. What one was called to do at one time may be very different to what one is called to do at another time. Each of us has to be listening for what we are called to do today. It is not that there is one moment of hearing a call and then that is the task for a lifetime – just think how such a static notion is untrue to the reality of how our lives unfold. Because vocation is unfolding we have the harder task of being continuously listening to what new vocation we have in the life we live at that moment.

5. Vocation is linked to our integrity.

   Vocation is not about doing a job, a specific common activity or a formal ministry in the church (although it may include any or all of these), but about being a person who is 'in Christ' and who seeks in every aspect of her/his life to act in Christ. I must become the person God calls me to become, and must act in my world honestly as that person.

6. Vocation is all embracing.

   It is always tempting to say 'my vocation is X' when there is a hint that any other vocation is excluded. But just as life can turn up all sorts of situations, so acting in Christ can take any number of forms. Because the whole of the creation is called towards the perfection of the kingdom, so every aspect of life is involved in the vocations of those of us who live and work in that part of the creation.

7. Vocation may embrace a formal ministry, but ministry is not to be confused with liturgical abilities or canonical status. In every church there will be people who have the skills within the body of Christ to serve their fellow Christians with the public skills they need as a church. These skills will then fall within the specific vocations of the members of that church, but every member of that church has a vocation whether or not it is a specific skill for the community.

Sixth Sunday of Ordinary Time

Introduction to the Celebration

My friends, assembling here for the Eucharist is a part of our week – one more of the things we do regularly in our lives like working, relaxing, shopping. But it is also something that is very different, for the values of this assembly are not those of our everyday lives but of the Christ: here it is the poor, the hungry, and those who mourn who are valued. Let us reflect on this clash between the values we take for granted for much of our lives and the very different values that come from the wisdom of the Lord.

Rite of Penance

Lord Jesus, for those times when we have not sought to serve you in the poor. Lord have mercy.

Lord Jesus, for those times when we have not heard your command to feed the hungry. Christ have mercy.

Lord Jesus, for those times when we have not given comfort to those who weep. Lord have mercy.

Headings for Readings

First Reading

The prophet warns those who turn their hearts from the Lord; and he reminds those whose heart is focused on the Lord that they are the blessed ones.

Second Reading

Jesus has risen, he has conquered death; and because he has conquered death, so too shall we who have entered his death and new life at our baptism.

Gospel

Jesus presents us with the challenge of his Way of Life in contrast with the Way of Death.

Prayer of the Faithful

President

Fellow disciples, let us unite our prayers with Jesus our great prophet and place them before the Father of mercies.

Reader(s)

1. Let us pray for all who are poor, that God will be with them and move our hearts to share with them. Lord hear us.

2. Let us pray for all who are rich, that they will see the limits of their riches and share them justly. Lord hear us.

3. Let us pray for all who are hungry that they may be satisfied and that God will empower all who work to avert hunger. Lord hear us.

4. Let us pray for all who have a fill of the earth's riches that they may discover the way of truth and distribute their riches with those who have not enough. Lord hear us.

5. Let us pray for all who weep, that God may console them and move us to oppose those who cause suffering. Lord hear us.

6. Let us pray for all who cause weeping and hurt, that they may have a change of mind and heart. Lord hear us.

7. Let us pray for ourselves, and all disciples, that we may have to strength to follow the Christ in our choices. Lord hear us.

8. Let us pray for all Christians who are suffering persecution that they may be strengthened and know the nearness of God. Lord hear us.

President

Father, your Son opened our way to the fullness of your life and taught us how to follow that way; hear our needs and empower us as disciples of Jesus Christ, our Lord. Amen.

Eucharistic Prayer

There is no Preface or Eucharistic Prayer that picks up the theme of today's gospel in any particularly appropriate way.

Invitation to the Our Father

To set out on the way of discipleship is to seek to act as daughters and sons of the Father, and therefore we now pray:

Sign of Peace

As disciples we have declared our willingness to build the
world shown to us by the Christ and that building starts with
our willingness to work for peace. Let us declare that now to one
another.

Invitation to Communion

As poor and needy people we are called to share in the Lord's
banquet; happy are we to be called to this supper.

Communion Reflection

Lord,

In our poverty, you have provided us with the riches of your
table;

In our hunger, you have given us yourself as our food and drink;

In our sadness, you have granted us a taste of the heavenly banquet.

Lord,

May we learn from this experience of sharing at your table:

To give from our riches to those in need;

To share our food with the hungry;

To bring joy to all who despair and live in fear.

Lord,

May this food and drink

Strengthen us to be your disciples now,

And in times of trial,

And, onwards, to life eternal.

Amen.

Conclusion

Solemn Blessing 14 (Ordinary Time V), Missal, p 373.

Notes

This is a day when having a collection for the poor – the origin of
the collection during the liturgy – gives a real expression to the
discipline demanded by Jesus in the gospel.

COMMENTARY

First Reading: Jer 17:5-8

This is a little summary of Israelite wisdom expressed in an elegant two-handed couplet or saying. The first is a curse, the second, a blessing. They are to be read together 'as two sides of one coin' which sum up the way of wisdom. In dedication to the Lord, and unconditional faithful service, lies the path to blessedness (the way of life); and its opposite in human behaviour leads to desolation (the way of death).

The authorship of this section has been much disputed, but that debate misses this central point: here is an authentic expression of the faith of Israel, and it is within that tradition of holiness that we, as Christians, understand the gospel's message. However, we should be careful not to imagine that we have adopted this wisdom without serious alterations. In this passage, the ultimate expression of a divine curse is barrenness – being unable to procreate. This fits with other places in Jeremiah where the classic expression of desolation is the absence of the joyful sounds of marriage (Jer 7:34; 16:9 and 25:6) and the marker of divine restoration of the people is the return of this joyful sound (Jer 33:10-11). But while Christianity uses this tradition as a metaphor for the end times (cf Marriage Feast of the Lamb in Apoc 19), it has not seen real human marriage, but celibacy, as the mark of special divine favour and as the 'special' gift. For Jeremiah such a notion of a gift would have been unimaginable as contrary to the first command of The Law (Gen 1:28) and the many with such a 'gift' would be visibly cursed.

Psalm: 1

The blessed man, the *beatus*, is the one who follows the Law, meditates on it, makes it the basis of life, and then reaps the rewards of that life in heaven: his future will be like [earthly joys]; it is not a case that his future will be these earthly joys.

Second Reading: 1 Cor 15:12, 16-20

As extracted here from the larger section in the letter dealing with resurrection, what we have is a series of basic Christian slogans:

God does raise the dead; he has raised Jesus; Jesus is the first of those who fall asleep; therefore, we can look forward to resurrection.

This reduction of Paul's letter to the size of a lection does not really produce any understanding of his theology of resurrection; but it was made necessary as to read it in a meaningful way would require a much longer pericope than is ever found for an epistle reading on the Sundays of Ordinary Time.

As laid out, this reading's value lies in that it repeats in the assembly some of the basic phrases used by Christians to express their faith in the resurrection – and this is no small service from this lection.

First Reading > Gospel Links

The relationship here is one of type and then the perfection of the type (what in older theological textbooks was called the *modus eminentiae*). Prophets are those who utter warnings and blessings; therefore both Jeremiah and Jesus do so; but while Jeremiah is a great member of the genus 'prophets', the Christ is both the perfection of that genus and the one who transcends it.

Gospel: Lk 6:17, 20-26

The focus of today's gospel is vv 20-26, 'the Lukan beatitudes', with v 17 included simply as a scene setter. This simple act of editing does, however, mean that 'beatitudes' are intended to be read differently in the liturgy than in the gospel. In the liturgy they are to be read as a dominical oracle revealing the mind of the Christ, and the context is simply an introductory device equivalent to the old '*in illo tempore*' – and we are expected to react with the liturgy knowing that anything said *in illo tempore* is something that is said as true in every time and season and place.

The so-called 'Lukan beatitudes' are less well known than those in Matthew and are also far more 'crusty'. It is this 'edge' that deserves notice. There is a radical separation between the now-times and the end-times; what appears successful now may ultimately be useless, that which is despised now may ultimately be what has value. There is a corresponding separation between the values of the world and the kingdom, expressed in terms of the values of those who accept that Jesus is Lord and become disciples, and those who do not. This theme of the values of the New People, almost invisible in Matthew, is made explicit in that the clash of values is expected to lead to the disciples having to suffer for their commitment to the coming kingdom. The disciples will be hated, denounced as criminals, abused, and avoided: this is far from the cosy world of Mt 5 which makes it one of the most used pericopes in the liturgy for all sorts of 'special Masses'!

This clash of values/worlds/kingdoms is then reinforced by the presentation – in the classic style shown in the reading from Jeremiah – of a blessing linked to its converse, a curse. In effect, what we have is four groups (the poor; the hungry; the weepers; the persecuted Christians) and two accounts: first, what those on 'the receiving end' of suffering now will receive at the eschaton; second, what those who on 'the giving end' now will be given at the eschaton. The full force of this approach is lost in the Jerusalem Bible translation which shrank from having 'woes' and put in the anodyne 'Alas for you' which destroys the deliberate shock that the cursing/blessing format demands and which Luke intended. The word in Greek is *ouai* – and has usually been translated as 'woe to ye' in English – but the best translation I have seen is 'how horrible it will be for you'. So the text needs correction if it is to carry its message.

This gospel is at the heart of Luke's teaching on discipleship: it is a radical choice that puts the members of the church at odds with the larger society and with their times. The church is, therefore, never to feel at home in the world and the present condition. It exits in the world and the now in that same mysterious tension in which the Christ exists in the world.

HOMILY NOTES

1. Luke presents us with the stark choice that disciples of the
    Christ must face. There are two contrasting universes: the
    world of the kingdom of God, and the world of those whose
    vision is earth-bound. Our lives are bounded by our imagin-
    ations: there is the world of those who see this world as the
    gift of the Father's goodness which will return to the fullness
    of life in him; and there are those who see this world as the
    means of their self sufficiency (and God is an after-thought or
    simply a limitation on their plans). This is the searching ques-
    tion every disciple has to ask about her/his own identity.
    None of us is simply an inhabitant of one or the other world:
    we are all sinners. The question is whether we are aware of
    the challenge and prepared to begin moving in the direction
    of the Way of the Lord.

2. How do we grasp such a momentous choice? How can 'we
    get our heads around' this clash of values that is at the heart
    of discipleship?

3. Luke's series of blessings and curses are like snapshots:
    These pick our the choice in terms of:

*   The poor – covering everything to do with possessions.
*   The hungry – everything to do with care for society and
    humanity.
*   The weepers – all who are hurt and everything to do with
    violence.
*   The persecuted Christians – awareness of the demands of the
    Christian lifestyle.
    These snapshots are the equivalent of 'before and after' com-
    parisons in modern advertising: the choice is made plain by
    being reduced to its essentials.

4. In the communities where Luke preached, this choice was al-
    ready known by heart by his audience for they had learned
    that every disciple had to choose between two Ways: one led
    to life and the other led to death. And the decision to follow
    the way of life meant doing things that non-believers would

think stupid, and not-doing things that everyone else took for granted.

5. This constant choice confronting the followers of the Way is made even more uncomfortable for us hearing this at the liturgy. We have not gathered at some preaching 'service' to hear God's word and then to reflect on it. We are gathered already at Christ's table, we are in his presence and so have already made our choice that we want to be with him in this life and in the life to come, but – and it is a very big 'but' – are our lives away from the table consistent with being an intimate follower and companion of Jesus?

Seventh Sunday of Ordinary Time

Introduction to the Celebration

When we gather for the Eucharist, Jesus welcomes us with his love and forgiveness. Sinners, we are called to share his supper: he shares his love with us without limit. But if we are recipients of forgiveness and love, he also calls us to be compassionate to others as the Father is compassionate to us. Let us thank the Father for his mercy, and let us ask him to be especially merciful to us because we are so often unmerciful to others.

Rite of Penance

Lord Jesus, for those times when we have not loved our enemies, done good to those who hate us, blessed those who curse us, prayed for those who treat us badly. Lord have mercy.

Lord Jesus, for those times when we have not turned the other cheek to those who hurt us or given to those who have asked for our support or have only given in hope of return. Christ have mercy.

Lord Jesus, for those times when we have not acted as sons and daughters of the Most High, lacked compassion, condemned others, or refused pardon. Lord have mercy.

Headings for Readings
First Reading

David refuses to kill his enemy although he could have done so; he refrained because he knew that there was a higher divine law to be obeyed.

Second Reading

As human beings we all have life, as Christians we share in Christ's life-giving spirit; as human beings we are fitted out for life on earth, as Christians we are fitted out for life in heaven.

Gospel

Today's gospel presents us with two messages: first, we must love our enemies, being compassionate as our heavenly Father is compassionate; and second, we must be generous to one another by refraining from judging others, being willing to offer pardon, and sharing our riches with others.

Prayer of the Faithful

President

Sisters and brothers, the words of the Christ have put before us a new vision of what it is to be a daughter or son of the Most High, let us pray for the gifts we need to change our lifestyles so as to become the people Jesus calls us to become.

Reader(s)

1. That this community will grow to love its enemies. Lord hear us.

2. That this community will grow to do good to those who hate us. Lord hear us.

3. That this community will grow to bless those who curse us. Lord hear us.

4. That this community will grow to pray for those who treat us badly. Lord hear us.

5. That this community will grow to present the other cheek to those who slap us. Lord hear us.

6. That this community will grow in not refusing the tunic to those who take our coat. Lord hear us.

7. That this community will grow in not asking back our property from those who rob us. Lord hear us.

8. That this community will grow to lend to the needy without hope of return. Lord hear us.

9. That this community will grow in compassion. Lord hear us.

10. That this community will grow to be less judgemental. Lord hear us.

11. That this community will grow to become slower to condemn. Lord hear us.

12. That this community will grow in its willingness to grant pardon. Lord hear us.

13. That this community will grow in its rejection of vengeance. Lord hear us.

14. That this community will grow in its willingness to forgive. Lord hear us.

15. That this community will grow as givers of God's gifts. Lord hear us.

16. That this community will grow to become the people of everlasting peace. Lord hear us.

President

Father, all compassionate and all merciful, hear our prayers made in union with Christ Jesus, our Lord. Amen.

Eucharistic Prayer

Eucharistic Prayer for Masses of Reconciliation I fits perfectly with today's gospel.

Invitation to the Our Father

Because the Father is compassionate to all, we can now stand in his presence and pray:

Sign of Peace

The Lord called us in the gospel to love our enemies, to do good to those who hate us, and to bless those who curse us; in this spirit of the Lord's love and reconciliation let us greet one another with the kiss of peace.

Invitation to Communion

The Lord is full of generosity, he gives us his love and invites us to share in his life; happy are we whom he welcomes to his banquet.

Communion Reflection

Use the Prayer of St Thomas Aquinas (Missal, p 1020) as it picks up the gospel's themes in a Eucharistic context.

Conclusion
Solemn Blessing 13, Ordinary Time IV (Missal, p 373) suits the day well.

COMMENTARY

First Reading: 1 Sam 26:2, 7-9, 12-13, 22-23
This reading is a selection of verses from one incident in the long tale of the rise to power of Israel's second king, David, in a vicious and bloody rebellion and civil war. This take runs from 1 Sam 18:6 to the end of the book. This entire section is an account of open warfare connected in one way or another with Saul and his activities – he is progressively portrayed as a 'bad thing' – and this only ends with Saul's ultimate military failure when his badness is finally revealed by his suicide (31:4). As the passage stands in the Lectionary it does not provide any particular angle for exegesis except to note that it has – even in the edited form which we read – all the elements of ancient military epic narratives: each incident is written from the perspective of an audience who will ask at the end of the incident: 'So what happened next?' Unfortunately, this particular narrative device is not one that is suited to the reading of the tale in chunks at the Eucharist.

Psalm: 102
This is the perfect text to prepare for the gospel.

Second Reading: 1 Cor 15:45-49
This is another element in Paul's development of an understanding of Jesus and his place in the history of salvation by setting up a comparison between the time of the creation (Adam) and the time of the new creation (Jesus). It takes the form in this case of seeing Jesus as 'the new, and final, Adam'. But while elsewhere in Paul's writings the relationship he wants to explore is one of contrasts (e.g. in Romans: from Adam came death, from Jesus came life), here it is one of complementarity: Adam was a living soul, Jesus a life-giving spirit; Adam was fitted for the earth, Jesus was/is fitted for heaven; Adam is the key to earthly living, Jesus to the life of heaven.

First Reading > Gospel Links

The links today are tenuous: David does not assassinate Saul but this is neither through love of neighbour nor forgiveness but for fear of the consequences of sacrilege. Yet the fact that he stays his hand is intended in some way to illustrate the gospel's call of love. The only possible way to construe the relationship is one of the superiority of the New Covenant's demands in contrast to those of the Old; yet this 'replacement theology' was one that the compilers of the Lectionary were anxious to avoid.

Gospel: Lk 6:27-38

Today's reading is a long passage that is, apart from one or two details, found also in Mt but in a very different arrangement: 5:39-42; 44-48 for Lk 6:27-36; and Mt 7:1-2 for Lk 6:37-42. This difference in arrangement of these ideas is a key for understanding today's lection, for what is found in the Lectionary is the whole of one section (Lk 6:27-26) usually given the name 'On love of one's enemies' and which has a very definite conclusion within the gospel tradition: 'be compassionate as your Father is compassionate' (v 36). Then comes the opening two verses of the next section in Luke (6:37-42) which is usually entitled 'On judging'. So let us begin by acknowledging that the text as it is given to us, has by its clumsy use of scissors given us a problem of preaching: we have one and a half snippets rather than one or two; and it is clear that Luke thought of this as two items of the Lord's teaching within his own preaching. Moreover, this has been compounded in the printed Lectionary, p 858, where the second paragraph in the text begins not on the beginning of the second item ('Do not judge ...'), but with the concluding verse of the first item: 'Be compassionate ...' So the first item lacks its rounding off conclusion, while the second seems to be an illogical association of ideas! The muddle arose by the selection of 6:39-41 for Sunday 8 (which had to be adapted to its truncated status by having 'also' omitted from its first line, but, at least, the parable can stand alone) and then the compilers found that there were two verses of Dominical instruction that were being 'left out', so they extended this Sunday's readings, but in the process forgot that their tacking on of two verses destroyed the integrity of both passages.

So what does one do? A simple expedient would be to drop the last two verses or move them to be the opening of the lection for next Sunday (where they really belong), but neither solution is simple as there will be many in the congregation with texts and what is printed in a book has automatic religious authority. So the simplest thing is to treat it as two items: conclude the first with its own conclusion and then pause for a good 'dramatic pause' (c. 5-7 seconds) and then begin the second part: 'Do not judge ...'

The difficulty of today's passages is not exegetical, but relates to our humanity. The difference between Jesus's teaching and the preaching of most religious systems is that he wants us to act towards others as the Father acts towards us. But being God-like in our loving – that is in our relationships to all whom we meet – is the call to perfection.

HOMILY NOTES

1. Any comment on today's gospel can only serve to take away from its stark demand: the Christian must act towards others as the Father acts towards us his creatures. St Thomas pointed out that God alone can be absolutely generous, but it is the Lord's generosity we are called to imitate. This is a day for meditative silence introduced by some formula such as: 'Today's gospel sets before us the Christian standard of behaviour towards others. Let us reflect on how we fall short of it and consider how we can grow towards its call.' Bring the minutes of silence (one needs at least three minutes to let people settle down and actually free their minds to reflect) with the call to profess the creed: 'Let us stand and affirm our commitment to the God who is love and who calls us to love our neighbour.'

2. If you intend to use the meditation option, then read the gospel slowly as 'words of wisdom' – both passages were ini-

tially used in the churches in this way as 'sayings' before being given a narrative location within the story of Jesus's teaching by Luke and Matthew.

3. The Prayers of the Faithful given above are deliberately longer than usual on the assumption that you opt for a space for reflection rather than a homily. If you do preach, then they need to be cut back or the liturgy will be too wordy.

Trinity Sunday

Introduction to the Celebration

This feast is unique in that the focus of our celebration is not an aspect of the history of salvation, but reflection on the nature of God as we believe it has been revealed to us as Christians. Thus every Sunday is the Sunday of the Trinity, every feast, every action has a trinitarian dimension, and should any prayer be uttered or homily preached which does not include that core of faith – at least tacitly with a conclusion such as 'through Christ our Lord' – then we are apostates, have ceased to be Christians and become some sort of vague deists or unitarians who value the 'message of Jesus'. At the outset of the celebration it is worth reflecting that today's focus is the very essence of Christian identity. We have just stated that we are acting 'In the name of the Father ... ' and that is a declaration of our basic faith, not just an opening formula. Our aim in today's liturgy should be to become more sensitive to the trinitarian cues that run right through our religion.

Rite of Penance (but see the Notes section below)

Lord Jesus, you have shown us the way to the Father, Lord have mercy.

Lord Jesus, you are Son of God and Son of Mary, Christ have mercy.

Lord Jesus, you have sent the Spirit among us for the forgiveness of sins, Lord have mercy.

Headings for Readings
First Reading

We identify the Wisdom of God as the Word, the Son, 'through whom all things were made.'

Second Reading
Through Christ we look to the Father in the Spirit.

Gospel
The Son, our Lord, received all from the Father, and he sends us the Spirit.

Prayer of the Faithful
President
Gathered into Christ by the Spirit, let us petition the Father.
Reader(s)
1. That we may seek the way to the Father. Lord in your mercy, hear our prayer.
2. That we may bear witness to his Son, Jesus Christ, in our lives. Lord in your mercy, hear our prayer.
3. That we may rejoice in the strength of the Holy Spirit. Lord in your mercy, hear our prayer.
4. That all who seek the truth with find it. Lord in your mercy, hear our prayer.
5. That all who seek justice shall be satisfied. Lord in your mercy, hear our prayer.
6. That all the dead may find joy in the Father's house. Lord in your mercy, hear our prayer.
President
Father, hear your people's prayers for we ask them in the power of your Holy Spirit, and in the name of Christ Jesus, our Lord. Amen.

Eucharistic Prayer
Preface of the Holy Trinity (P43) (Missal, p 446). Eucharistic Prayer II is ideal for today as it presents the trinitarian pattern of all prayer in two opening sentences which taken together are among the most elegant, and concise, statements of trinitarian faith in the whole of the Latin liturgy: 'Lord you are holy indeed, the fountain of all holiness. Let your Spirit come upon these gifts … that they may become for us the body and blood of our Lord, Jesus Christ.'

However, it is worth noting that while P43 is directed to be used today, many people find it a cold statement of doctrine. If you want a preface that is equally explicit in its statement of trinitarian faith, but which expresses the mystery in terms of the history of salvation – what is sometimes referred to as 'the economic trinity' – then look at Preface of Sunday in Ordinary Time VIII [P36] (Missal, p 439).

Invitation to the Our Father
In the power of the Spirit and the words of the Son, let us pray to the Father.

Sign of Peace
We have been baptised into the life of the Father, Son, and Spirit. Here strife and ill-will have no place. Let us express our desire to become more God-like in our lives by exchanging a sign of peace with one another.

Invitation to Communion
Through sharing in this meal we have a share in the divine banquet. Blessed are we who are called to this supper.

Communion Reflection
Our God is the God of all humans.
The God of heaven and earth.
The God of the sea and the rivers.
The God of the sun and moon.
The God of all the heavenly bodies.
The God of the lofty mountains.
The God of the lowly valleys.
God is above the heavens,
and he is in the heavens,
and he is beneath the heavens.
Heaven and earth and sea,
and everything that is in them,
such he has as his abode.

He inspires all things,
he gives life to all things,
he stands above all things,
and he stands beneath all things.
He enlightens the light of the sun,
he strengthens the light of the night and the stars,
he makes wells in the arid land and dry islands in the sea,
and he places the stars in the service of the greater lights.
He has a Son who is co-eternal with himself,
and similar in all respects to himself;
and neither is the Son younger than the Father,
nor is the Father older than the Son;
and the Holy Spirit breathes in them.
And the Father and the Son and Holy Spirit are inseparable.
Amen.

Bishop Tírechán, c 700

Dismissal

Every good gift comes from the Father of light,
May he fill you with his blessings. Amen.
The Redeemer has given you lasting freedom,
May you inherit his everlasting life. Amen.
The Spirit inspired different tongues to proclaim one faith,
May he strengthen you in faith, hope and love. Amen.
May almighty God bless you …

Notes

1. We encounter God, Father, Son, Spirit, in our baptism, therefore this is a good day to being with the Rite of Blessing and Sprinkling with Holy Water (Missal, p 387). However, if you have used this rite regularly during Eastertide, then perhaps today is the day to simply use the *Kyrie eleison* Rite of Penance.

2. There is no day in the year when the mystery of faith can be so easily betrayed by making it into a conumdrum than today. So if you hear youself using numbers ('three in one, one in three') in your words, then stop. If you hear yourself saying something

like 'to understand the trinity', 'it can be explained like ...', then stop. If you find yourself mentioning triangles, or shamrocks, or Möbius strips, then stop at once.

3. In the face of the mystery of God we often try to cope by using more and more words: if there is one day of the year to keep it simple and have few words, it is today.

COMMENTARY

First Reading: Prov 8:22-31
Second Reading: Rom 5:1-5
Gospel: Jn 16:12-15

The Christian belief about God is an all-embracing confession whose ramifications only emerged over many centuries in the life of the church as it recalled, prayed, celebrated, reflected, taught new generations, and saw-off various false prophets. This is the phenomenon of the development of doctrine by which the understanding that exists within the tradition (i.e. the living mind of the church as it believes now and teaches, while looking back through its life right to the time when the documents such as today's readings were written) is always greater than any particular moment or text. Thus what we believe is not 'based' upon a collection of texts, rather each text is a testimony (to a greater or lesser extent) to the faith of the church which is a whole, a unity. Given this, if one wanted to read our trinitarian faith into these readings we would destroy their integrity as texts; while to read them as if they 'justified trinitarianism' or 'supported' it, would be to deny the integrity of the tradition of which texts are only particular expressions. Moreover, the latter approach would be theologically perverse as it would imply a fundamentalism that 'everything is in The Bible', and that that book is the revelation.

This means that for this Sunday the usual skills of the exegete are of little value, and so to offer here a commentary on these texts would be inappropriate. It might be objected that the texts have a meaning apart from this feast and this could be commented upon. Yes, but such a commentary would exist in the abstract, while the texts are being read in a specific liturgical context: the recollection of our faith as seen within the fullness of the tradition.

First Reading > Gospel Links
Two readings without any intrinsic connection as readings. They are linked within a larger theological framework where they are assumed to be wholly consistent.

HOMILY NOTES

1. There is almost a tradition of beginning homilies today with: 'this is the most difficult sermon of the whole year', or 'this is a mystery and I was never good at dogma in the seminary', or some such deprecating remark which is ostensibly intended to emphasise that God is mystery, and defensively that actually speaking of 'things divine' is more demanding than commenting on the practical implications of belief. However, what is actually communicated is that what follows is really rather irrelevant and that you are only going through with the homily because it's your job. In that case, no matter what you say, the congregation have switched off. Every teacher knows that if you tell a class that the next topic is awfully hard to understand, it is a self-fulfilling prophesy; equally, if you tell the assembly that this is all very complicated, then they will decide that it is probably something they can live without – as they have successfully done until now. In any case, what it required is not a mini-version of Augustine's *De Trinitate*, but a recollection that to believe as we do, is to believe that in Christ we are caught up into the life of God, he shows us the Father, and sends the Spirit to dwell with us. Your task is not a lecture in dogma (so avoid 'arithmetical theology' such as '1 God, 2 processions, 3 Persons, 4 relations, 5 notions'), but to bear witness in the assembly to what we believe to be the basic dynamic of life revealed in Christ.

2. One useful way to raise awareness of that dynamic is to draw

people's attention to the basic structures of the prayers we use in the liturgy.

3. But, first, it is useful to recall what we do not believe. We do not address a 'God' as if it is 'us' and 'him over there', as if our prayers were like letters to a distant ruler. That is a model of the God-humanity relationship that belongs to many religions (indeed it is a constant distraction for us too), but it does not reflect our basic confession. To talk of God as the 'wholly other' is to forget that Jesus Christ, the Son, wholly God, is wholly one with us.

4. We believe that we were brought into the life of God by Christ, when we were baptised into him. The Son reveals that he is distinct from the Father, he comes from the Father, he returns to the Father. The Son gathers us and the whole creation into his kingdom which he presents to the Father. The Son sends us the Spirit, the Spirit enables us to grow 'in Christ' and to call the Father, our Father. We see this in the opening prayer today: 'Father, you sent your Word ... and your Spirit ... through them we come to know the mystery of your life.' This pattern of 'from the Father', 'through the Son', 'in the Spirit', and 'to the Father' can be found in virtually every prayer in the liturgy. A slightly larger example would be Eucharistic Prayer II. We address the Father throughout the prayer, who as the fountain of holiness sends us the Spirit. The Spirit enables us to remember Christ. Then we actually remember Christ and his thanksgiving/offering (the institution narrative) which he made to the Father. Through the Son we stand in the Father's presence and serve him, and ask him that as we 'share in the body and blood of Christ' we might 'be brought together in unity by the Holy Spirit'.

5. To be baptised and to believe means that we enter into the trinitarian life of God, we profess this when we recite the creed. But the creed in its reciting form is derivative of the three-fold, question-and-answer form of baptism. This trinitarian aspect can be brought out more effectively today by replacing the recited creed with a renewal of baptismal promises as on Easter Day (Missal, p 220).

The Body and Blood of Christ
(Corpus Christi)

Introduction to the Celebration

Since the very first days of the church – before St Paul had set out on his journeys or any of the gospels were written – our brothers and sisters have been gathering every week for this sacred meal. But when we routinely do anything, we often lose sight of just how wonderful it is. So today we are reflecting on just how wonderful it is to be called by the Lord to gather in his presence, to be his guests at his table, and to eat and drink from his wonderful bounty. In this banquet we become one with Christ, and are transformed into being his Body, and his Blood flows in all our veins giving us the strength to be his witnesses in the world and the life that never ends.

Rite of Penance

Option C vi (Missal, p 394).

Headings for Readings

First Reading

We see in the bread and wine offered by the priest Melchizedek the foreshadowing of Christ's perfect offering.

Second Reading

At the heart of belonging to the Christian community is gathering to break the loaf and drink the cup – this is what Paul was taught, this is what he in turn handed on, and so it has continued down to our gathering here today.

Sequence

The *Lauda Zion* (optional) is a theological gem; but see the notes section below.

Gospel
Christ gathers his people around him, and feeds them.

Prayer of the Faithful
President
We have gathered for the Lord's banquet. Now as his priestly people let us present our needs to the Father.
Reader(s)
1. For ourselves gathered at this holy meal. Lord hear us.
2. For friends absent from this meal. Lord hear us.
3. For all Christians, may we be united around the Lord's table. Lord hear us.
4. For all who are hungry. Lord hear us.
5. For all who are excluded from the world's riches. Lord hear us.
6. For the dead, that they may share the banquet whose foretaste we now celebrate. Lord hear us.
President
Father, in this holy meal we encounter your Son and recall his passion. Fill us with your grace, and grant our needs through that same Christ, our Lord. Amen.

Eucharistic Prayer
Preface of the Holy Eucharist II (P48) has a narrative quality that makes it more accessible than P47; moreover, the emphasis of P48 is more on the actual celebration than P47 and therefore is more suitable for today. Eucharistic Prayer I should be used as it picks up the link to Melchizedek in the first reading.

The Our Father
Gathered as the body of Christ around this table, let us pray to our common Father, Our Father ...

Sign of Peace
In Christ we are united into his body around this table; disharmony and strife have no place here. Let us show this now to one another.

Invitation to Communion
We are his people when we recognise him in this, the breaking of the loaf. Happy are we who are called to this supper.

Communion Reflection
They knew it was the Lord, Alleluia,
In the breaking up of the loaf, Alleluia.
The loaf we break is the body of Jesus Christ, our Lord, Alleluia,
The cup we bless is the blood of Jesus Christ, our Lord, Alleluia,
For the remission of sins, Alleluia.
Lord, let your mercy rest upon us, Alleluia,
Who put all our confidence in you, Alleluia.
They knew it was the Lord, Alleluia,
In the breaking of the loaf, Alleluia.

O Lord, we believe that in this breaking of your body and pouring out of your blood we become your redeemed people;
We confess that in taking the gifts of this pledge here, we lay hold in hope of enjoying its true fruits in the heavenly places.
(From an early medieval hymn for during the fraction, found in an eighth-century Mass book from Ireland)

Conclusion
Prayer over the People 18 (Missal, p 382) is suitable.

Notes
1. The focus of this feast
This used to be one of the most colourful days of the year, its focal point being the great procession. Its emphasis was the divine presence in the Blessed Sacrament: a King entitled to public acknowledgement and adoration. The Mass became a thanksgiving for the Blessed Sacrament: the Mass was a doing (the 'sacrifice') and the 'sacrament' was the precious possession which we were so glad to have. While this emphasis, and the attendant confusing theology, have been abandoned, it tends to resurface today where the Blessed Sacrament is approached as if it were a primary part of Christ's gift to the church, rather than as the se-

quel to our encounter with him in the actual banquet in which we break the one loaf and share the one cup.

Our focus today should be to hold a mirror up to our weekly assembly: a day of reflection on why we gather for the Eucharistic Meal each week, and our aim must be that we depart from this assembly with an enriched awareness of the significance of encountering the body of Christ in the assembled community, in the shared memory, and in the loaf and cup.

It is worth noting that this feast is, since 1970, *Corpus et Sanguis Christi*. This change in name is significant as our gaze has shifted from the monstrance as the key image of this day, to the table prepared for us around which we gather.

2. The sequence

This worked well when sung in Latin, simply read in English it sounds pathetic. Moreover, since people are not expecting it, they do not know whether to listen seated or standing, or whether to join in or not. Its value is that it marks out this day as special. If done with clear directions ('Let us stand for the sequence') and read by a small group (three/four female voices) in the manner of a Greek chorus, it can be an excellent item in the liturgy. If simply 'read' by the reader, it is just noise adding another brick to the wall of words that separate people from a sense of participation. This is an optional item and so it is a place where the musicians and readers can express their artistic creativity.

COMMENTARY

First Reading: Gen 14:18-20

This text, of obscure origin, serves to identify Jerusalem as a place of sacrifice throughout the whole history of the people. The figure of Melchizedek is that of an ideal king-priest, which from the outset Christians were using as a type for their understanding of Christ as the great High Priest (cf Heb 5:6-10; 6:20; 7:1-11).

Second Reading: 1 Cor 11:23-26

The appropriate celebration of the Eucharist was one of Paul's concerns for the community at Corinth. Along with the *Didache*, this is our earliest reference to the Eucharist; and it reminds us that the keryma, which would later be fixed in our written gospels, was originally repeated at these assemblies – the celebrating of Eucharist is a primary Christian reality, the texts are secondary.

First Reading > Gospel Links

There is no link between the two readings; rather the first reading is linked to today's feast. This link is both one of 'prophecy-fulfillment' and of 'antetype and reality'. Melchizedek is a type of priest-king who offers thanks in bread and wine. This action is remembered not in its own setting in Genesis, but as foreshadowing another act in the time of the Christ (prophecy-fulfillment) and then that later act is more fully understood (i.e. it is by Jesus who is a priest-king) by looking back at who/what Melchizedek was (antetype-reality). This use of Gen 14 today is consistent with the use of the passage in early Christianity (e.g. its use in Heb 7) and has been a constant theme in the Latin liturgy (see Eucharistic Prayer I).

The gospel adopted a completely different approach to the feast to that of the first reading.

Gospel: Lk 9:11-17

From the beginning the Eucharist was understood within the pattern of Christ's meals/feedings, so already when this story was incorporated by Luke into his text, it had Eucharistic significance: his meal is one of miraculous abundance for all.

HOMILY NOTES

1. The whole point of today is to cause us to reflect that we encounter the mystery of Christ in events which belong simultaneously to this world and to the world to come. As Jesus Christ is the sacrament between the mystery of God and our

humanity, so he has left us the sacraments, above all this meal, as the means by which we encounter, here and now, the future banquet of heaven. The Eucharist is the 'mystical meal' (the language of the eastern churches), and the *sacrum convivium ... pignus futurae gloriae* (Aquinas). Thus sacraments are something that are best understood through experiencing them, rather than hearing lectures upon them. So rather than try to deepen some mental awareness about the Eucharist with a homily, enhance the actual quality of the celebration. Here is an action plan:

2. (Step A) If you live in an area where drinking from the cup is not standard (e.g. Ireland), then introduce it today. (Step B) If you live where communion 'under both species' is normal (most English-speaking countries) then procure some of the very large breads that allow for a genuine fraction. The key to the symbolism of the Eucharistic meal is not bread as a generic substance, but a single loaf of bread. This has simultaneously the notion of scattered grains gathered into a unity – one loaf – and the notion of each person having a share (literally: participating) in that loaf which is Christ. (Step C) If you are actually doing in the liturgy what we say we do (breaking the loaf, drinking the cup) then arrange for the congregation to stand around the table, become actual *circumstantes*, for the Liturgy of the Eucharist. The normal arrangement is that of a sanctuary which is akin to the teacher's part of the classroom or the stage in a theatre, and those in the audience / class area watch on and answer invitations to speak. Yet we are always talking about being 'gathered around the Lord's table' – so give people the actual liturgical experience.

3. The experience of the liturgy should act as a pointer, through faith, from what happens here to another reality. When the liturgy is celebrated in a minimalist, token fashion it is its own undoing. Then what actually happens (you go into a pew, listen to words, see the altar up there, walk up to communion, taste a little round pre-cut wafer that does not seem like bread, and then move off) must first point to what

should happen here (look at the liturgy's formulae), before it can point beyond this dimension to the mystery. When your liturgy demands this double pointing (we got away with it pre-1965 in Latin for the linguistic inaccessibility was a mystical screen, an *iconostastis*, which made just being there enough), it sends out a signal that it is just a ritual of words. And when the Eucharist appears to be just that, then people vote with the feet – and they are doing so!

Eighth Sunday of Ordinary Time

Introduction to the Celebration

We are the people of the resurrection: we proclaim to the world the good news that Jesus has conquered evil, sin, and death; and we gather here each Sunday to celebrate that resurrection and encounter the risen Jesus in our fellowship around his table. But if we are to proclaim this new life, then we need to become a people who have sought to overcome our shortcomings, who have asked pardon for our sins and failings, and who are modeling our own lives on Christ. If we are to show a new life to others, we must be living it ourselves.

Rite of Penance

O Lord and teacher, for the times we have gone astray and have been blind guides to others. Lord have mercy.

O Lord and teacher, for the times we have seen the speck that is in our sister's or brother's eye, but not noticed the log that is in our own eye. Christ have mercy.

O Lord and teacher, for the times our hearts and mouths have produced evil. Lord have mercy.

Headings for Readings

First Reading

The wise person does not judge by the outside but tests the true quality of people by judging their words over time and noting what is good and abiding and what is not. This wise person is a model for the well-trained disciple.

Second Reading

We are the people who believe in a new life that cannot be destroyed by death. This is why we are a people of hope and a people who challenge the ways of death and despair when we meet them.

Gospel

We are called to become fully trained disciples: then if we have a good heart with a store of goodness, we will produce goodness; but if not we may be hypocrites who lead others astray and produce wickedness.

Prayer of the Faithful
President

We must become fully trained disciples of our teacher, and one of those practices which we must be skilled in is praying as a group for our needs, the needs of all our Christian sisters and brothers, and all humanity. So now let us pray together as disciples in union with our master.

Reader(s)

1. For the whole People of God, that we may grow as disciples and witness to the Way of the Lord. Lord hear us.

2. For the People of God who form this church, that we may have the generosity of spirit, of our time, and of our material resources to become fully trained disciples. Lord hear us.

3. For all those sisters and brothers the Lord has called to a ministry of training disciples, that they may have the wisdom this task demands. Lord hear us.

4. For all who work in the ministry of teaching, both those who are Christians and those who are not, that they may be guided by the truth. Lord hear us.

5. *Specific local needs and topics of the day.*

6. For all those disciples who have followed the Way of the Lord in this life and have died, that they may rejoice in the fullness of Christ's life. Lord hear us.

President

Father, your Son is our Way to you. Hear the prayers we put before you in communion with him who is our way, our truth, and our life. Amen.

Eucharistic Prayer

Preface of Sundays in Ordinary Time I (P29) emphasises the

notion of us being a people who have been specifically called by God. Any of the first three Eucharistic Prayers fits the theme.

Invitation to the Our Father
The well-trained disciples are those who have learned from the Son the importance of regular prayer together to the Father. As such, let us say:

Sign of Peace
As disciples we are called to live in communion with one another; let us express now that communion to one another.

Invitation to Communion
The first disciples learned the way of new life from Jesus, gathered about him at table; now we are his disciples around this table; happy are we to be gathered here.

Communion Reflection
We have put on Christ.
We have drawn strength from the Bread of Life.
We have drawn joy from the Cup of Salvation.

We have put imperishability upon our perishable nature.
We have put on immortality upon our mortal nature.
We have joined our Lord in his victory over death.

We have shared in the meal of discipleship.
We have entered the company of the saints.
We have joined the fellowship of the Lord.

Conclusion
May the God of all wisdom grant you the sight to see the way that leads to a world of justice, love, and peace.
May the God of all mercy grant you generosity to grow to be fully trained disciples following the path of the Christ.
May the God of all goodness grant that each day of the coming week you may bring forth good from the store of goodness in your heart.
May almighty God bless you …

Notes

The theme of discipleship runs through today and, in particular, the notion that discipleship requires decision and action. The disciples are apprentices: people engaged in active learning, developing skills, getting ready to play an ever-increasing role. This is very different from the very passive images that accompany the notion of discipleship when it is thought of as 'followers': 'followers' conjurers up images of being passive, waiting for decisions to be given them, rather than decisive people who work at their tasks independently. So this could be a good day for the various groups within the community that help to form disciples into greater awareness or more specific forms of ministry 'to display their wares' before the rest of the community.

COMMENTARY

First Reading: Sir 27:4-7 (The 1981 printing uses the out-dated Latinate form 'Ecclesiasticus')

This is a snippet out of a much longer selection of words for the wise on how to act with wisdom and not be a fool. People are found out to be good or bad when they are put in trying situation or when they are tested: the very language we use in English ('trying,' 'testing') shows how we still know this to be wisdom. This reading is a complement to the gospel, for Jesus saw himself in succession to many strands within the tradition of Israel and one of these is the tradition of the wise teacher – a tradition in which Jesus the Son of Sirach also saw himself.

Second Reading: 1 Cor 15:54-58

This is the concluding blast of encouragement to the Corinthians: resurrection is the destiny of the Christians, so be steadfast. What is the basis of this final hope? Jesus has conquered death. The imagery is that of putting on a garment where that is the symbolic expression of taking on a new task or beginning a new life. This is imagery that we do not often use in our society – though there are still vestiges of it in graduations and coronations – but which we still widely use in the liturgy: the white garment at baptism, vestments at ordinations, habits at professions. But to put on a garment in these symbolic systems is not to take on something that is extrinsic to us (e.g. the newly baptised putting on the white garment is not simply 'suiting up' for a job or function), but actually becoming that new reality: to put on immortality is to become immortal in nature, to put on Christ is to become one being with Christ, it is to exist in Christ. Paul uses language that is rooted in human ritual – every non-modern western culture uses putting on as a means of becoming other than what the person was formerly – and in the liturgical traditions of Israel (e.g. the vestments of the High Priest), but which for many people today (for whom symbols are merely tokens or 'pointers') does not constitute a potent means of understanding.

First Reading > Gospel Links
Both readings are in the single continuum that is the wisdom tradition. Both are about forming a righteous God-fearing man who produces good. In both there is the assumption that this is the result of a process of formation, and both use the notion of the tree being known by its fruit. The actions of a man reveal his inner moral disposition.

Gospel: Lk 6:39-45
This is a selection of statements on judging and on the test of goodness that come from Luke's 'Sermon on the Plain' (Lk 6:20-49). The material that goes to make up this collection of 'sayings' (cf Lk 7:1) can almost all be found somewhere in Matthew, and because of this it is usually said to come from that early collection of sayings that was widely used in the early church to which we give the name 'Q'. While the exact nature of Q is a source of endless fascination for academics, it is important not to forget the basic lessons we should draw from the fact that there was such a collection. First, the actual snippets of teaching that Jesus gave at various times to his disciples were treasured by the community, and repeated within the preaching as his basic

teaching. Second, these pieces of wisdom, what we could look on as 'long sound-bites', were gathered up in some manner in a collection of sayings that was the equivalent of a modern collection of filing cards: each a distinct unit of teaching (we see this in the various ways that they have been used by Matthew and Luke), and the whole collection constituted the wisdom of the Christians: their distinctive glimpses on how we relate to God, what life was about, and how we should live and act. Third, this collection of materials formed the basis out of which the preachers formed their larger stories that located and explained that teaching within the larger context of who Jesus was and is, and how he related to the tradition of Israel. We have in common use two of those preachers' uses of the material: Matthew and Luke. Fourth, when we read Matthew or Luke we are getting their distinctive 'slant'/'take'/'spin' on how these teachings of Jesus should be understood and should form the basic story of the church – it is this individual use of these common materials within the tradition of the whole church that constitutes their individual theologies, just as mine or your re-use of the material today constitutes our distinctive theologies.

So the task is to take the three items in this passage and see how they present a composite picture of Christian action.

1. The parable of the blind leader: vv 39-40.
2. Fix yourself before criticising others: vv 41-42.
3. The test of goodness: vv 43-46.

Taken together they form a picture of the fully taught disciple: well trained, not a hypocrite, and a source of goodness. But each, singly, is a piece of wisdom that can be applied over and over again in the transactions of our lives. These statements constitute a reservoir of practical Christian wisdom.

HOMILY NOTES

1. The word 'disciple' (as we commonly use it) can be a very slippery word. We are apt to make it simply the equivalent of 'follower' and then we can think of the followers of a sport or

of a football team. A follower might be very intense, even obsessive, in her or his following, or might be someone who just drifts along with interest in someone, some group or some idea: it is really up to you and your level of interest in what you are following. Another word likened to disciple/follower is 'devotee': this is someone who is very interested in someone or something, but there is the element of fun or hobby about it. The devotees are 'into' something because it is of interest and amazement – or simply amusement – to them.

2. Discipleship must involve something sterner: disciples have had to speak up for the poor, the oppressed, they have been persecuted for their claims about the name of God, they have had to speak up for peace and justice and, more recently, a responsible attitude to the material creation. So getting a better grasp of what it means to be 'a disciple of Jesus' is important, because it is a lot more than just being a religious groupie.

3. Today's gospel has an important clue: it talks about a teacher and a fully trained disciple. Training, the sort of thing that goes on in a class with an outcome, seems far removed from the happy, indulgent world of religious ideas. One would want one's house wired by a 'fully trained electrician' not by someone who liked fiddling with bits of wire and screwdrivers, but surely religion is all about feelings and emotions and does not require training! Likewise we all want fully trained physicians to treat us when we are sick and even the hint of lack of training swiftly brings a law suit, but do we have to take following the Lord that seriously?

4. It worth noting that the word we use for disciple (*mathétés*) is sometimes translated as 'student', and our word 'discipline' comes from the attitude that disciples are to adopt to the skills they are seeking to acquire. Probably the best word we have today for a *mathétés* today is 'apprentice'. The apprentice is expected to be with the master, know the solutions that the teacher knows, and then eventually to be able to operate on her/his own, and indeed impart the skills to another ap-

prentice. While our word 'follower' can often point to someone who is passive and who follows the crowd, the notion of
an apprentice is active; the apprentice is expected to be un-
dergoing training and acquiring skills. While our word 'disciple' has pious overtones and indicates my doing 'my sort of
thing', we think of an apprentice as becoming proficient in an
objective skills-set that are useful not only to the apprentice
but to those who meet the apprentice.

5. So if we think of following Jesus as entering an apprenticeship, what sort of skills should we be picking up, and what
   training regime should we expect?

6. The first Christians did think of the process of becoming a
   Christian to be that of an apprenticeship, and even had little
   booklets on the process that contained mnemonics (the
   Christian equivalent of '30 days hath September') that could
   be learned off by heart. Here are few key elements:

• They had to learn to pray as part of the group and to pray
  regularly each day. The prayer they had to learn by heart was
  the Our Father and they said it three times daily: dawn, mid-
  day, evening. They thought of themselves as a single people
  all praying together when they prayed at the same time; that
  is why the prayer contains only plurals: 'forgive us our trespasses' even if in our individualistic society we imagine it is
  'forgive me my trespasses'.

• They had to learn self-denial and care for the poor. This was
  fostered by the community fasting twice a week on
  Wednesdays and Fridays.

• They had to think of themselves as past of a community gathered at table thanking the Father once a week: the origins of
  what we call 'Sunday Mass'.

• They had to learn a style of life that led to risen life, and learn
  to reject a style of life that was seen as leading to death.

• They had to listen to the memory of the community because
  through that they heard the words of the Christ.

7. The gospel reminds us that we are called to become 'fully
   trained apprentices'. The tradition of our community is full

of wisdom on how we can become trained. Jesus reminds us that 'the good person draws what is good from the store of goodness that is in his heart,' but to start as an apprentice is a serious decision.

Ninth Sunday of Ordinary Time

Introduction to the Celebration

Today we recall that when we address Jesus as 'the saviour' we are actually addressing him as 'the giver of healing'. He is the One promised who would come among a people in need of healing and wholeness and bring health. We see this today in the story of the miraculous healing of the centurion's servant when he came and asked Jesus for his help. Let us now reflect on our own need for healing and forgiveness.

Rite of Penance

Lord Jesus you answered the call to come to the centurion's servant in his need. Lord have mercy.

Lord Jesus you praised the faith of the humble centurion who recognised the power of your word. Christ have mercy.

Lord Jesus you restored the sick servant to perfect heath. Lord have mercy.

Headings for Readings

First Reading

Solomon prays before God asking that God will hear the cries of every human being – from whatever background – who calls out for help in distress.

Second Reading

Paul begins his letter to the Christians in Galatia by reminding them how they have fallen away from the manner of behaviour that should characterise the community of Christ by listening to those who sow dissention in the community.

Gospel

The centurion is not one of the people of Israel, but God's mercy and healing extend to all who call on him in faith.

Prayer of the Faithful
President

As a community we have a duty to pray for the sick and to care for them, so now let us make our prayers known in the presence of the Father from whom all healing comes.

Reader(s)

1. For all who are sick in our community, that they may healed. Lord hear us.

2. For all who are in distress of body, mind or spirit, that they might receive wholeness. Lord hear us.

3. For ourselves, that we will become a more caring community who are increasingly aware of the Lord's call that we help all who are sick. Lord hear us.

4. For all health care workers, that the Lord will give them his strength and joy. Lord hear us.

5. For all engaged in medicine and medical research, that God will grant them the understanding they need to use their talents with wisdom. Lord hear us.

6. For all humanity, that we might grow in respect for the wholeness of human beings. Lord hear us.

7. For all who have died, that they may be brought by Christ to the wholeness of the resurrection. Lord hear us.

President

Father, you sent your Son among us to bring us healing and give us the fullness of life. Hear our prayer for ourselves, our sick brothers and sisters, those who care for them, and for the healing of the whole human family, and grant what we ask in Christ Jesus, our Lord. Amen.

Eucharistic Prayer

One option today is to use the Preface from the Rite of Anointing within Mass, *Pastoral Care of the Sick*, pp 114-5. Then use the special additions given there with either Eucharistic Prayer I or II or III. Thus the theme of healing found in the Liturgy of the Word can be repeated in the Liturgy of the Eucharist.

Invitation to the Our Father
Gathered in Christ our source of healing, let us pray to the Father:

Sign of Peace
The Lord's gift to us is reconciliation and healing. Let us show our willingness to be reconciled and to promote healing and wholeness in this community by offering peace to each other.

Invitation to Communion
Behold the Lord has come among us. Let us join in the words of the centurion: Lord I am not worthy ...

Communion Reflection
If you have focused on healing in today's liturgy, then one way of linking this celebration of the Eucharist to the on-going care of the sick in the community is to now bless some oil to be used with the sick during the coming days. This is a ritual that is virtually invisible to most people (unless they are recipients of anointing) and so is very prone to false understandings. The nature of the prayer of blessing makes it suitable for the time of thanksgiving after communion. Use a glass container with an amount of oil that makes the blessing visible to the community. The formula can be found in *Pastoral Care of the Sick*, p 109 (formula A is better in this context).

The act of consecration can be introduced with words like: 'During the coming weeks I shall have to anoint many of our sisters and brothers with oil in the name of the Lord. I want now to bless this oil in the midst of the whole community so that it can carry our prayers as a community to each sick person.'

Conclusion
Use Blessing B from Rite of Anointing within Mass, *Pastoral Care of the Sick*, pp 117-8.

Notes

The Sacrament of the Sick is one of the 'Cinderella sacraments': normally hidden and then, when seen, misunderstood. Today is an opportunity to help promote not only a deeper understanding, but to let people see that the care of the sick is an aspect of the life of the community and not just of the priest who 'administers' the sacrament.

COMMENTARY

First Reading: 1 Kgs 8:41-43 (This is a faulty citation in the Lectionary: it should be 1 Kgs 8:22, 41-43.)

As this reading is found in the Jerusalem Bible Lectionary it is incomprehensible not just because of colloquial translation but also on account of faulty punctuation. The lection's core is 8:31-43 which is part of the final section of Solomon's prayer at the dedication of the temple in Jerusalem, but the lection is opened by the preamble to the prayer: 1 Kgs 8:22.

So the scene is this. The temple is now finished and is being dedicated. Solomon, its builder, has entered it and as the Lord's anointed he intercedes for the building that it might be the place where God – whose real dwelling is in heaven – might be able to hear him (8:23-29), his people (8:30-40), and even able to hear those who come from foreign parts as they know that here is the Lord's temple (8:41-51). It is part of this prayer that we read today, and its purpose is to show that the Old Testament 'christ' (the king) would intercede for those who came from afar seeking the Lord's aid, so how much more will the last Christ intercede in the very presence of the Father.

The phrase 'hear from heaven where your home is …' is meaningless. Either read the entire text from the Revised Standard Version, or replace the phrase with 'hear his prayer in your heavenly dwelling place … '

Second Reading: Gal 1:1-2, 6-10

Paul's rationale for his letter to the Galatians is that they have gone so quickly off-message. However, given the importance of the letter's teachings on so many aspects of Christian belief and practice, perhaps we should be grateful they needed this letter.

First Reading > Gospel Links
The link is that of a consistent idea expressed in both testaments: there is a place for the foreigner in the plan of God. The New is in continuity with the Old.

Gospel: Lk 7:1-10
This is Luke's variant on a healing miracle also found in Matthew (8:5-13). The major difference is that while in Matthew the centurion himself comes up to Jesus, here is the model of the humble God-fearer from the nations who approaches through the appropriate intermediaries: the elders (*presbuteroi*) of the community. This fits Luke's scheme for the good news being able to reach out to all nations but beginning with Israel. The notion of the *presbuteroi* of the community interceding with the Lord for healing would have had resonances in the early Christian community – as we know from the Epistle of James – of their own practice with regard to prayer for the sick.

HOMILY NOTES

1. Today's gospel brings before us the whole realm of healing.
2. In the modern industrial world this is often seen simply as the domain of technology. Being well, staying well, and getting repaired when something has gone wrong is a matter of having the right physical regime, the correct skill set in the form of therapists and technically skilled experts, and the appropriate resources and machinery. Health is big business and is the great triumph of our science-based knowledge. This skill base should not be scoffed at: imagine the pain of an ulcer before modern drugs; imagine the agony of other conditions before modern surgery. Medical skill is a tribute to our God-given human genius; and let us thank God and praise God that we now have these skills.
3. However, technology can all too easily be seen as self-suffi-

cient. When that happens the spiritual side of our humanity becomes simply 'the bit left over' when the 'real work' of healing and health care are finished. We see this whenever we hear a phrase like: 'The doctors have done all they can, so they sent for the priest to give the last rites.' Built into that statement is a subtle atheism: healing is really a material process, but if it does not work, then you can try anything (religion and ritual included).

4. Yet, even health care workers acknowledge – sometimes grudgingly – that healing and health is something that involves the whole person and always has a spiritual (spiritual with a small 's') dimension. Humans are spiritual beings, not machines with souls, so when we are sick it is the whole person that is ill; and we know that when the person is ill, often the body is sick or prone to sickness.

5. We Christians have a very distinctive view of health and wholeness and sickness and healing. We view the universe as a fundamentally friendly place that was made by God in goodness, and that in God's plan health and wholeness have been there from the start. Equally, we believe that God loves the world and sent his Son among us as our saviour. And, the word 'saviour' and 'health-giver' are, for us, essentially the same word. Just look at the Latin word *salus*: it means 'health' in everyday speech, and only in theological jargon is that rendered 'salvation'. At the end of time, the Lord's Anointed will bring healing and wholeness to the whole creation. Jesus is, in the words of the prophet Malachi (4:2), 'the sun of righteousness' that rises over us 'with healing in its wings'.

6. We know that healing and wholeness are more all embracing than drugs or skills: it requires the grace of God, it requires a new vision of light and life, it requires the embrace of the community to show to the suffering individual that they are valued, and it requires reflection and prayer. Prayer, both that of the individual and of the community, makes plain our need for healing before God. Moreover, it acknowledges our

fundamental dependence on God: healing, no matter how skilled we are, will always be more than we can do for ourselves.

7. We believe that Jesus has come and brought healing among us: the miracle story today is a glimpse into the world that he promises us all. He brings wholeness, health, reconciliation, and has sent the Holy Spirit to give strength to us in our weakness. This is why we pray for our own inner healing at every gathering for the Eucharist. This is why we recall the sick at our gatherings. This is why we share our Eucharist each Sunday with the sick and housebound by sending them a share in our sacred loaf.

8. This is why we have the Sacrament of the Sick – it is not 'last rites' nor some sort of magic for when 'all else has failed' – but is rooted in our believe as a community that we are all somehow ill when one is sick, and that all in the community have a role in bringing healing to each. Hence, the early Christian practice of sending for the presbyters when one member is sick, anointing the person with oil in the Lord's name and praying for healing and forgiveness.

9. In a world where the human is often threatened by technology, where the sick cry out, and where there is a constant need for the restoration of wholeness, we are a people with a message of good news, and we catch sight of this in today's miracle account.

Tenth Sunday of Ordinary Time

Introduction to the Celebration

We look to Jesus as the Lord: he is the Son of the Father, the conqueror of death, who has visited us from on high to redeem us. In today's gospel we see this in his raising a young man from the dead in Nain. We recall this incident from our memory of Jesus not because we expect miracles to happen like this every day, but because they remind us that the life Jesus gives us is not bounded by death. He gives us a new way of living in this world and the promise of the fullness of life with the Father in the world to come.

Rite of Penance

O Great Prophet, may we encounter you in our needs. Lord have mercy.

O Great Prophet, may we hear your words: 'Do not cry!' Christ have mercy.

O Great Prophet, may we hear your command to rise on the last day. Lord have mercy.

Headings for Readings
First Reading

In this reading we hear the story of God's prophet Elijah who takes pity on a widow whose son has died and who asks God to restore the boy to life.

Second Reading

Nowhere else in his letters does St Paul tell us as much about himself as here: what we are going to read can be seen as his attempt at autobiography.

Gospel

In this reading we hear the story of God's prophet Jesus who takes pity on a widow whose son has died and who himself restores the boy to life.

Prayer of the Faithful

President

We are here today because we believe that in Jesus's coming God has visited his people: Jesus our Great Prophet is among us. Now in union with the Son let us make our needs known to the Father.

Reader (s)

1. That all may know the Great Prophet through the witness we bear to him in our lives. Lord in your mercy, hear our prayer.

2. That we may grow in our awareness of the presence of Jesus Christ among us making us God's people. Lord in your mercy, hear our prayer.

3. That all who mourn may know the comfort of God's presence in the midst of human sadness. Lord in your mercy, hear our prayer.

4. That all who despair may gain new courage from our good news of Christ's victory over death. Lord in your mercy, hear our prayer.

5. *Specific local needs and topics of the day.*

6. That all who have died may hear the call to arise to the new life of the kingdom. Lord in your mercy, hear our prayer.

President

Father, you have sent your Son among us to be our Great Prophet bearing witness to you and our Great Priest presenting our prayer to you. Hear your disciples now for we make these prayers through Jesus our Lord. Amen.

Eucharistic Prayer

The Preface from the Rite of Anointing the Sick within Mass – along with the inserts for Eucharistic Prayers I, II, and III (*Pastoral Care of the Sick*, pp 114-5) are very suitable today to express our faith in Jesus who brings healing and joy to the sorrowful. None of the Prefaces for Sundays in Ordinary Time pick up, in a specific way, the gospel's theme.

Invitation to the Our Father
We have been made a people of joy through our encounter with the Lord; now let us joyfully pray to the Father:

Sign of Peace
Jesus has brought us joy and healing, reconciliation and peace: let us express the joy and peace to one another.

Invitation to Communion
To all who encounter him, Jesus comes with healing and new life; happy are we who are called to his supper.

Communion Reflection
Lord Jesus, you bring life in the midst of death.
Lord Jesus, you bring healing in the midst of sickness.
Lord Jesus, you bring joy in the midst of sorrow.

Lord Jesus, you give us the food of life.
Lord Jesus, you share with us the cup of salvation.
Lord Jesus, you invite us to the banquet of heaven. Amen.

Conclusion
Solemn Blessing for Ordinary Time IV (Missal, p 373) is suitable.

Notes
Nain or Naim?
If you look at the Lectionary, p lii you will see the gospel for this Sunday described as 'The Widow of Naim'; but when you read it (p 865) you see that 'Jesus went to a town called Nain.' The confusion arises because in the Latin (both in the Vulgate and the so-called Neo-vulgate), from which the introduction to the Lectionary is translated, this place is called Naim. But in Greek it is called Nain, and this is reflected in the modern place-name:

'Nein'. This form is then found in the body of the Lectionary where the translation is based on the original. How this blunder occurred in Latin is lost in the mists of time, but the form does persist in older Vulgate-inspired books. It is a pity it has been perpetuated in the Lectionary's introduction.

COMMENTARY

First Reading: 1 Kgs 17:17-24

This story is part of the Elijah cycle of miracles that simultaneously show the power of the prophet to have his prayers heard, and his own prowess as a holy man whose prayers the Lord heeds. This story was a part of the imagination of Luke's audiences and they would have grasped the contrast between Elijah and Jesus at once: Elijah was the prophet of mighty deeds, but these only occurred through his intercession; Jesus must be a still mightier prophet, and indeed a prophet who is one with God since he can simply command the dead and they obey him. Incidentally, these Elijah stories remained a common part of the western Christian imagination down to the time of the Reformation because these were the stockroom for the miracles of the saints retold in hagiography. While Luke knew his audience would be able to use this story to see how much greater Jesus was than Elijah, later Christian writers used it to show that the saints were as good as Elijah but only approaching Jesus by way of intercessory imitation.

Second Reading: Gal 1:11-19

This is not autobiography for its own sake, but this account of Paul's life is given to justify his claim to be an apostle (Gal 1:1) and so someone whom the Galatians should heed rather than abandoning his words in favour of another perverted gospel (Gal 1:6-7). His proof is not only the events of his life (who he met and where he went) but his conviction about the providence of God who was preparing him from the time he was in his mother's womb.

First Reading > Gospel Links

The relationship here is one of parallel narratives. Begin by noting the parallels: both stories are about resurrection, both have a central actor, both have the same supporting actors of a widow and her son. Now that we have noted the similarities, we see that what links them today is in how they contrast: Elijah acts on behalf of God, Jesus acts directly as God. Here we see a liturgical use of texts that is wholly consistent with Luke's own use of his scriptures in forming the story of the widow of Nain. This is a good example of the christocentric reading of the Old Testament that is such a feature of the Lectionary.

Gospel: Lk 7:11-17

This touching story of compassion for a widow who has lost her only son is found only in Luke. The miracle is not a demonstration of who he is or of miraculous powers as such: the divine power over life and death is only seen because it is called forth by human need. This is power as mercy, not power as might. The response is a series of confessions of faith: 'A great prophet has arisen among us' (see also Lk 1:76) and 'God has visited his people' (see also Lk 1:68). Taken together these statements are foundation stones of Luke's christology. This then becomes fully visible in 7:22 in the answer Jesus gives to John the Baptist's questions: the sick are healed, the deaf hear, the dead are raised up … These are the kinds of 'proof' – not acts of cosmic retribution – that Jesus offers that he is the one 'who is to come'. And in showing God's power in this way, and the kind of messiah that God has sent, Jesus is giving us a very different 'picture' of God to that which many were expecting (including John the Baptist himself). So this miracle is both a 'christology' – telling us about how we should view the Anointed One – and a 'theology' – telling us how we should view the relationship of God to the creation.

HOMILY NOTES

1. We can read the gospel today at two ways. First, we could
    read it as a miracle story and wonder whether we think it is
    likely that it could happen, or likely that it did happen. This
    is a concern of skeptics on the one hand who think all talk of
    miracles is bunkum; and the concern of fundamentalists on
    the other who want to be able to 'prove the bible is true' and
    wrap the whole thing up in a neat little box. These two
    groups may thoroughly dislike one another, but they share
    many assumptions, not least of which is that there is little
    room for mystery: that sense that the fullness of the truth is
    greater than the sum of the facts and bits and pieces that we
    know about. The second way of reading this gospel concen-
    trates on what it tells us of the style of an encounter with the
    Christ: the lives of a sorrowful people are enhanced. Sorrow
    becomes joy, death becomes life, mourning has become
    dancing.

2. It is always easy to divide people into two groups and then
    see an opposition between them (e.g. those who can do, do;
    those who can't, teach), but there are times when such group-
    ings correspond closely with our experience. We meet people
    who are life-enhancers (people who bring joy and ease to
    their surroundings, who will help, who will listen, who will
    share knowledge, burdens, and sufferings) and we meet life-
    diminishers (there is always a problem, they are always too
    busy with their own things to worry about others, and who
    when they leave after being with us we feel exhausted and
    'down'). Let us take that experience of these two types and
    ask this question: do we think of our encounter with God as
    one that is with a life-enhancer or a life-diminisher?

3. It is both easy and common to imagine God as the ultimate
    life-diminisher: the killjoy, the moral keeper of tabs, the
    wrathful raw power. God becomes a projection of the worst
    qualities of human power and must be appeased and served
    in the most servile manner. All powerful, but also small
    minded, keeping track of little regulations and just waiting to

pounce, and small-minded also in that if the rules are kept and the various 'security tests' passed, then we can escape!

4. But if a good person we meet is someone we would describe as a life-enhancer, then God who is goodness itself must be the ultimate life-enhancer! This we see, presented with gentleness and sympathy and compassion and mercy, in today's gospel. Jesus would not gives signs or miracle when he visited Nazareth, as his authority as the Son was not there for display of power. But he did show his authority over life and death in Nain where suffering called forth his mercy.

5. Many people say they find it hard to believe in miracles. OK. However, we are often so battered by human meanness and encounters with life-diminishers that we find it hard to believe that there is ultimately goodness in the universe and that the encounter with God is an encounter with life-enhancement. Believing this – what we call 'faith' – is often more difficult than whether or not we think miracles can occur. So today we are called to look upon Jesus and restore our faith in the loving goodness of God. The God who in love created us, in love sends us the Christ, and who desires us to enjoy his love.

Eleventh Sunday of Ordinary Time

Introduction to the Celebration

Today is one of the very few times in the year when the actions of women towards Jesus are at the centre of our recollection. We recall that Jesus was supported and helped by women in his work as he moved around Palestine. We also recall the incident when an unnamed woman anointed his feet with oil, kissed his feet, and wiped away her tears with her hair. Her sins were forgiven because she had shown such love.

Now we are gathered at table with the Lord, let us pray that our love will be such that our sins may be forgiven.

Rite of Penance

Jesus, our Lord, you accepted into your friendship all who came to you in love and who made you welcome at their table. Lord have mercy.

Jesus, our Prophet, you saw into the hearts of those who sat with you and of those who came near you. Christ have mercy.

Jesus, our Saviour, you forgave the sins of the woman who showed great love, and let her depart in peace. Lord have mercy.

Headings for Readings

First Reading

David repents of his sins, and because of this repentance he is forgiven.

Second Reading

The key to new life is to entrust our lives to Jesus, the Anointed One.

Gospel

In this gospel we hear about women that were close to Jesus: first, a woman who came to him while at supper and had her sins forgiven; then, about a group of women that travelled with him or provided back-up support for his mission.

Prayer of the Faithful
President
Sisters and brothers, as those who follow Jesus today, let us unite our voices with his and ask the Father for our needs.
Reader(s)
1. For the church, that there will always be many women and men to carry on the proclamation of the kingdom. Lord hear us.
2. For all who hear our proclamation, that the Spirit will dispose their minds and hearts to receive the Word of Life. Lord hear us.
3. For this church gathered here, that each of us will be empowered to be a witness to the gospel. Lord hear us.
4. For all Christians, that we will be moved by the Spirit to provide generously from our means to support the coming of the Kingdom. Lord hear us.
5. *Specific local needs and topics of the day.*
6. For all who have died and who in their time proclaimed the kingdom, that they may be welcomed into its fullness. Lord hear us.
President
Father, you sent your Son among us and have shared with us his ministry of proclaiming your kingdom. Hear us now and answer us for we pray in Christ Jesus, our Lord. Amen.

Eucharistic Prayer
Eucharistic Prayer for Masses of Reconciliation I fits nicely with the first part of today's gospel.

Invitation to the Our Father
Sisters and brothers, as those called to proclaim the kingdom, let us pray:

Sign of Peace
The Lord has brought forgiveness and peace to those who gather

for his supper; may we now rejoice in that acceptance by proclaiming it to one another.

Invitation to Communion
When the Lord sat at the Pharisee's table he brought forgiveness
to those who appealed to him. As we come to his table may we
too receive his love and mercy.

Communion Reflection
The hymn 'This day at thy creating Word' (Breviary, vol III,
[140]) can be read as a poem: it is a very elegant expression of the
theology of Sunday.

Conclusion
Prayer over the People, n 23 (Missal, p 383).

Notes
The gospel today presents the president with a difficult choice.
The lectionary's standard reading is Lk 7:36-8:3, with the option
of a Shorter Form: 7:36-50. The longer form is made up of two
distinct pericopes from Luke (and both are only found in his
gospel): the story of the Woman with the Ointment (7:36-50);
and then the narrator's comment about the women engaged in
ministering to Jesus (8:1-3). Normally the better course is just to
read one pericope and concentrate on it, and avoid introducing
extraneous materials; and this policy would argue here for using
the Shorter Form. However, if that course is taken, then the account of the ministering women is lost from liturgical reading
and from preaching; and these contain a memory of Jesus not
found elsewhere in the canonical gospels.

    In the past this would not have posed a problem for these
few verses were usually brushed over as of little significance.
Today, they provide a valuable insight into the place of women
in the ministry of Jesus and the early church, which can form
part of the 'hidden history' of women. One of the stock criti-
cisms of Christianity today is that it is not a woman-friendly reli-

gion; preaching on this text may help the assembly to see that the situation is not as black/white as either the critics of Christianity suppose, nor as clear-cut as those who hold that that the position of women in Christian ministry is definitively settled. Therefore, there are strong pastoral and apologetic reasons for using the standard form of the gospel. And in the homily notes, the concentration is upon the second of today's sections: 8:1-3.

COMMENTARY

First Reading: 2 Sam 12:7-10, 13

There seems to be some definite break in the sense when one comes to the end of this reading (a feeling of 'have I missed something?') for the last sentence does not follow from the previous four verses. The reason for this is that the crucial linking verses have been removed because they state that God will bring evil on the house of David as a punishment. Now the formulators of the lectionary were correct not to include such verses, but since it destroys the sense of the reading it would have been better if they had sought a completely different reading.

One cannot comment meaningfully on the reading as given. What we have is salacious details of David's greed and venality. Then a statement that the Lord forgives him which is taken by the liturgy as a slogan that, we are to assume, is intended in some way to prepare us for the gospel.

This is one of the days on which the lectionary really lets us down in its choice of first readings.

Second Reading: Gal 2:16, 19-21

This is a snippet out of the complex argument about righteousness and individual sins that is central to this letter. However, as excerpted here it is really little more than basic maxims about the life that is ours through commitment to Jesus.

First Reading > Gospel Links
The link is very tenuous. Both readings are interpreted as having a focus on repentance. If that is how you see them, then there is a continuity of theme: in every time there is need for repentance. The linking of First Reading > Gospel really has broken down in any meaningful way on this occasion.

Gospel: Lk 7:36-8:3
Two completely separate pieces of his narrative are placed one after another simply because the first story concerns Jesus and a woman, so that forms the cue to Luke to inform us of the women in the support group around Jesus.

The woman forgiven her sins brings out several Lukan themes: Jesus accepting a welcome to sit at table, his rejection of the notion that God's mercy is limited to the religiously observant and up-right, and that love is the centre of the law. It also provided Luke with an opportunity to show Jesus as a prophet and as one who can on his own authority forgive sins. Luke is here assembling a snapshot of who Jesus is seen to be in this instance: the Anointed One (i.e. the Christ), the Prophet, the Forgiver, the Saviour.

Traditionally, this woman who anoints his feet in this scene is identified with Mary Magdalen (hence 'maudlin' [using the Middle English pronunciation of 'Magdalene'] for a crying woman, and 'Magdalen Homes' for 'fallen women'). Not only is this identification (1) wholly unfounded; (2) a recollection of an attitude to women pursued in the name of the church that is a horrible blemish in our history; (3) but shows with what little care this gospel passage was read: it is essential to Luke's message that this woman is without a name for she is representing all humanity before the Christ – and an individual name would distract from that role. So make sure you do not refer to this woman as 'Mary Magdalen'.

By contrast with the anonymous woman of the first part, there are three women named as being part of the entourage or support network of Jesus. The named women were obviously well remembered in the early church. However, Mary from Magdala apart, who is remembered as a pastiche of several women in the gospels, neither Joanna nor Susanna passed into hagiographic memory while the work done by women that is recalled here by Luke was almost wholly forgotten.

HOMILY NOTES

1. How do you imagine Jesus moving around Palestine? It is usually an all male affair: Jesus in the lead, and twelve men following on behind. It is the same group that we think of around the table in the famous picture of the Last Supper by Leonardo da Vinci. Indeed, this is the way Jesus and his group have usually been painted: a group of twelve men around Jesus, and then that small group meet other people such as Pharisees, women, tax collectors, the crowds that came to listen, and then the occasional other named individual. Indeed, the group around Jesus is so small and so focused on the twelve that we call them in everyday speech, 'The Twelve Disciples' or 'The Twelve Apostles' or simply 'The Apostles' and mean by that name the twelve men that went about with Jesus.

2. When we read the gospels a little more carefully we see a much richer picture than that popular memory; and the end of today's gospel is one of those few times when we publicly read at the Eucharist one of those little details that can so alter how we imagine Jesus and his first followers.

3. Let us begin with noting the diversity of the women mentioned today. There is this woman called Mary from Magdala (traditionally she has been amalgamated with other women named 'Mary' and with a few un-named women also). She might be seen as a typical hanger on to a religious reformer as she has been cured by him. She is obviously travelling with Jesus, but there is no indication that she was one of those who could provide for the needs of the group. Then there are Joanna and Susanna who are clearly wealthy, and very independent minded women (e.g. we are told about

Joanna, but not what Chuza thought about Jesus), who were also influential in society. Then we are told that there were many other women, and that these women provided 'out of their own needs' for what was needed to support the group, Jesus and his followers, who were making their way around Palestine 'bringing the good news of the kingdom of God' to the towns and villages. In modern jargon it is these women – and their wealth and generosity – that are 'the grass-roots support' or 'the logistic support infrastructure' for the coming of the kingdom.

4. So how can we have a more adequate picture of Jesus with his first disciples? We could think of it as four concentric circles around Jesus. The largest group is made up of all those – women and men – who listen to him and accept his message that the kingdom of God is coming close to them. Then in the next circle there are those – women and men –– who are devoted to him. They provide the support structure that allows him and his followers to move about preaching. They must have provided support in many ways – shelter, food, hospitality, and also money. Many of the women mentioned in today's gospel belong to this circle. Then there is the circle made up of men and women who travelled around with Jesus. This group was not only his support team, but the community that encapsulated in its manner of living the new way of life that belongs to the New People of God. It is with this group we have to imagine Jesus sitting down each day at table and it is from this group that some were sent off preaching two by two. All the people – women and men – in the second and third circles are, as a group, named 'the disciples'; while those from this group who were sent off on missionary tasks were called the 'apostles'. Lastly, we come to the small inner circle of twelve men known simply as 'The Twelve'. This group was chosen by Jesus to be for the New People of God what the twelve sons of Jacob (i.e. the fathers of the tribes) were for the original People of God.

5. So we have (1) Jesus and (2) his symbolic group of 'The

Twelve,' then (3) we have 'The Disciples' that went around with him on his preaching mission: men and women whose number we do not know and only a couple of whose names we know, then (4) we have more 'Disciples' that enabled the preaching group to stay on the road; and then (5) those who accepted the news of the kingdom.

6. The whole picture – although it is far more complex – shows a marvellous array of ways of being at the service of the gospel. And, without those women who were fully part of the ministry of Jesus, the good news would not have been proclaimed.

7. We use phrases like 'the church founded on the apostles' and 'the apostolic church' and we think of twelve men; when we use such phrases we must include Mary from Magdala, Joanna the wife of Chuza, Susanna, and the many other women mentioned by Luke.

Twelfth Sunday of Ordinary Time

Introduction to the Celebration

We have gathered here as we call ourselves 'Christians' – literally 'followers of the Anointed One'. But what does it mean to follow the Anointed One of God? Today we get a stark answer to that question: 'If anyone wants to be a follower of mine, let him renounce himself and take up his cross every day and follow me.' Let us begin our assembly by reflecting on how well we follow him.

Rite of Penance

Lord Jesus, you are the Christ of God who has called us to be your disciples. Lord have mercy.

Lord Jesus, you are the Son of Man who suffered for our sins. Christ have mercy.

Lord Jesus, you are the Son of Man who rose on the third day to give us life. Lord have mercy.

Headings for Readings
First Reading

This is the prophecy that the Father will send a prophet to Israel who will suffer: they shall look on him whom they have pierced.

Second Reading

What is at the heart of our identity: race, colour, sex, social status, money? All these things distinguish people and discriminate between people. But we have been transformed by the Christ in baptism: we are a new people and such distinctions make no difference.

Gospel

We are the people who confess that Jesus is the Christ, the Son of the living God.

Prayer of the Faithful
President
Friends, because we confess that Jesus is the Christ of God we can now in union with him stand and ask the Father for our needs.
Reader(s)
1. For the whole of God's holy Church, that we may know the Christ in the depths of our minds, and hearts, and lives. Lord in your mercy, hear our prayer.
2. For the whole of God's holy Church, that we may have the courage to confess Jesus as the Christ to all humanity. Lord in your mercy, hear our prayer.
3. For the whole of God's holy Church, that we may change our lives to make ourselves ever more Christ-like. Lord in your mercy, hear our prayer.
4. For the whole of God's holy Church, that we may have the strength to take up our cross each day of our lives. Lord in your mercy, hear our prayer.
5. *Specific local needs and topics of the day.*
6. For the whole of God's holy Church, that all who have died confessing faith in Jesus the Christ may be united with him and all the saints. Lord in your mercy, hear our prayer.
President
Father, we are gathered here in Jesus, your Anointed One, and with him we ask for all our needs. Hear us, and help us through that same Anointed One, our Lord. Amen.

Eucharistic Prayer
Preface of Ordinary Time II [P30], (Missal, p 433).

Invitation to the Our Father
The Christ of God has made us daughters and sons of the Father, and so we pray:

Sign of Peace
The Christ has established the reign of peace by coming among us. Let us rejoice in this gift of peace.

Invitation to Communion
The Christ has called us to be his people and to share with him in
his holy supper, Lord I am not worthy …

Communion Reflection
Silence is an activity! It is keeping quiet. And for many people it
is an activity that is anxiety producing – some background
sound is considered essential in supermarkets to make people
feel comfortable (and when people feel comfortable, they have
less fears of spending on what they do not really need). Yet,
without silence and reflection, the mysteries of faith cannot
speak in the depths of our being. So introduce the silence with
'Let us pray' and give enough time for people to get over the
first moments of 'just waiting', then the second phase of anxious
coughing and shuffling, to the time of actual quiet.

However, a structured silence is also a stillness: so make sure
that there is no one wiping cups and patens, locking tabernacles,
or bringing baskets to the door for a retiring collection. If you
have a silence, then distractions and movement must also be
avoided.

Conclusion
The Son of God has transformed creation by coming among us
as the Christ; may he fill you with every blessing. Amen.
The Son of God has transformed creation by coming among us
as the Christ; may he give you strength to carry your cross each
day during the coming week. Amen.
The Son of God has transformed creation by coming among us
as the Christ; may he share with you the fullness of everlasting
life. Amen.

Notes
Since today the gospel focuses on the basic confession of faith,
this is a suitable day on which to alternate the declaratory form
of the creed with the question-and-answer baptismal form. That
which forms part of the Renewal of Baptismal Promises on

Easter Sunday (Missal, pp 220-1) is a convenient formula for today.

First Reading: Zec 12:10-11

This text is problematic in its readings, but this is resolved in the liturgy by reading it as it is found (both textually and in meaning) in Jn 19:7. Jn reads 'They shall look on him whom they have pierced', but the Hebrew has a different slant, and this problem is fudged in the Jerusalem Bible by saying 'They will look on the one whom they have pierced.' Here in the liturgy the reading is a prophecy of the passion of Jesus. From the House of David will come one who is sent by the Lord; he will be pieced in the sight of the citizens of Jerusalem; there will be great mourning, but this man will, by being pierced, open a fountain that will wash away the sin and impurities of Jerusalem (cf Jn 19:34: 'But one of the soldiers pierced his side with a spear, and at once there came out blood and water'; read within the scene of the crucifixion in John where the cross is located near the city such that the citizens can go and look at Jesus on the cross: cf Jn 19:20).

Second Reading: Gal 3:26-29

The Greco-Roman world was one of strict stratification and demarcation: of 'highers' and 'lowers,' of 'insiders' and 'outsiders'. The new community was to overcome this and was thus to model the equality of all in the presence of God and within his love. This was a central plank in the kerygma: the new open welcome to all that Jesus had practised in his meals, and which Paul was extending to the gentiles, was a great attraction of this new community. A community that defines itself by inclusion rather than exclusion and which declares that boundaries are not absolutes is a rare phenomenon, but such was part of the 'sales pitch' of the Christians. It has, of course, proved controversial from the very start and the need for stratification within the community made itself felt almost at once. Yet it has remained a potent memory that in every age has prompted groups of

Christians to either shun social distinctions or to work to overcome discrimination in many ways. However, it is a complicated
memory: someone might, for instance, argue on the basis of this
absence of demarcations in the New Israel that there cannot be
any difficulty with having women ordained to preside at the
Eucharist. And, if this reading's vision of the ideal church were
to be accepted as the basic image of church, then they would
have a point. But, as a matter of fact, such an absence of stratification is impossible in any group that has definite functions
which must be performed; hence, this reading has been understood eschatologically rather than ecclesiologically by most
Christians over the centuries.

First Reading > Gospel Links
The first reading is aimed at announcing the theme of Lk 9:22
('The Son of man must suffer many things, and be rejected by
the elders and chief priests and scribes, and be killed, and on the
third day be raised') using a text that was first used by
Christians in the late first century (Jn 19:37). In John the relationship between Zec 12:10 and the Christ-event is one of prophecy-
fulfilment; and it is this pattern that is at work in the liturgy
today.

Gospel: Lk 9:18-24
This is the scene conventionally labelled 'the confession at
Caesarea Philippi'. It is found in all three synoptics. But Luke's
version is the most distinctive, by far the shortest, and the most
stark. In Mark this is the very centre of his whole story and there
is the complaint of Peter that draws out the cry from Jesus: 'Get
behind me, Satan!' Then in Matthew we have all that is in Mark,
plus the Petrine commission: 'You are Peter and on this rock I
will build my church.' Indeed, Matthew's text has been used so
often that this reading from Luke is virtually unknown, and
when it is known we silently conflate it with Mt/Mk.

Read Luke and note the starkness:
(1) There is no location given – Caesarea Philippi is mentioned

in Mark (who is followed by Matthew) but this detail is omitted by Luke – this is just an event that has happened on the road as part of the following of Jesus by his disciples.

(2) There is just Jesus and 'disciples' – note there is not even a reference to 'The Twelve'; the scene is one of Jesus with the followers (i.e. the church who are listening to Luke) for Luke has made this an archetypal encounter. Peter is only there to give the essential answer; he is not the focus of Jesus's attention as he is in differing ways in Mark and Matthew.

(3) There is no banter: the conditions of discipleship are given as statements of what life will be like.

(4) Just in case there is any mistake about the nature of discipleship, Luke adds a single word to the text of Mk 8:34 (which Matthew takes over from Mark without change): 'daily' – discipleship will not just involve taking up a cross or some spectacular suffering which one might well avoid, but it will mean taking up the cross every day.

Luke takes a scene and story that is localised as part of the memory of the times of Jesus in Mark and Matthew, and universalises it for the experience of the church. This is the Christ of God speaking to every community in every time about whom they are following and what that following will involve.

HOMILY NOTES

1. Who is Jesus? On this question hangs not only the whole of Christian theology, but every aspect of our life of faith. 'Christology' – which is the attempt to provide the answer to the question – is not an abstract academic study within a theology course, but the constant activity of believers: when we celebrate, when we act or write or paint or sculpt, when we engage in social activities, in all of these there is implicit christology. Every action of the church in some way says or betrays how Christians in their hearts and lives – as distinct from their repeated rhyming off of creeds or formulae of orthodoxy – answer the question. Some of those statements and actions might show him as merciful; others might show

him as a killjoy or as a tyrant (but in the spiritual realm). Then there are attitudes that are tantamount to docetism: he never really became an individual human in the midst of the circus of life; and there are attitudes that are tantamount to reducing Jesus to a moral philosopher or a 'God-like' chap. And, there are actions of Christians that imply he is irrelevant to the actual living of life in society.

2. So we have our two starting points: (1) who is Jesus is as much a question for our gathering today as it was in the assembly in which Luke was telling his story; and (2) there are as wide a diversity of opinions among those who have heard his words as ever before. It is a rare occurrence when a situation in the gospel and a situation in a community today have such complete congruence.

3. But how do we make this question small enough to say something focused in the course of a homily? Perhaps one could begin with a seemingly frivolous question: what is Jesus's surname? Is it 'Christ'? This is quite a common practice in indices in books on the history of ideas where Jesus is referred to as a kind of populist philosopher: 'Christ, Jesus, pp n, n, n.' Funnily enough, this is not a new phenomenon: it is Luke who records that the followers of Jesus were called 'Christians' in the Greco-Roman world, and many Romans such as Tacitus and Pliny thought so as well and assumed that 'Chrestus' or 'Christus' was simply the name of the originator of our cult. The trend continues today when people say 'you followers of Christ'; and we are often just as guilty when we say 'we are followers of Christ'. But the word 'christ' is not a name, but the basic title by which we acknowledge who Jesus is.

4. Our confession of faith is: 'Jesus is the Christ.' He is the individual we call 'the anointed one'. Chosen by the Father to enter into the totality of our human experience, Jesus is Lord; and he is the Son giving to all reality a worth such that it can exist in the presence of God. To say 'Jesus is the Christ' is to say that all humanity is offered the chance to be transformed

into the divine image. It is a wholly different way of looking at the world and at the human condition. And if we really see the world in this new way – as countless brothers and sisters of Jesus have down the centuries – then we will react in a wholly different way to human joys and human sorrows. All that is good and noble can lead us towards holiness; all that is sordid or sad can be transformed.

5. However, a small start would be to stop using 'Christ' as if it were a surname – that is the practice of those who have not encountered Jesus but just heard about him – and begin using it as the our basic confession of faith: Jesus is the Christ. Amen.

Lectionary Unit IV

Towards Jerusalem

This unit is devoted to the first part of the 'Travel Narrative' and its theme is the qualities Jesus demands of those who follow him.

It runs from Sunday 13 to Sunday 23, and contains eleven Sundays. Its sections/themes are:

Sunday 13	*The journey begins*
Sunday 14	*The mission of the seventy-two*
Sunday 15	*The Good Samaritan*
Sunday 16	*At the meal in the house of Martha and Mary*
Sunday 17	*The friend in need*
Sunday 18	*The parable of the rich fool building barns*
Sunday 19	The need for vigilance
Sunday 20	Jesus brings 'not peace but division'
Sunday 21	Few will be saved
Sunday 22	True humility
Sunday 23	The cost of discipleship

The sections of the gospel referred to in italics in this chart are incidents that are only found in Luke's gospel and so are texts that are only preached upon on those Sundays in the Three-Year Cycle, whereas Luke's text on the other Sundays may be verbally very similar to texts met elsewhere in the gospels and consequently read on other Sundays over the three years.

Thirteenth Sunday of Ordinary Time

Introduction to the Celebration

Coming together week after week we can forget that we have each made a decision to follow Jesus and to make the growth of his kingdom our goal in life. But we get distracted, we lose focus, we get tired, and we even get lost from time to time. Now as we gather around the Lord at his table we ask the Lord to re-focus us on what is truly important and to give us the food to sustain us on our pilgrimage of life.

Rite of Penance

Lord Jesus, you set out with your disciples for Jerusalem to fulfil the Father's will. Lord have mercy.

Lord Jesus, you rebuked your disciples when they spoke of vengeance. Christ have mercy.

Lord Jesus, you have called us to follow you above all other commitments. Lord have mercy.

Headings for Readings
First Reading

Today we are going to hear a story about how one prophet passed on his mantle to his successor: the new prophet, Elisha, knew at once that his life had changed.

Second Reading

We are the people who are called by Christ to walk in the Spirit and to love our neighbours as ourselves.

Gospel

The Lord turns his faced towards Jerusalem, as this was his central task in life. But travelling our road with Jesus will make many demands on us.

Prayer of the Faithful

President

We are called to become fit to be members of the kingdom of God. Let us ask the Father for the help we need to begin our lives of following the Lord and building the society of God in our lives.

Reader(s)

1. For the strength to renew our discipleship. Lord hear us.

2. For the courage to accept in our lives the Lord's call to follow him. Lord hear us.

3. For the perseverance to continue in the Lord's way. Lord hear us.

4. For the gift of wisdom to know the path of true freedom. Lord hear us.

5. For the gift of hope to enable us to keep walking on our journey of discipleship. Lord hear us.

5. *Specific local needs and topics of the day.*

President

Father, grant us those gifts for which we ask and grant that we may not be found unfit to enter your kingdom with Jesus, our Lord. Amen.

Eucharistic Prayer

There is no preface or Eucharistic Prayer that is particularly suited to this day.

Invitation to the Our Father

Gathered as the followers of the Son, as we walk forward in the Spirit, let us pray to the Father:

Sign of Peace

For us who are called to journey with the Lord as his followers, the whole law is summed up in 'love your neighbour as yourself'; let us now express this love to one another.

Invitation to Communion
Jesus has called us to be his followers, and now he calls us to share in his supper.

Communion Reflection
Christ has set us free; he has conquered death; he stands among us now, here, today.

We stand united with one another and with him.

We must not submit again to a yoke of slavery to selfishness, possessions, power, or sin.

We have been called to freedom, sisters and brothers; we have been called to use our freedom wisely, and through love be servants of one another.

Our whole law is fulfilled in one word, 'You shall love your neighbor as yourself.'

We are called to walk by the Spirit, and do not gratify the desires of the flesh.

Christ has set us free; he has conquered death; he calls us to walk in the Spirit, and he beckons us to stand with him in the presence of the Father.
Adapted from the Second Reading

Conclusion
None of the Solemn Blessings or of the Prayers over the People is particularly fitted to this day.

COMMENTARY

First Reading: 1 Kgs 19:16, 19-21
The background to the moment of the investiture of Elisha is that Elijah has complained to Yahweh in an encounter with him on Mount Horeb that he is alone as a prophet in his battle against Baal-worship in Israel. The Lord replies that he is not alone because there are thousands of faithful people in the land. But Yahweh will also choose a successor: Elisha. Elijah then commissions Elisha to whom has passed the task of restoring purity to the cult of the Land.

Second Reading: Gal 5:1, 13-18

This is a section out of a much longer discourse in Galatians on preserving freedom from the law. Not to accept this liberty from the law is to ignore the Spirit; and to keep disputing about this freedom from the law is to ignore the new manner of life that should be at the base of their community. They do not need to worry about the law because they have the indwelling Spirit which counteracts the dangerous human tendencies that the law sought to curb. This text – with its notion of an indwelling Spirit which makes rules and practices unnecessary to the practice of Christian life – has been at the basis of most Christian antinomian movements throughout history.

First Reading > Gospel Links

The relationship here is one of parallel narratives. The gospel's final verse contains echoes of the passage in 1 Kgs: Elisha wants to say farewell to his parents, but he also leaves the plough immediately; by knowing the story of Elisha we are in a position to appreciate the imaginative background to the gospel story.

Gospel: Lk 9:51-62

This gospel is made up of several elements. The first element is the story of the Samaritan villagers who show hostility to this group of Galileans passing through their territory on the way to worship in Jerusalem. The very fact of passing through that area was tantamount to saying that the only place for '[true] Jews' (because the Samaritans also claimed the name 'Jew') to worship is in the temple in Jerusalem, and implicitly to assert that their cult in their temple was a false one. Jesus, by rebuking the disciples who want to call in an air strike, shows himself to be living by his own command to love one's enemies.

The second element is the sayings on the nature and cost of discipleship. Here Lk 9:59-59 is paralleled in Mt 8:19-22, but the Lukan text is made much sharper by the addition of verses 60-62. What we have is three 'words of wisdom' – rules of thumb –

for disciples. And, following a convention with such 'words' (our word 'proverb' does not really convey the idea), they are models of hyperbole: a point so exaggerated as to be bizarre, but precisely because of this they are memorable and lodge themselves in the imagination of the hearers. We might express it with a tag like: 'Discipleship is demanding.'

However, many people have become so accustomed to hearing utterances of Jesus as if they were first uttered yesterday, that becoming attuned to the teaching methods of his distant world is almost impossible for them, and in recent centuries this has often led to literalist interpretations (e.g. in the rules of enclosed nuns on attending family celebrations) that miss the point that Jesus was making: the demands of discipleship are there day in and day out – not just in these extreme situations.

HOMILY NOTES

1. This gospel (or, at least, the last four verses of today's gospel) not only sounds harsh – leave the dead to bury the dead – but to go against both a basic instinct to sympathise and help those who mourn, and against what Christians have preached as a 'corporal work of mercy': to bury the dead. But the place to start is not with this saying of Jesus but with some basic characteristics of human behaviour to which this is a saving antidote and a nugget of holy wisdom.

2. The first instinct is the 'get it for me now' instinct: we want results instantly and without waiting. We become then fixated on the immediate, today, quick wins, and visible results. This is not a new characteristic that has been produced by the speed of modern living for it is at the heart of many philosophies that we can be so intoxicated by what see directly before us or feel or taste, that we loose sight of the more important realities. Gregory the Great in his *Pastoral Rule* noted this phenomenon when he said that one type of fool was the person who going on a long journey down a road was so distracted by the dogs barking at him from each gate that he forgot the destination and only noticed the various dogs. It is

this instinct that the advertising industry taps into with glossy images and promises of instant satisfaction: you don't have to wait; it will happen today, heaven is an instant (and a little cash) away.

The other instinct seems the opposite of the first: procrastinate, wait till we have a bit more time or energy, put things on the long finger. This only seems the opposite instinct; in fact, it really is the same problem: important big things can wait, while I concentrate on little and palpably gratifying quick wins. Fixing the gutters of the house is neither cheap nor that satisfying for no one will tell you how much they like the repair, it is hassle and expensive and disruptive: all that stuff needs to be moved, the tradesmen found, the cash saved up, and then you have to be around to answer questions and make decisions and … Well, they have lasted this long, they can last a bit longer, or at least till after the holidays or the big birthday or the winter or till next year! This is characteristic of us humans as much as thinking that instant coffee is really coffee simply because it is quicker and easier to make! How often do we hear that a disaster has crept up on people as they left it too late to do something. There is a deep-rooted laziness in us that finds tackling the bigger, less obvious issues so difficult as to overwhelm us. So we avoid them and concentrate on immediate things of the senses as a substitute for real action.

3. This laziness has been given various names down the centuries in various religions. For western Christianity the most famous name was given to it by Augustine, 'concupiscence,' and he saw it as a direct result of the sin of Adam and Eve that had established itself in our genes, as it were. But while it is probably best to steer clear of the whole edifice of the theology of Original Sin in relation to this, and certainly in a little Sunday homily, there is still the fact – known to both governments and advertisers – that we have this laziness within our make-up, irrespective of what name we give it or how we explain its origins.

4. This laziness reaches its greatest depth when it comes to the things of the spirit: the decision to take discipleship seriously, to begin building the kingdom of God, to live as witnesses to the presence of God. This is made all the more difficult as to desire the kingdom of God necessitates that we start building the society of God with those we live with, work with, and interact with. But the change and action needed seems too big, so let's put it off till a little later, next year perhaps, or when life has settled down a bit. That moment, by the way, when life settles down a bit (and when we can make a more considered decision) is identical with the moment when the earth finally settles in our grave.

5. Today's sayings by Jesus: 'Leave the dead to bury the dead, but you go and preach the kingdom of God' and 'No one, having put his hand to the plough and looking back, is fit for the kingdom of God' alert us to this fact of our nature. The kingdom must begin now, and it is difficult, and it is a shock to the system. And, when we look around we can see just how many of us stand and pray 'thy kingdom come' yet at the same time putting our part in that coming off until 'some-time in the future'.

6. However, once we listen to the proddings of the Spirit in our hearts, that we should begin this work of building the king-dom, then the Spirit helps and gives us strength to set out on the new road of discipleship. It is this help we receive to take our part in the reconciliation of the world to the Father through Jesus that we often refer to as 'grace'. God invites us to follow and then helps us respond to the invitation: but it is easier to say this than to make this an urgency in our lives. The plough is before us, the challenge is to take hold of it and use it to carve out a new furrow that plays its part in the re-newal of the creation.

Fourteenth Sunday of Ordinary Time

Introduction to the Celebration

When we think of Jesus preaching we think of people flocking to hear him, just as today we gather to re-affirm our identity as his people gathered now at his table. But in today's gospel we hear of people being sent out from Jesus to prepare his way before him. We gather now, but we are also the people he has charged to prepare his way in the world today. To be a disciple is not only to follow, but to go ahead of the Lord announcing his presence. Let us reflect on these twin aspects of being Christians: following the Lord, and presenting the Lord to the world. We are called not only to be 'disciples' but 'apostles'.

Rite of Penance

This is a day when the Rite of Sprinkling with Holy Water is especially suitable as it contains a recollection of baptism and its universal call to be the presence of the Christ.

However, it that is not possible, then these Kyrie-petitions may be useful:

Lord Jesus, for the times when we have acted without justice. Lord have mercy.

Lord Jesus, for the times when we have ignored the poor. Christ have mercy.

Lord Jesus, for the times when we have exploited others. Lord have mercy.

Headings for Readings

First Reading

The prophet looks forward to the time when joy will come to Jerusalem and she will rejoice when the Lord reveals his hand.

Second Reading

Paul tells his hearers that the most important demonstration of being a Christians is that one had become a new creature in Jesus Christ.

Gospel
This is the story of the sending out of seventy-two of the disciples who were to announce that the Lord was coming their way as he journeyed onwards toward Jerusalem.

Prayer of the Faithful
President
As a people called to follow the Christ, and as a people charged to prepare the way for the Christ, let us now place our need before the Father.
Reader(s)
1. For the whole church of God, that it may prepare the way for the coming of the Lord into our world. Lord hear us.
2. For the work of the People of God, that the Lord of the harvest may send labourers into his harvest. Lord hear us.
3. For this church gathered together, that we may be given the courage to profess our faith in Jesus. Lord hear us.
4. For all who are in darkness or despair, that the Lord may come into their lives. Lord hear us.
5. For all people of goodwill, that they may hear the promptings of God in their lives. Lord hear us.
6. *Specific local needs and topics of the day.*
7. That all who have died may rejoice that their names are written in heaven. Lord hear us.
President
Father, Lord of the harvest, your Son travelled towards Jerusalem to intercede for all humanity. Now in his name we ask you for our needs; hear us, we pray you, for we make our prayers in union with your Son. Amen.

Eucharistic Prayer
No Preface or Eucharistic Prayer is especially suitable.

Invitation to the Our Father
Jesus invites us to pray to the Lord of the harvest for labourers to advance the coming of the kingdom, so let us pray to the Lord of the harvest now:

Sign of Peace
The greeting and gift of those sent out by Jesus was to be 'Peace to this house'; now let us offer the gift of peace to one another.

Invitation to Communion
Those sent out by Jesus were to rejoice that their names were written in heaven. Happy are we who are called by name to take part in this supper.

Communion Reflection
Concentrate on the simplicity of this time of year (see Notes), rather than having a formal reflection.

Conclusion
Solemn Blessing of the Holy Spirit (Missal, p 371) fits this day well as it focuses on the church being sent out in the power of the Holy Spirit.

Notes
Summer Holidays
By this time of year the community is about to go (if it has not done so already) into 'summer recess'. The choir is on holidays, the school which has recently been centre stage with Confirmations and First Communions is now not to be seen, there are more changes in the rotas for the various ministries than usual, and on sunny days many people just do not seem to be able to fit in 'going to Mass'. This often gives the liturgy during the period between mid-June and mid-September an appearance as if it is running on 'low power'. However, one can look on this time as an opportunity to have a quieter, deliberately more reflective liturgy. It can be a valuable time to experiment

with other ways of celebrating, and a time for those parts of cat-echesis that take time and will really only work with smaller groups than usual.

A more intimate Sunday liturgy – making a virtue of the smaller numbers and the fact that there is not some special event to be celebrated – can often give people a whole new under-standing of being gathered around the table of the Lord, sharing his loaf, and cup, and so becoming the one body of Christ. Table, Loaf, Cup, the TLC of our sacramental life, can so easily be over-laid with so much else that they become invisible on the average Sunday, but on these summer Sundays they can be made to stand out with simplicity and clarity.

COMMENTARY

First Reading: Isa 66:10-14

This is taken from the final section of the Third Isaiah which is concerned with the new temple – the final presence of God among his people – in Jerusalem. This is a reading we usually encounter in Advent and that is a guide to how it is read within the church whenever it appears in a lectionary: the anointed one is come, and this is Jesus. He is the new and final temple, and therefore at his coming Jerusalem – which, personified, is mother of the people – can rejoice. The development of the christology of the temple (see for examples of this: Mk 15:38 and parallels; Jn 2:20-21 and synoptic parallels; the place of the temple in Luke's infancy narrative; and the imagery of the temple in Hebrews) owes a major debt to reflection on this section of Third Isaiah.

Second Reading: Gal 6:14-18

This is part of Paul's farewell and blessing at the end of the let-ter. It contains one final shot at those who want to emphasise 'the law': they are not to be heeded as it is the death of Jesus on the cross – hence that is all he is prepared to boast of – that justi-fies the people.

Such a statement then usually provokes a question about 'what does 'justify' mean?' This question is not really an issue of exegesis but a conundrum from late medieval systematic theology and only becomes problematic if one assumes there is a perfect opposition between the notion of grace and works, and then this is referred back into Paul. It is better to avoid the whole question and pose a different one: what brings us as a people into the presence of the Father? The obedience of our head, and that obedience was demonstrated perfectly in the death on the cross.

First Reading > Gospel Links

This is a case of prophesy and fulfilment: the prophet looks forward to the final presence of God; when this is announced there will be rejoicing; Jesus has come and now that coming is to be announced, so the time of rejoicing is come.

Gospel: Lk 10:1-12; 17-20

This story in Luke shows us the variety of ways each evangelist molded the tradition he received to formulate his narrative within his individual overall theology. Most of 10:1-12 can be found somewhere in Matthew, but here it is gathered into one story. Then there is the cursing of Chorazin and Bethsaida for their unbelief (also found in Matthew), and then the return of the seventy-two which completes the story (10:17-20) which is only found in Luke. However, while Luke's aim was to join all this material into a unified and memorable story, there were, and still are, several bad junctions between the various bits that he used. Perhaps the worst such junction was the portion of information on Chorazin and Bethsaida (verses 13-16, paralleled in Mt 11:21-23 and Mt 10:40) which broke up the story of the seventy-two, and which has very wisely been excised from the lection today to give a much more harmonious and comprehensible text. However, other bad junctions remain: for instance, only Luke mentions Jesus sending out seventy-two to prepare the way, yet once these are sent out (and one has no suspicion that there is any shortage of people to send out), we are immediately told to pray that there would be enough labourers for the harvest! (an item that makes perfect sense in the location it occupies in Matthew at 9:37).

The focus of Luke's story can only be appreciated within his overall preaching (gospel and Acts) which is to locate the life of the church within the pattern of the spread of the good news: from Christ, to Jerusalem, to the surrounding areas, then out to the ends of the earth. This task is the work of Providence in human history (therefore, no haversack, etc.); and it is into this, the mightiest work of God, that the church is inserted. The whole church is, in effect, the seventy-two. This good news is then encapsulated in 'the kingdom is near' and the apostles, i.e. everyone in the churches, can rejoice not in their powers or status as Christians but because their names are written in heaven.

One technical point may come up from those who hear this gospel, if read from the lectionary today: how many were sent out? The Lectionary follows the Jerusalem Bible here which on this occasion opts for 'seventy-two' (and which thereby is in agreement with the Vulgate which reads *septuaginta duos*), in contrast to which most modern translations (e.g. RSV, NRSV) read 'seventy.' The problem is that the textual evidence is almost perfectly divided between the two numbers, so much so that some modern Greek editions go for this fudge: 'seventy [two]'. The question that should be asked is which of the two numbers is more likely to be particularly symbolic for Luke? To that question, 'seventy' wins hands down, and there are almost no examples of 'seventy two' being a symbolic number. However, I personally am very glad that 'seventy-two' is in the lectionary text. The retention of this textual curiosity may provoke some of its hearers to ask interesting questions about the ecclesial origins and nature of the texts we read.

HOMILY NOTES

1. For much of the twentieth century, many of the key words in the vocabulary of lay organisations in the church was related to the word 'apostle' such as 'apostolate,' 'apostleship', or 'apostolic [activity]'. This is a word that we sometimes see less often today and words like 'ministry' and 'discipleship' have a greater prominence. This is, in itself, a very good de-

velopment for each of these three words, 'ministry', 'apostle-ship', and 'discipleship', each picks out a particular aspect of the whole complex of what we are called to do as Christians. An active Christian life always involves service to the community, it requires following and imitating, but it also requires a going out, a making present of the Lord in the world. It is this third aspect, this sending out, that is the focus today.

2. In the whole of the mystery of Christ there is a 'ripple principle' at work. The image is that of a stone entering a lake and then the effects go out in concentric circles, getting wider and wider, until they reach the very edge. The whole surface of the lake is transformed as the ripples spread ever outwards. This is 'like' the entry of the Christ into the creation and then the effect of his coming keeps spreading outwards over the whole of the world and the whole of time.

3. This ripple principle forms the overall architecture of Luke's preaching: the Lord comes among us, then he forms a group who are sent out bringing his message ever outwards, then the Lord ascends on high and his message spreads out through the apostolic preaching: first, in Jerusalem, then in Judea and Samaria, and then 'to the ends of the earth'. This gospel presents this pattern in a nutshell.

4. We today are called to bring the ripple effect of our encounter with Jesus Christ outwards. We are the group who have to show within the places we live that 'the kingdom of God is near.'

5. But there is a constant danger: we often think that 'the apostolic life' is something that we can delegate to a few specialists: full time 'apostles' or 'missionaries in foreign lands' or those who live 'the religious life'. Every individual is called in a specific way to spread the word and to bring the presence of Christ into the world – only some are called to do so in a 'high profile' way. We are called to be apostles in our baptism; we cannot delegate the responsibility. Rather we must search out the precise way that each of us is called to be an apostle – whether it is high or low profile – and how we

each can make ourselves better fitted to the precise place and moment in the history of salvation where each is called to be the rippling presence of God.

Fifteenth Sunday of Ordinary Time

Introduction to the Celebration

We live in the age of the sound bite: a snappy phrase that covers over a complex situation; and rarely in matters of faith is such a sound-bite possible. Yet today at our gathering to join the Lord at his table we are asked to recall one of the most famous sound bites of all time. A lawyer stands up to ask Jesus a question: 'Teacher, what shall I do to inherit eternal life?' And as the good teacher Jesus does not just feed him the answer but draws it out from him: 'You shall love the Lord your God with all your heart, and with all your soul, and with all your strength, and with all your mind; and your neighbour as yourself.' It sounds simple. But keeping both dimensions, loving God and loving neighbour is difficult; and an even bigger challenge is making sure that for us neighbour is more than the people we like, and so excludes all forms of sectarianism, racism, other barriers humans tend to set up between us and 'them'.

Rite of Penance

Lord Jesus, for those times when we did not love God with all our hearts, and souls, and strength, and mind. Lord have mercy.
Lord Jesus, for those times when we did not love our neighbour as ourselves. Christ have mercy.
Lord Jesus, for those times when we did not show compassion to those in need and when we treated people as outcasts and not as neighbours. Lord have mercy.

Headings for Readings
First Reading

God's law is not something exotic or bizarre. It is a call to live our lives in accordance with something that is near to us and written in our hearts: loving as we seek to be loved.

Second Reading
This is a hymn that was in use among the very first communities of Christians. It is a way of answering the question 'Who is this Jesus whom we are following?'

Gospel
This is the famous gospel of the Good Samaritan: it is a story we love, but it is one of the hardest messages in the whole gospel for us to make our own because the disease of setting up barriers between 'us' and 'them' is deep within most human cultures.

Prayer of the Faithful
President
Friends, we could dwell on many differences between members of this gathering, but we are made one in being guests at Christ's table. Jesus wants our unity here to be a sign to the whole world; he wants the love and welcome he shows us at his table to be a model for us in all our dealings. Let us pray that we will be more like the community Jesus calls us to become.
Reader(s)
1. That this gathering will renew its basic dedication to love God and neighbour. Lord hear us.
2. That this community will be a model of love for all who are outcasts. Lord hear us.
3. That this assembly will work to remove barriers between groups and promote understanding. Lord hear us.
4. That this church will empower some of its members to minister to the poor, the sick, and those suffering injustice. Lord hear us.
5. *Specific local needs and topics of the day.*
6. That this family of God may discover its own prejudices and work to repair the damage in our world. Lord hear us.
7. That our weekly gathering at this holy table to receive the Lord's generosity may be a beacon to all who are isolated, abandoned, and in need. Lord hear us.
President
Father, we are called to love you with all our mind, and heart,

and will, and to recognise every human being as our neighbour and love them as ourselves. But we know we can only carry out this command with your help. So hear us we pray and grant our needs in Christ Jesus, our Lord. Amen.

Eucharistic Prayer
There is no preface or Eucharistic Prayer that is particularly suitable as picking up the themes of today's readings.

Invitation to the Our Father
We express our love of the Father when we call on him in prayer; we express our love of neighbour when we forgive those who trespass against us, as we would want to be forgiven; so now we say:

Sign of Peace
We are called to love our neighbours as ourselves. Let us express that love for one another with a sign of peace.

Invitation to Communion
Because we are the people seeking to love God and our neighbour, the Lord welcomes us as his guests at his banquet. Lord I am not worthy …

Communion Reflection
Lord Jesus,
You have gathered us at your table.
You have made us one with you in sharing the one loaf.
You have shared your life-blood with us in common drinking.
You are the image of the unseen God.
You are the first born of all creation.
You are our head, we are your body.
You are the first born from the dead.
You have reconciled us to the Father.
You have given us peace.
Amen.

Conclusion
Solemn Blessing, Ordinary Time III (Missal p 372) in appropriate.

Notes
'Prejudice' is a pre-rational aspect of human behaviour: it literally means an opinion that is there before we sit down and think about something. So becoming aware of prejudice is often the first step to overcoming it. This is a suitable day for the liturgy group to take stock that no forms of racism or xenophobia are at work within the community. Does the group who 'do things' at the liturgy reflect the ethnic, cultural, and economic diversity of the community? Has there been a special effort made to ensure that newcomers have been positively shown welcome and inclusion? Could visitors describe as a clique or as unwelcoming this church community?

COMMENTARY

First Reading: Deut 30:10-14
Within Deuteronomy the purpose of this passage is to make the point that the Law was not something esoteric that required either some angelic or some apocalyptic figure to communicate it. Rather, it was something that was at one's fingertips because it was recited as part of the normal liturgy of the community.

However, this reading does not cohere with the gospel, and why exactly it was chosen – apart from being generically about the Law – to go with today's gospel is unknown. Certainly, given that the gospel quotes Dt 6, here an opportunity was lost to show links between the Old Testament and the New Covenant. Dt 6:4-9 (the 'Shema') with 6:3 as a context setting verse would have made a much better first reading for today.

Psalm: 18:8-11
This is the alternative psalm for today and it is to be preferred for it focuses on the law and the joy of the people, and this acts as a bridge from the first reading to the gospel.

Second Reading: Col 1:15-20

This is the early hymn that has been incorporated into the letter and whose christological sophistication sets at naught any theory that the earliest churches had only some 'simple' notion of Jesus as a 'good man of God'. The hymn sees Jesus as the Christ, and the role of the Christ is not simply that of the expected one in the history of Israel, but is the key to the whole creation (material and spiritual, and both human and angelic) from the Alpha-moment to the Omega-moment.

In a brief note one cannot even begin to examine this hymn's contents for it is at once a piece of liturgy – and so is doxological – and a credal statement – and so is doctrinal – and a precious link with the liturgy of the earliest groups – and so it has the inherent sacrality of a relic. Its nature demands that it is not just run through by a reader as just a piece of obscure prose. Announce it as a hymn, and then have it sung either by a cantor or by the choir. Because it is used in Evening Prayer as a canticle, there are numerous simple musical settings available.

First Reading > Gospel Links

The link is one of complementarity and consistency: the law is close to people in their lives, and this is revealed in all God's dealings with his people.

Gospel: Lk 10:25-37

This section can be split into two parts: verses 25-28 (the lawyer's question) and verses 29-37 (the story of 'the Good Samaritan'). The first section is common to all the synoptics, but the story is only found in Luke and it is clear that he wanted the whole scene (today's gospel reading) seen as a single piece. The opening section is the demand to have a rule of thumb that distills the whole law to its essence. The context demanded that the distillation be itself part of the law, and so Jesus's answer is made up of a combination of two quotations: first, Dt 6:5 ('you shall love the Lord your God with all your heart, and with all your soul, and with all your might'); and, second, a part of Lev

19:18 ('you shall love your neighbour as yourself'). However, Luke wants to show that this love of neighbour that Jesus preached was far more demanding than anything that was normally expected as part of the law. Luke knew that the whole verse of Lev 19:18 had a very restrictive meaning that would not sit at all well with the universalism of love that Jesus preached. The whole verse runs: 'You shall not take vengeance or bear any grudge against the sons of your own people, but you shall love your neighbour as yourself.' The neighbour is the people in your own group, camp, area: it is a demand that exists to stop local strife and vendettas of one sort or another. So the new meaning of love that Jesus preached and the new extension of the domain of fraternal care that was part of the Christian message needed a question to draw out its implications. Hence, Luke gives us the lawyer's question. The response is not a parable in the normal manner but a hypothetical case whose purpose is to elicit an awareness of the new Jesus-way of being a neighbour. However, there is a curious twist in the tail: it is not who we, the audience, think has acted in the new way of being a neighbour, but who would the one who had received help recognise as a neighbour. It is the action of love, not the boundaries of tribe, race, social status, or cult, which establish the boundaries in the kingdom.

HOMILY NOTES

1. The story of the Good Samaritan has become part of our overall culture: even people who reject Christianity or for whom the gospel is only a dim background noise can use the phrase 'a good Samaritan' and simply mean someone who helps out someone when they are in need. So the story has become simply the message to give a hand to anyone you come across in a crisis. The story's very familiarity hides its punch. And it is trying to get to its deeper challenge that is the task facing the preacher today: to take the familiar and show how little it is known.

2. We have several ideas in our minds about this scene and the story Jesus told to bring out in a concrete situation his teach-

ing. The first is that the message of the Good Samaritan is that one should be a decent person and help anyone in need. This is a valid and important point but that is not the message here. Then, second, we think of the hypocrisy of the priest and the Levite who were the public face of religion, and hypocrisy in professional religious is especially loathsome, so it is a warning about preaching and not practising. Again, this is a valid and important point but that is not the message here. Then, third, we tend to make the message of Jesus here the same as that of the Golden Rule – 'do as you would have others do onto you' – which is the basis of many codes of morality and which is found in the gospels (e.g. Lk 6:31: 'And as you wish that men would do to you, do so to them'). Yet again, this is a valid and important point but that is not the message here.

3. The story is not about how to treat others in a passive sense; it is to draw out that the call to inherit eternal life is the call to love others. This is a deliberate act of reaching out to others in need. And the question then becomes how far can you expect to reach out and from how far away can you accept the reach of love.

4. The priest and the Levite are both automatically insiders to the group: they should be obviously neighbours. They know the law and the prophets; they know they have a duty of service to the community of Israel. The Samaritan, by contrast, is the perfect outsider: by race for they were seen as half-breeds; they were invaders and thieves of land; and they were heretics.

5. Love of neighbour has to reach out beyond our bounds and accept love from beyond our barriers. It has to be greater than racism; it has to be greater than national boundaries and the hatreds that these produce; and it has to be greater than purity boundaries and the prejudices of religion and sectarianism.

6. Loving neighbour as self supposes that one can interchange one's position with any other human being, and be willing to both give and receive love.

7. We tend to praise the Samaritan and say that he was a good neighbour – and indeed he was for he showed mercy. But look a little more closely at the end of the story. Who exactly has found a neighbour? It is the beaten up insider who has discovered a neighbour. Where? In the one who showed mercy – despite the fact that he is one of those wretched Samaritans?

8. It is worth reading over the story again so that the homily's notes on the text can be fixed within the matrix of the story. The demands of loving God as a disciple of Jesus and so taking his message to heart are a lot more radical than the proverbial willingness to loan a cup of sugar.

Sixteenth Sunday of the Year

Introduction to the Celebration

Welcome! Today we recall a small incident in the life of Jesus. Going along a road he came to a village and was welcomed into a house. There one sister, having to get the meal, complained that the other just sat and listened to Jesus; and Jesus says that this second sister, named Mary, 'has chosen the better part and it is not to be taken from her'. This Mary is a model of discipleship for us. We are frequently busy with many things, but are we spending time listening to the voice of the Lord, are we reflecting on his wisdom, are we meditating on his goodness and wonder as we see it around us in the creation, are we recalling his gift of life, are we rejoicing in the presence of the Word made flesh?

Rite of Penance

Lord Jesus, we have not always made you welcome in our hearts and homes. Lord have mercy.

Lord Jesus, we have not always sat at your feet and listened to you. Christ have mercy.

Lord Jesus, we have not always chosen the better part. Lord have mercy.

Headings for Readings

First Reading

This reading and the gospel today are linked: they are both about visitors being welcomed at table. Guests suddenly appear before Abraham's tent and he recognises them as visitors from the Lord: at once he wants to make them as welcome as possible which means preparing a meal for them and sharing it with them.

Second Reading
Paul is happy for the church in Colossae because Christ is present in it and his wisdom will bring them to perfection.

Gospel
Jesus and his followers are welcomed into Martha's house and offered welcome: a meal is prepared. But while Martha is burdened with anxiety thinking how she will get the food on the table for her guests, Mary recognises that the event – having the Lord at her table – is more important than the practicalities: she sits and listens as an ideal disciple.

Prayer of the Faithful
President
Friends, it is Christ our Lord who gathers us for this sacred meal; he is our host who makes us welcome at his table. So now, in union with him present among us, let us place our needs before the Father.

Reader(s)
1. For the whole church of God, that every disciple will choose the better part. Lord hear us.
2. For this church, that we will grow in wonder at the mystery of God. Lord hear us.
3. For this gathering here now, that we grow in discipleship through this meal. Lord hear us.
4. For all who are hungry, that we become the channels of the Lord's bounty. Lord hear us.
5. For all who are down trodden and outcast, that Christians will make them welcome. Lord hear us.
6. For our sisters and brothers who have died, that they may be welcomed to the heavenly banquet. Lord hear us.

President
Father, you have sent your Son among us and this is our continual source of rejoicing. In your goodness hear us now, and help us grow as followers of your Son, through whom we make these and all our prayers. Amen.

Eucharistic Prayer
Preface of Ordinary Time V [P33] is very suitable as it dwells on
reflecting on the wonder of the creation and being thus brought
into the mystery of God.

Invitation to the Our Father
Around this table we are sisters and brothers in Christ Jesus, so
we can pray to our heavenly Father:

Sign of Peace
Through forgiving us, the Lord has welcomed us to his table; let
us now show our forgiveness and welcome to one another.

Invitation to Communion
Behold the Lord, behold him who sat at table with Martha and
Mary, and now bids us to share in his supper.

Communion Reflection
If the assembly has gathered around the table for the Eucharist,
this is a chance to just stand in silence and for all to be invited to
remember the food from this table – the actual real table physically there – is food for our pilgrimage of life. But is it also a reminder that heaven can be described as being at the Father's
table and banquet. Words like these would do:
'This food from this table [point to it or touch it] feeds us on our
pilgrimage of faith during the coming week, but it reminds us
that we will one day be gathered at the banquet of heaven.'
End the silence with 'Let us pray.'

Conclusion
The Lord has welcomed us to his table. May you extend that
love and welcome to everyone you meet during the coming
week. Amen.
The Lord has made us part of his body and given us his life to
empower us. May you remain in his love during the coming
week. Amen.

The Lord has made us companions in this meal. May you also be his companions in the banquet of the life to come. Amen.

Notes

Because today we recall one of those precious meal encounters that formed the basic preaching about the Eucharist, this is a day to focus in a special way on the Eucharist and to try to make its fundamental sacramental shape become starkly clear for people. The three fundamental shapes are that:

- We all are gathered around one table
- We all share a common loaf
- We all drink from a single cup.

Until the reform of liturgy by the Second Vatican Council this structure was all but hidden, but a key reason for the reform was to make this structure visible once again. Hence:

• 'Altars' against the wall with the people in rows behind the celebrant were abolished. The new table was to be such that it could be gathered around. This has not been as successful as was hoped as many thought that the reason for 'turning round the altar' was to allow what the priest was doing to be visible. So instead of changing our perception from a priest going up to an altar over there, to being gathered around a table, we have often kept the idea that it is the priest's place at the altar that has become now 'easy to see'. In effect, it is as if the table is arranged like the demonstration bench in a chemistry lab – people can watch what the priest was doing – but they are really just participating by observation at what is being done 'for them'. Moreover, the structure of many buildings did not really let the table be put in a central position: it was still off at one end of the gathering. However, the fundamental reason for instituting the change was to allow us to gather round the table – and, of course, if you are located there you can see everything.

• There is a new emphasis on the fraction and many places use large altar breads – often now around 150mm in diameter – that can be broken into many pieces. This has been the area where the renewal has faltered seriously, partly as the notion of 'getting communion' has not been renewed with a richer theology in many places, and partly because the basic symbolism demands the use of real bread, and the issue of continuing the medieval practice of unleavened bread has not been tackled by the Latin church yet.

• The Council began the practice of 'restoring the cup to the laity' and the permission to do this has been gradually extended in the law. Now this can be done on virtually every occasion that it is physically possible. However, it has often been forgotten that the basic symbolism is of a common cup, and many chalices do not really promote that symbolism.

One of the most frequently cited reasons why the full restoration of this basic shape has not taken place is 'the size of the congregation.' However, in many places congregation sizes are dropping which allows a more intimate approach. At the same time it is the lack of intimacy in our liturgies that is often cited as why 'Mass seems just a bothersome routine.' So this is a day when we can experiment with showing off the basic symbolism of the Eucharistic meal.

• Gather the assembly around the table in the fashion of a meal for the Liturgy of the Eucharist.

• Have a proper fraction if you can get some large 'breads' – ideally get one that is big enough for the whole group so that there is really a single loaf.

• Let all share the cup – ideally use only one cup.

COMMENTARY

First Reading: Gen 18:1-10

This reading stops mid-way through verse 10 of a story that goes on to vv 15-16; it is edited in this way in the lectionary so as to concentrate on the act of Abraham making the guests welcome, rather than on the reaction of aged Sarah to the news that she was going to have a son. Anyone reading the account for the first time would be struck by the inconsistency between the first verse – where it is said that the Lord (the word is a pointer to the J source for chs 18 and 19) appeared to Abraham – yet in the very next verse what he sees is three men. This becomes even more complex later when these three are 'messengers' or 'angels'. It is this combination that gives rise to the Byzantine icon known as 'The Welcoming (*philoxenia*) by Abraham' which is often referred to as 'the icon of the trinity'. However, for the reader the move from the Lord to three men makes people wonder have they missed something? The probable reason for this is to bring out the mysteriousness of the whole event.

We have a beautifully drawn scene: Abraham having a quiet nap but then confronted by busy, strangely silent, travellers. Yet without a word on their part, Abraham realises just what a significant event this is and so wants to welcome and entertain lavishly. Despite them being 'no warning guests', they get anything but 'pot luck'. Fresh bread in abundance: a loaf as big as a bushel would make, and each gets a whole loaf to himself. Then Abraham wants to kill a fine calf, just for them. The whole scene is deliberately over the top, we are expected to imagine that all this butchering and kneading and leavening and baking and roasting can be done in an instant! Nothing is too much for this hospitality because in welcoming these guests, the Lord himself is welcomed.

Second Reading: Col 1:24-28
This is Paul's defence that while they have only recently become the followers of Christ, the gospel is not something new fangled or alien: the mystery of Christ is deep within the creation and is only now being made plain. This mystery is not extrinsic to them, their needs and their hopes and desires, but that which brings them to perfection.

First Reading > Gospel Links
Both readings are seen as having a common theme: hospitality as part of entering the divine realm.

Gospel: Lk 10:38-42
This scene is found only in Luke, and is the story of one of a

series of meals which are related in his gospel. Each shows the
Christ with a different company, with a slightly different take on
the nature of the welcome he receives from the householder and
which he gives to those at table with him. For, while these meals
always take place in another person's house, it is clear that it is
Jesus's table: he is the host of the meal.

When this gospel was preached, the scene clues provided
would have immediately made the audience recognise this as a
meal of disciples and they would have read it eucharistically.
This is not something that comes immediately to us for two reasons. First, we have so developed the theological interpretation
of the meal, that we fail to see the meal under the theology. Yet
without the meal, there is nothing to be a sacrament of anything!
Second, we make a radical distinction – even when we are trying
to study the early church – between the meals of the community
and 'The Eucharist'. But this distinct item of practice, along with
its name, did not emerge until the second century. However, we
still read the gospels as if only the Last Supper (and possibly
Emmaus) relate to the Eucharist; while all the other meals are
just informal settings so that Jesus could preach. This distorts
Luke. For him to be a Christian disciple was to belong to the
community and its common practices at the core of which was
the weekly gathering at table in continuity with the practice of
Jesus. In this gathering, the medium was the message. So every
meal story was a teaching about the importance of being at the
meal with the Lord.

It is from this perspective of the praxis of Luke's audience
that this text is interpreted in the homily notes. However, while
the 'message' of this scene is tied up with the contrast between
the actions of Martha and Mary, it should be noted that the trad-
itional interpretation (going back to John Cassian) that it is the
contrast between two ways of life, the active and the contempla-
tive, is an imposition upon it from 'spiritual' interpretation. This
is not a charter for a two-tier church, nor a plan for a pecking
order between various religious orders in the church. The contrast concerns ways of behaving at the meal, and the reference to

the 'better share' (*meris*) uses the exact same term used for the share (i.e. the broken parts of the loaf) each member of the community had in the Lord's loaf.

HOMILY NOTES

1. The scene in the gospel could not be simpler – it appears. Jesus happens to be going down a road and meets a village and accepts hospitality, there is some talk, and then, for the gospel teller, he moves on getting ever closer to the 'centre stage' in Jerusalem. But the early Christians froze this moment in their memories as something significant; and we have been recalling it ever since. Why?

2. Somehow this encounter was, for Luke, a vignette capturing something essential about Jesus. It somehow gave in a 'snap shot' something that was true of all encounters with the risen Lord. But how can we grasp the essence of this story and see how it might – as part of the kerygma – characterise our encounters with Jesus?

3. The place to start is with the common elements: a village, a house, a meal, sitting at table, discussion. This is one more of these meal events – particularly prominent in Luke – that remind us that Jesus was 'a party animal'. The meetings with those who were his followers and those who would listen are often shown to take place around the dining table. This was not just 'a quick bite on the way from work' – his gathering of people around him at meals was at the very heart of the Lord's work. To learn about Jesus and to be with him is to eat with him; and his meals model the perfect new community and offer a taste of the welcome of the Father in the final banquet.

4. We think of communities as 'cities' and churches as 'parishes' with hundreds of people. We usually think of our gatherings not being in a house – the 'House Mass' or 'Station Mass' is an increasingly rare phenomenon – but in special formal buildings called 'churches' and then they are often built to fit hundreds. We tend to think of 'getting Mass', not of 'sitting

around the Lord's table.' And, we may see the table when we gather but we call it an 'altar'. Gathering for any meal around a table where we talk may be something done only rarely as we eat 'fast food' or food off trays in front of a screen. So our gatherings do not immediately remind us of the meal in Martha's house; and reading of that meal seems very distinct from sitting here on Sunday. Two factors create the separation: the first is sheer scale – we think of large groups and many such gatherings each Sunday; and second we use a language and a formality that obscures some of the basic shape of our encounter with the Lord at his supper

5. We should recall that for most of our history Christians have lived and worshipped in very small villages. In an ancient city like Corinth the Christians would have had a village-like existence and met in groups of 50 at most, and so would have had a real meal experience. This is what Luke knows and experiences and what his audience knows and experiences. To meet for the meal / the Eucharist is the central act of the disciples' week as Christians. There they gather to be participants in the presence of the Lord as their welcoming host. There they share his food and his life and listen to his words. There the key is to be focused on the Lord – Mary – rather than focused on the mechanics of the meeting and the meal – Martha.

6. The gospel today reminds us that the Word has become flesh, and he sits among us. He shares his table with us – the most basic human experience of welcome and sharing. We are disciples and sit with him and listen and learn from him so that we can grow to be fully-trained disciples.

7. Luke's message today could be summed up as: To know Jesus is to eat with him.

8. There is always a surprise at Jesus's meals: have you noticed this is a house that is owned by a woman? This is most unusual in the ancient world. Have you noticed that Jesus accepts women as full table companions – they can sit with him and talk with him? Again, not something that was at all usual

in the ancient world. But Jesus broke down all the barriers to welcome at his table for that welcome was intended to show the welcome of the Father at the heavenly table.

Seventeenth Sunday of Ordinary Time

Introduction to the Celebration

We are assembled here, not as a bunch of individuals, but as distinct members of a single body. This is something that we recall in a special way today when we read a story about the first disciples asking to be taught how to prayer together. We are the people who can call God *our* Father, who gather now to thank him and praise his name, who gather to ask him for our daily needs, and who ask him to forgive us as we forgive others. We need to pause now and recall our need of forgiveness for ourselves, and Jesus's call to us to forgive others.

Rite of Penance

Lord Jesus, for the times when we have not prayed and have not offered thanks to your Father. Lord have mercy.

Lord Jesus, for the times when we have not forgiven others who have trespassed against us. Christ have mercy.

Lord Jesus, for the times when we have been too busy to remember the demands of being disciples. Lord have mercy.

Headings for Readings
First Reading

Here we read a very strange story about Sodom and Gomorrah: two very sinful cities. But the punch line of the reading is at the end: if there are even ten holy people in the city, the Lord would not destroy it. The message is this: the prayers of the People of God sanctify the whole community.

Second Reading

Our reading from the early Christian letters today continues to be taken from the Letter to the church in Colossae. The topic of this section concerns what it means to be one of the baptised.

Gospel
The first Christians recited one prayer, the 'Our Father,' three times a day. Here we have a story accounting for the origins of the prayer to which they attached such importance.

Prayer of the Faithful
President
Sisters and brothers, our Lord has told us that when we ask, the Father will provide our needs, so now as Christ's holy people let us stand before the Father and intercede for our own community, for the whole church, for those in need, and for all humanity.
Reader(s)
1. That we may become a community that prays each day. Lord hear us.
2. That the whole People of God may offer an acceptable sacrifice of praise. Lord hear us.
3. That our example may help others to learn to turn to the Father in their needs. Lord hear us.
4. That all in need may learn to trust in the Lord's goodness. Lord hear us.
5. That we who stand here may know that we are called to be the agents of the Lord's care for those with any need. Lord hear us.
6. That Christians may be generous to those in need as the Father is generous with us. Lord hear us.
7. That all who have died may join in the perfect praise of heaven in union with the angels and saints. Lord hear us.
President
Father, we approach you with our needs because Jesus your Son taught us to pray to you and to present you with our petitions. Hear us, for we tell you our needs in union with your Son, our Lord. Amen.

Eucharistic Prayer
Preface of Sundays in Ordinary Time VI [P34] (Missal, p 437) picks up the gospel's theme of the Father's constant care through the gift of the Holy Spirit.

Invitation to the Our Father
John taught his disciples to pray, and Jesus taught us, so as the disciples of the Christ we can now stand in the Father's presence and say:

Sign of Peace
We ask the Father to forgive us as we forgive. Let us show our forgiveness of one another now with a sign of peace.

Invitation to Communion
We have gathered at the Lord's table to offer thanks to the Father. Happy are we who are called to this supper.

Communion Reflection
The readings today are relatively long and the liturgy can all too easily become overburdened with words. So perhaps a structured silence is what is needed. Introduce it with something like: 'Let us now prayer together in silence for a moment that we become a community of prayer.' Break the silence formally after one minute with: 'Let us pray.'

Conclusion
Any one of Solemn Blessings for Ordinary Time is suitable, but none is especially suited to this day.

COMMENTARY

First Reading: Gen 18:20-32
This was probably one of the last bits to be added to the text of Genesis during the process of its formation. The scene is inserted just before the story of the destruction of the city of Sodom and the rescue of Lot (19:1-29), and has much more sophisticated theology than is found in the story of the destruction. We have a scene where Abraham is bargaining with God because Abraham knows what God intends to do and wants to make sure that there is no 'collateral damage' when God sets out to wreak vengeance. The story is about God as the Just One who will not let the righteous suffer with the wicked.

We find this a crude theology: it seems an insult to the divine love to imagine that he might become so exasperated with the sinfulness of the surroundings that he might destroy everyone and everything, and then this reading merely presents mercy as 'We few righteous will escape.' However, even this notion of God being so discerning as to rescue Lot and his family marks an understanding of God's interest in people that is far in excess of that found in many cultures where 'Bad things happen because there are bad people and God gets angry.' So before we dismiss this story as simplistic, we should note that there are some far more crude notions of justice, be it divine or human, active in our world.

This reading also presents a notion that the presence of the righteous intercedes for the security of the whole city. This is a theme which is transformed later when Jesus's death is seen as the intercession that spares sinners from the divine wrath.

Psalm: 137
This psalm's text is so obscured in The Grail translation, and so cut-about in the Lectionary's selection, that any link between its original text and its use today is irrelevant. In this liturgical context its significance is that it is the praise of a community at prayer gathered in a sacred place: the community's gathering place being analogous to the temple. However, even this theme, which in some ways fits with the gospel, only applies to the first stanza as set out in the Lectionary.

Second Reading: Col 2:12-14
This is one of the key explanations used in the Pauline churches as to what is the significance of baptism. The bath which marks the group's boundary is the means by which the individual undergoes death, not of his/her pre-Christian self, but of the Christ. The new life in the community is then not just a new lifestyle, but the actual risen life of the Christ.

First Reading > Gospel Links

The link is based on the notion of the constancy / consistency of God in his dealings with his people: God listens to the prayers of his people for deliverance.

Gospel: Lk 11:1-13

This story of the disciples asking for a lesson in prayer methods is only found in Luke; in Matthew (6:9-13) the 'Our Father' is given in the context of an instruction forming part of the Sermon on the Mount. So the first point to note is that in our memories we combine this occasion in Luke, with the text that is found in Matthew. We see this common memory harmonising the two texts in many introductions to the 'Our Father' in the liturgy.

Second, the text here seems 'simpler' than that which is known in the tradition or found in Matthew; and therefore (because we assume everything develops in a sequence from 'simple' to 'complex', it is often glibly stated that therefore this Lukan version is 'more original' or even 'closer to the words of Jesus'. This often leads to attempts to derive the familiar form from this one in Luke, and it is an endeavour that invariably calls for ever more subtle moves to seem convincing. The place to start is not with the written gospels – either Matthew or Luke – but with the community of the church which preserved the memory of Jesus during those crucial early decades before papyrus and ink could freeze the shape of the memory.

That Jesus taught some prayer that was distinctive in its approach to God is certain, as all the evidence coheres that there was a common Christian prayer formula and that it addressed God as 'father'. That this was taught orally can be observed in two ways. Firstly, the well-rounded cadences and doublets (e.g. 'thy kingdom come, thy will be done') point to a text rounded off to allow for easy committal to memory. Secondly, the prayer has some minor variations in the various languages and in the manuscripts, and these variations show that oral transmission was the norm and that scribes followed their memories rather than their exemplars when copying Matthew. The most famous of these slight variations is the doxology ('for the kingdom, the power and the glory are yours now and forever') which was omitted in Latin. Moreover, we know that the prayer, in virtually the shape we know it, was part of the training of new Christians before the time of our gospels: we find it in the *Didache* (but with one or two tiny changes which prove that the scribe was neither copying from memory or from Matthew). So we can conclude that before 70 AD this prayer in our familiar form was being learned by heart as part of the basic formation of every Christian.

Since it was such a basic element of the *Didache* (the training), it had to have a place in the kerygma (the preaching). Consequently, Matthew incorporated it into his most formal sermon exactly as it was recited in Greek in the churches in which he preached. Luke, however, opted to explain its importance with an origin story, and either knowing or recognising that it was well smoothed for memory based recitation, gave it a more archaic feel in his text. His construction – which has never been a reciting text anywhere – is therefore the first commentary on the prayer in so far as his text highlights what Luke saw as its most important features.

He then takes the opportunity to present some other teaching on prayer and the Father's answering of prayer. First, he has the parable of the friend at midnight (11:5-8) – which is only found in Luke – which contrasts God's concern with humanity with what one could expect from even base motives. Second, he has the statements on how the Father will answer those who ask for their needs. The interesting difference here with Matthew (7:11) is that while in Matthew the Father gives good things to those who ask him, here the Father gives the Holy Spirit to those who ask him. This fits with Luke's overarching theology that it is the Spirit who dwells in, gives life to, and directs the church.

HOMILY NOTES

1. This is a day when we really must learn from our history as the community founded on Jesus.

2. The written gospels that we treasure came into their written form in the last third of the first century. Mark was probably written in the late 60s, John in the 90s, and very probably Matthew and Luke sometime in between. There are many subtle arguments moving the dates a bit this way or bit that way, but this is a broad consensus, and does for our purposes. The key fact is that the written gospels are not only at least a generation after the first disciples – a generation being about 25 years – but they are in the different cultural setting of the Hellenistic cities rather than rural Palestine.

3. Now we can ask a key question: was it a book or books that kept the people together and gave them identity during these early years, or was it something else? The simplistic answer is to think of Christians as, to use an oft-repeated but wholly inappropriate phrase, 'people of the book': so the key to Christian identity is that they accept 'The Bible' or 'The Gospels' or some such set of writings. But Jesus is the only religious leader in history that never wrote a book or dictated a book or even ordered a book to be written (writing in sand is hardly a good example of a desire for written records!).

4. What kept the community in being was its regular practices as a community and its memories recalled in community. To be a Christian is to be a member of a group, the community of the People of God, not to be just one more individual who buys into a philosophy or a spirituality.

5. How can we find out about these key practices? We can see them in three ways: first, we see them in a wonderful little guide for training new members which predates our written gospels and is given the rather off-putting title of The Training (the *Didache*). It is wonderful as it tells us directly what they had to do as a group. Second, we see these practices referred to now and again in the letters that are in the New Testament, most of which predate our gospels. Third, we see strange echoes of the practices in our gospels – they are 'strange echoes' as they usually are presented as an event which the first hearers of gospels would immediately see as

the 'original event' that is the background and authorisation for what they are actually doing.

6. So what were these key practices? The first, and most important practice, was that they gathered each week as a group – and the groups were probably no more than 25-50 people in size – and ate together the meal of the Lord. In the midst of a proper community meal, they thanked the Father for sending his Son to gather up the scattered flock of Israel and celebrated this re-gathering 'Jesus-style' by each getting his/her share in the one loaf and then each drinking from a single cup of blessing as they all had a single life-force surging through their veins. At this gathering they recalled the memory of Jesus and welcomed new members through baptism. This practice would become our Sunday Eucharist – the actual meal disappeared, and the memories were fixed by being written down. Over the centuries there have been other changes that have made the basic facts of eating and drinking less obvious, but one can still make out the pattern.

7. During the rest of the week they had fixed community practices. Fasting on Wednesdays and Fridays, and giving to charity were the two material practices of prominence. We see this given an 'echo' in the gospels in scene when Jesus tells the disciples to fast but not show off that you are fasting, to give alms but not ostentatiously, and to pray but not where everyone will see you (Mt 6). There was also a practice that was carried out each day: three times each day they recited the prayer we call the 'Our Father'. This was done probably at morning, noon, and in the evening. It is this practice that is being given an origin point and 'authorisation' in the words of Jesus himself, and a specific purpose, in today's gospel reading.

8. There is a strange aspect to this prayer that we usually miss when we say it during our Eucharists. It is the prayer of a group even when someone says it privately: it is a prayer to '*Our* Father, … give *us* this day … forgive *us our* trespasses as *we* forgive those who trespass against *us*, and lead *us* not, but

deliver *us* from …' What this tells us is that in those very first generations even when the group had not gathered together, the individuals had such a common sense of being part of the People of God, that they saw the fact that they were all praying at the same time (even if the individuals were physically apart) meant that they were offering a single group prayer. At morning, noon, and evening, even when alone, the Christians prayed as the single body of Christ to their Father.

9. This need for prayer at fixed times, and indeed to recite the Our Father, continued as part of the Liturgy of the Hours but this (with odd exceptions) is now something confined to 'professional religious people.' (You could show a volume of the Breviary as a visual aid at this point.) And, in any case, this is a far too cumbersome prayer for someone racing to get out in the morning, get the kids out, and get everything else done. However, saying the 'Our Father' – the bedrock of regular Christian prayer – is not too difficult: it does not require formally sitting or standing, it does not need so much time that a household needs to be ordered around the prayer, and it does not need a book.

10. Many Christians have today lost three precious understandings. First, Christians have, to a large extent, lost the sense of the importance of formal prayer at regular times. Yet all human experience of religion – just look at the regular prayer times in Islam – not to mention our experience from the very first days of the church shows us that regular formal prayer is essential to preserve our sense of God. Second, Christians have often lost the sense that when we pray as Christians it is not my prayer and your prayer, but *our* prayer in Jesus. The sense of a common time uniting separated people is something that used to be reinforced by the Angelus Bell just as in Islam it is done by the voice of the muezzin, but we need to recall that when we prayer simultaneously we are praying as one body and I pray at this time to join my prayer with that of the body. Praying simultaneously is a non-computer-based 'virtual community'. Third, to be a Christian is to be a disciple,

a disciple is one who learns over time and takes on the practices, the discipline, of the master. The master prayed regularly – as we hear about Jesus in today's gospel – so must we.

11. A recovery of the practice of everyone saying the 'Our Father' morning, noon, and evening is the basis of a renewal programme for the whole church, that does not need a single meeting or handbook to get it started.

Eighteenth Sunday of Ordinary Time

Introduction to the Celebration

My friends in Christ, our culture is one where sudden death rarely visits us and where we are encouraged to place our trust in material wealth as never before. But today we have the stark reminder that this world is passing. A moment will come when this life is no more. It is that moment that calibrates our value system of what is true wealth: a vast hoard of money, or riches in God's sight. Let us reflect on our values, on where we place our trust, and ask for mercy.

Rite of Penance

O Master, for the times when we have failed to guard against avarice. Lord have mercy.

O Master, for the times when we have placed our trust in material wealth. Christ have mercy.

O Master, for the times when we have not set our hearts on being rich in the sight of God. Lord have mercy.

Headings for Readings

First Reading

This is the famous warning – vanity of vanities, all is vanity – about seeing this world and its work as an end itself.

Second Reading

We are the people who acclaim that Christ has died, Christ is risen, Christ will come again. Therefore, St Paul reminds us, our lives must reflect being the people who proclaim this mystery of faith.

Gospel

One of the hard questions we have to ask ourselves as followers of Jesus is whether we are placing too much store on material things. Is our desire to grasp more and more possessions or to be rich in the sight of God?

Prayer of the Faithful
President
As people who are in need of God's help, let us stand before the Father and ask for our needs and the needs of all humanity.
Reader(s)
1. That we may not be deluded by material wealth. Lord hear us.
2. That we may care for the poor. Lord hear us.
3. That we may work for a just distribution of the creation's resources. Lord hear us.
4. That we may have the courage to reset our values. Lord hear us.
5. *Specific local needs and topics of the day.*
6. That those who have already been called in death, may rise in glory. Lord hear us.
President
Father, your Son taught us to set our hearts on your kingdom and to seek what is wealth in your sight; grant us the values of the kingdom through Christ our Lord. Amen.

Eucharistic Prayer
Preface of Sundays in Ordinary Time V [P33] (Missal, p 436) stresses that we are the stewards, not the owners, of the gift of the creation, and so we should use it with wisdom.

Invitation to the Our Father
The kingdom, the power, and the glory belong to the Father so, conscious of the Christ's call to recognise where true treasure lies, let us pray:

Sign of Peace
Peace is one of the treasures of the kingdom; let us acknowledge to one another that this is a value we are pursuing.

Invitation to Communion

To all who sought wisdom from him, our Saviour invited them to learn the new ways of the kingdom by sharing his table with them. Now we are called to share this table and learn his wisdom. Happy are we who are now gathered here.

Communion Reflection

Christ has died, Christ is risen, Christ will come again.

We have been raised with Christ,
We must seek the things that are above,
where Christ is, seated at the right hand of God.

Christ has died, Christ is risen, Christ will come again.

Let us set our minds on the things that are above,
not on things that are on earth.

Christ has died, Christ is risen, Christ will come again.

We have died in Christ at our baptism, and our lives are hidden with Christ in God.
We look forward to when Christ, who is our life, appears,
then we also will appear with him in glory.

Christ has died, Christ is risen, Christ will come again.
Based on the Second Reading

Conclusion

Prayer over the People 20 (Missal, p 383), which can easily be read as three separate verses inviting the response 'Amen' and would thus be transformed into a Solemn Blessing, is well suited to today.

COMMENTARY

First Reading: Qoh 1:2; 2:21-23

The sections on vanity – and the portion we are reading is only one such item from many – can be read in two ways. First, they can be read as world-weary cynicism: why bother, it will all end in dust anyway. Or they can be read as a warning to avoid the delusions of matter and its illusion of stability and security. Given that this text has been read, used and preserved by theists down the centuries, and it is in that context that it is being used now, it is this latter approach that constitutes its exegesis.

Psalm: 89
This psalm picks up the wisdom theme from the first reading and anticipates the gospel; the alternative (Ps 94) has nothing to recommend it in the context of today's Liturgy of the Word.

Second Reading: Col 3:1-5, 9-11
The community of the baptised (i.e. those 'brought back to true life in Christ') must, in the time before the eschaton, live in a new manner. Then, following in a well-known method of teaching among the early Christians borrowed from contemporary Jewish practice, we are given a list of things to avoid as not belonging to the Way of Life. Not only that, but Christians must also have a new way of relating to one another given the new image of God that is given to them in baptism – so that there is now no room for earthly distinctions. The deepest identity of each is with one another, and they all share the new 'image of God' which is Christ Jesus.

First Reading > Gospel Links
Based on a similarity of teaching between the wisdom tradition's identification of the fool, i.e. the un-wise man, who trusts in materials things – which is silliness – and the identification of the fool in the gospel who believes that material possessions bring ultimate safety.

Gospel: Lk 12:13-21
This passage, the parable of the Rich Fool, is found only in Luke's gospel, but draws together some basic elements from the wisdom tradition on the foolishness of placing final trust in the security of material possession. This wisdom tradition is more sophisticated than the proverbial 'You can't take it with you' or 'There are no pockets in a shroud' which could be simply be a

variant on 'Eat, drink, for tomorrow we will be dead' (cf 1 Cor 15:32). Rather the purpose of the wisdom is that one imagines that one can have control over one's environment or that material advantages bring long-term security. In the face of the contingency of human life, and of matter, the wise person has to place their long-term trust in God.

HOMILY NOTES

1. Going to extremes is always easy; and preaching extremes has an elegant simplicity as every demagogue knows. Striking a balance and acting with wisdom and prudence is more difficult and more tiring. Today we have to reflect on one of these tensions: between possessing in this life, and having 'treasure in the sight of God'. The tension can be expressed in any number of ways: between care of this life and care of the life to come; having concern for the creation and concern for eternity. It is the great 'either/or' of umpteen sermons.

2. But this gospel avoids making one extreme the position of Jesus. The one who has gone to the extreme is the man in the parable. He is a fool because he has concentrated on the earthly at the expense of the heavenly.

3. Let us think about the extremes for a moment. One extreme is to be so wholly focused on heaven that one is 'no earthly use'. The other extreme is to be so enmeshed in material pursuits that one becomes just another material object. The first gives away everything, but human poverty might be just as great after this extreme gesture as before. The other is indifferent to human suffering and poverty, and the world is as badly off after that person as before.

4. The really difficult calling of the whole church and of each of us individually is to embrace the tension, and seek to wisely judge between extremes each day. This is not only the wisdom of prudence, but it is more difficult because it calls on us to think about situations carefully, and it is tiring for we have to keep at the task day-in and day-out.

5. We have to find the balances between:

> Love of Self / Love of Others
>
> Appreciating the material creation / Knowing its limited existence
>
> Bodily health / Penance
>
> Service to neighbour / Prayer and Reflection
>
> Enjoying God's gifts / Fasting
>
> Liturgy as ritual / Liturgy as working for justice

'Both-and' is more demanding than 'either-or.'

6. The ecological movement has a great slogan: 'Think Global; Act Local.' We as Christians can wholly endorse the idea: we have to keep the big picture in mind (the creation comes from God and is returning to him – that is our version of 'Thinking global'); but while we are within the process of living in this world, we have to pay careful attention to the demands for our responsible action that are close to hand (action in the creation here and now is our 'Acting local').

7. It would be useful if Christians could come up with a slogan to go alongside 'Think Global; Act Local'; the best I can think of is: 'Think of Heaven; Work on Earth' – perhaps your assembly could come up with a really snappy slogan.

Nineteenth Sunday of Ordinary Time

Introduction to the Celebration

The gospel today reminds us that we must 'stand ready' for the return of the Lord. We must be people who are 'dressed for action' and have our 'lamps lit' and be those who are 'found awake'. Let us reflect on how we are often not quite up to the mark or have 'postponed till later' the call to witness to Jesus.

Rite of Penance

Lord Jesus, for the times we have not been ready to follow you with our lamps lit. Lord have mercy.

Lord Jesus, for the times when we have not been ready to open the door at your knock and welcome you into our lives. Christ have mercy.

Lord Jesus, for the times when we have not been ready to welcome you when you came among us in unexpected ways in the poor and needy. Lord have mercy.

Headings for Readings

First Reading

The People of God were united by the trust they placed in God, by remembering in common God's mercy, and by offering sacrifice together.

Second Reading

We refer to Abraham as 'our father in faith'. Now in this reading we see how a group of early Christians reflected on this to remind them that faith involves placing our trust in realities that are unseen for the time being.

Gospel

This gospel reminds us that we must be a people who stand ready for the return of the Lord.

Prayer of the Faithful

President

Friends, gathered here as a royal priesthood in Christ Jesus, we can stand and place our needs before the Father.

Reader(s)

1. That this little flock will not be fearful, but ready to do the Father's will. Lord hear us.

2. That the whole Christian body will be alert to the coming of the Christ among us in umpteen unexpected ways. Lord hear us.

3. That all in poverty or need will find hope through our willingness to sell our possessions and give alms. Lord hear us.

4. That all who fear for the future or who have lost hope may get new strength from our courage. Lord hear us.

5. *Specific local needs and topics of the day.*

6. That all our brothers and sisters who have died may be welcomed by the Son of Man and brought into the heavenly banquet. Lord hear us.

President

Father, you sent your Son to call us to be disciples. As we journey along our path we place our trust in you and our needs before you, hear us and answer us through Christ Jesus our Lord. Amen.

Eucharistic Prayer

Preface of Sundays in Ordinary Time I (Missal, p 432); and Eucharistic Prayer I should be used as it takes up the theme of the second reading: 'Abraham, our father in faith.'

Invitation to the Our Father

As a people who stand waiting for the coming of the kingdom, let us now pray:

Sign of Peace

We are made sisters and brothers in Christ by his gathering us around this table. Let us express our love for each other in the sign of peace.

Invitation to Communion

The Lord has come among us, has gathered us, and now he feeds us with the food of heaven. Happy are we who are called to this, his supper.

Communion Reflection

It seems to come as a great surprise every time a survey on Mass attendance is conducted that figures are falling. As with any social change among Christians, the causes are complex. However, one constant note is the desire for greater intimacy in liturgy. This is strange as many people find the sense of community in Pentecostal 'worship services' more intimate than the setting of the Eucharist. This is strange precisely because there can hardly be a more intimate setting than being gathered around a table. But most celebrations of the Eucharist are still plagued by the legacy of centuries of incomprehension by virtually everyone present which led to a dichotomy between meaning and symbol. On the one hand, there was the activity of the priest seen in terms of a perfect sacrifice towards God with people simply present; on the other, there was 'taking communion' which was the fact of obtaining the ultimate spiritual commodity by those who were fit and worthy to receive it. That the Eucharist was an intimate activity of thanking the Father in union with Jesus, while the community was transformed into Christ in his sacred meal, was lost sight of almost entirely in practice and catechesis. But if the Eucharist is not normally intimate, then it somehow fails to take into account the nature of the incarnation; and, sadly, Christians seek ritual intimacy elsewhere. So trim back on words, and put the energy into creating a real table fellowship. Then in the intimacy, and the concomitant informality, of being actually at a table, breaking up a loaf and sharing it with one another, drinking from a single cup passed from one to another, see if people can reflect on what Jesus has called them to share without the leader having to supply words.

Conclusion

Solemn Blessing for Ordinary Time IV (Missal, p 373) picks up several themes of the readings.

Notes

The Shorter Forms of the Readings

Today is unusual in that there is a shorter form both of the second reading and of the gospel. In both cases these are to be preferred. In the case of the gospel the longer text, although it is continuous in Luke, is a combination of several items within Luke's tradition, and this gives too many starting points (each quite substantial in nature) for a focus at a celebration of the Eucharist. The shorter form provides more than sufficient material for a gathering for the Eucharist to ponder upon.

In the case of the second reading the shorter form is to be preferred but for a different reason. On every Sunday in Ordinary Time the second reading is something of an intrusion between the first reading and the gospel, and today's longer form is so long that it unbalances the whole rhythm of the Liturgy of the Word.

COMMENTARY

First Reading: Wis 18:6-9

The final section (18:5-19:22) of the Wisdom of Solomon is a reflection on the last plague suffered by the Egyptians, the first Passover night, and the exodus from Egypt. In this passage we have an account of how the people were to treat this memory as the basis for their liturgy; and thus we have an account giving witness to the importance of the Passover celebrations as being at the heart of the liturgical year in some strands of Judaism at the time of Jesus.

Second Reading: Heb 11:1-2, 8-12 [longer form: 8-19]

Abraham journeyed to find a land in which to dwell. However, this reading uses this to state that there is no permanent dwelling on earth – he lived in Canaan as if in a strange land.

The city would be built by God, and this the author intends us to see as heaven, and it is that city's citizens that are Abraham's true descendents. This reading is a fine example of how the early church re-read the Old Testament and, by giving it a 'spiritual' interpretation, used it to explain, expand, and expound their own beliefs.

First Reading > Gospel Links

The link is most obscure. One possible link is that the first reading deals with the commitment to liturgy and faithfulness, and there is a notion of faithfulness in being 'ready' for the Lord's return.

Gospel: Lk 12:35-40 [longer form: 32-48]

While this material is not found only in Luke, it is so transformed by him that it can be treated as if it were found only in his gospel. Verse 35 marks the beginning of a section on watchfulness and faithfulness so that the disciples are ready for the moment when 'the Son of Man' returns. However, the internal elements seem to concern those who are the servants and stewards of the community: if they do their task well and persevere in it, then they will be rewarded with a reversal of roles. Having been servants of the master's table, then they will be given seats and waited upon by the master. Meanwhile, they must be careful in how they carry out their tasks for they do not know when he will return.

We can read this gospel in two ways. First, it can be read as a general warning 'to be alert' for the Lord's return – a theme found in many places in the gospels. Second, as a warning intended primarily for those with special positions in the churches where Luke preached that they be good servants of those churches.

HOMILY NOTES

1. This is one of those Sundays when the readings are not really suitable for exposition in a homily of between five and ten

minutes. That does no mean that there is not much that could be preached upon in them; rather it is a case that to give a homily that would offer something to an average congregation, while building directly on the readings, would probably need longer than is usually available. So one way around this is to link the gospel to another text which can be expounded in the space of five-ten minutes.

2. The gospel says we have to be ready for the Son of Man to come again among us? So who are we who must stand ready, with our lamps lit? An answer is provided in Preface of Sundays in Ordinary Time I:

   We are the people freed from sin by Christ's cross and resurrection. We 'stand ready' every time we celebrate this paschal mystery, as we are doing now.

   We are the people who have been called to the life of glory, we are united with Christ Jesus in baptism.

   We have become a chosen race, a royal priesthood, a holy nation, a people set apart.

3. And if this is who we are, then standing ready means that we have certain tasks entrusted to us.

   Everywhere we must proclaim God's mighty works. Why? Because we have been called out of darkness into the wonderful light of God.

Twentieth Sunday of Ordinary Time

Introduction to the Celebration

Dear Friends, each week we gather in union with Jesus, the Christ, the Anointed One, the Son of the Father, the Word made flesh and listen to his words, share his table, and join our lives with his great act of thanksgiving to the Father. But how often do we ask ourselves have we an adequate image in our minds of who it is we are following as Christians? Today the readings pull us up short and ask us to deepen our understanding of Jesus. We often think of Jesus as 'the man of peace'; but today we hear that he is a prophet who came to bring division rather than peace. We sometimes reduce our understanding of Jesus to being some kind of moral teacher with a few 'general simple truths', but today we hear that Jesus, the Son of God, is 'the pioneer and perfecter of our faith, who for the joy that was set before him endured the cross, despising the shame, and is seated at the right hand of the throne of God.' Now, assembled in his presence, let us ask him to give us a deeper understanding of himself and his good news.

Rite of Penance

Lord Jesus, you are our Saviour, our Redeemer, and our Source of Life. Lord have mercy.

Lord Jesus, you are our Way, our Shepherd, and our path to the Father. Christ have mercy.

Lord Jesus, you are our Wisdom, our Guide, and King of Heaven and Earth. Lord have mercy.

Headings for Readings

First Reading

The prophet is one who in serving God brings trouble among the people of God on earth.

Second Reading
Jesus now has taken his place at the right of God's throne in heaven, there he intercedes for us his people.

Gospel
The coming of Jesus is the arrival of the time of decision: our bonds to one another in him may sometimes even cut across our family ties.

Prayer of the Faithful
Use the Sample Formula for General Intercessions for Ordinary Time I (Missal, p 1002).

Eucharistic Prayer
There is no Preface or Eucharistic Prayer that is particularly suited to the readings of this day.

Invitation to the Our Father
Jesus has taken his place at the right of God's throne and he now invites us to pray:

Sign of Peace
Let us acknowledge the bonds of love that link each of us who have been born anew in Christ Jesus.

Invitation to Communion
The Lord comes among us and calls us to recognise ourselves anew as members of this family around his table.

Communion Reflection
Take the list of titles relating to Jesus and use each of them as a litany with the response: 'Thank you for sharing your life with us.'

Conclusion
If you have focused on how we perceive Jesus, then the Solemn

Blessing for the Advent Season (Missal, p 367) will serve equally well for today as it focuses on the Christ-event in a way that none of the others do.

First Reading: Jer 38:4-6, 8-10

This is one incident in the much longer section of the book that deal with the sufferings of Jeremiah that take place before the fall of Jerusalem in 587 BC. There are several similar incidents in the part of the book (in 37:11-21) where Jeremiah's crime is that he is sowing dissention among the soldiery ('weakening the hands of the warriors') in the face of the forces coming against them.

Psalm: 39

The second stanza of this psalm as given in the Lectionary today picks out the experience of the prophet ('He drew me from the deadly pit …') in the first reading, and interprets this as the basis for the prophet trusting in God. However, it does not relate that reading to the gospel.

Second Reading: Heb 12:1-4

We have to think of the whole letter as a great imaginative stage which combines (1) the imagery of the royal court with its careful gradations of exclusiveness and separation which serve to emphasise the power and aloofness of the king, with (2) the imagery of the temple with its decreasing circles each of which is more sacred than the one larger than the previous circle. Now there at the centre, at God's right hand, is Jesus who is the one who has endured hardships and opposition from sinners. So he is the source of consolation for his followers who are now suffering. But because they can hear the letter being read to them, then they have not yet had to suffer to the extreme extent that Jesus did (i.e. they have not yet been put to death).

First Reading > Gospel Links

The link is intended to be the similarity of situation between Jeremiah (whose work leads to him causing disaffection among the soldiers) and Jesus (whose work will cause division). However, the most memorable section of the first reading is the rescue of Jeremiah, not what led to his imprisonment; and the similarity between his actions and what Jesus says in the gospel is pretty far-fetched. This is a Sunday where the link simply does not work, and one suspects that the compilers were at their wit's end to find a passage to accompany the gospel, and this was the best they could find.

Gospel: Lk 12:49-53

Although this statement by Luke is more fulsome, this material is also found in Mt 10:34-36, and has been a source of anguish to preachers for centuries. If one accepts this as a basic verse within a christology, then the result is a messiah who comes to lead just a few people who accept his message in a form that revels in any clash with the times and the cultures in which people live. On the other hand, if one relegates these verses it could appear that one is praising peace at the price of compromising the word of God. Moreover, it was only with the advances in hermeneutics in the twentieth century that this sort of dilemma was successfully transcended.

But very briefly, we can view these collections of sayings (in Matthew and Luke) in this way. First, the starting point is the actual opposition to Jesus during his ministry, which has continued into the time of the church in opposition to those who embrace its teachings about Jesus. The fact is the opposition, and with this the fact that friendships are being broken and so are bonds of loyalty within families. Second, this is acknowledged in words by Jesus and the format of these words is a form of exaggeration that makes the point that the opposition is inevitable. He not only accepts it has happened, but knew 'all along' that it would happen; indeed, he wishes it to happen as it would make sure that people were coming to a decision about discipleship.

The problem with this text is that the statements taken as 'words from the bible' or 'the plain words of Jesus' can, within a popular biblical hermeneutic, be taken as a justification for assessing religious ideas as being those which are most likely to provoke opposition in the larger society. This effectively confuses the necessary counter-cultural stance that Christians need to take on specific points with an attitude of being awkward 'for Jesus', on the assumption that the larger society is inherently sinful and corrupt.

HOMILY NOTES

1. A homily at a Sunday Eucharist is not a suitable occasion to tackle the difficulties of today's gospel; the backgrounds of the average congregation are too diverse to assume any of the levels of understanding to deal with this complex gospel theme; and even if the congregation has a great many people who have a good familiarity with the gospels and their exegesis, there is not the time in a homily to grapple with these five verses. However, one can use the gospel reading as a peg to hang an exploration of the question 'Who is Jesus?' that is accessible to an average assembly. In this case one reads the gospel as a 'wake-up call': so you think you know about Jesus and his message? Well, just look at this text with its prediction of family strife which is so much at variance with much Christian preaching on the family. So you think you know his message of peace, then look at what this text says. So you think that the Christian gospel can be boiled down to some general set of 'great moral truths' – which are more or less the same in every religion but it just so happens that we hear them in the 'Jesus version,' then now look at this text and ask if Jesus fits neatly into your box.

2. If the congregation is a small one, then one can ask them to list all the different names and titles we give to Jesus. The resulting list then can form the basis for the homily. However, if the gathering is large, uncomfortable with the idea of participating in the homily, or is just generally reticent, then you

can provide a list of your own. The idea is to note the complexity of the list, and then see how the various names / titles / designations relate one to another.

3. Here is a list I have drawn up. I have come up with 50 names / titles in no particular order: Jesus Christ; the Christ; Christ; Messiah; Anointed One; Son of David; Son of Man; Son of God; Light; Light from light; Fisher of men; Shepherd; Man; King of the Jews; Sacred Heart; Prince of Peace; Son of Mary; Logos; Word; Word made flesh; Bread of life; The Crucified; The Man of Sorrows; Second Person of the Trinity; Guide; Carpenter's son; Alpha and Omega; Saviour; Conqueror of sin; Redeemer; King; the Infant of Prague; King of Kings; God; Priest; Prophet; Lord; Liberator; Son of the Father; High Priest; Master; Rabbi; Teacher; Healer; Lamb of God; Victor over death; Sovereign; Brother; Friend; 'the pioneer and perfecter of our faith'. We could keep going as any number of other images and titles have been given to Jesus within the life of the People of God; but probably in this list you will find all the common ones.

4. When we take any such lists we notice that (1) they can be seen to belong to various frames of reference; and (2) that all these names have to be co-coordinated to one another.

5. Just to keep it neat, I break these into seven boxes:

First, we have names that are used by Jesus or of Jesus in the four gospels: the Christ (= Messiah; Anointed One); Son of David; Son of Man; Man; King of the Jews; Son of Mary; Bread of life; Carpenter's son; King; Prophet; Lord; Master; Rabbi; Teacher Lamb of God.

Second, we have names that have been used since the first generations of Christians: Son of God; Light; Shepherd; Prince of Peace; Son of Mary; Logos; Word; Word made flesh; Bread of life; The Crucified; The Man of Sorrows; Alpha and Omega; Saviour; Conqueror of sin; Redeemer; King; God; Priest; Prophet; Lord; Son of the Father; High Priest; Master; Rabbi; Teacher; Healer; Lamb of God; 'the pioneer and perfecter of our faith.'

Third, we have names that are derived from our reflection on the history of salvation: Messiah = Anointed One; Son of David; Son of Man; Prince of Peace; The Man of Sorrows; King; King of Kings; Priest; Prophet; Lord; High Priest.

Fourth, we have names that have to be linked with one another if they are not to be found wanting: 'Son of God' with 'Son of Mary'; 'Man' with 'God.'

Fifth, we have names that are used in the church's formal expression of faith: Light from light; Second Person of the Trinity; Redeemer.

Sixth, we have names that come from popular devotions: Sacred Heart; Infant of Prague.

Seventh, we have informal names, but which capture essential aspects of our faith: Shepherd; Guide; Carpenter's son; Liberator; Teacher; Healer; Brother; Friend.

6. The ways we could group the names is endless; just as we could keep adding to the list. The need for all these names is that the person at the centre of our faith exceeds all our understanding. A mystery is not a puzzle, but a reality so beyond our understanding that we have to keep trying to grasp it, now this way, now that. But these various glimpses must always be used in 'both-and' mode, rather than in the 'either-or' mode, of understanding. The 'either-or' mode is suitable for ordinary everyday objects of understanding; but if 'to understand'/'to appreciate' another person we might meet every day in the flesh we need to use the 'both-and' mode, how much more is this true of our seeking the one who came 'to bring fire upon the earth.'

7. No group's list, nor individual's list, will be the same as any other, but what is included and what is missed out may provide a glimpse into that group's or individual's level of religious awareness and spirituality.

Twenty-first Sunday of Ordinary Time

Introduction to the Celebration

We have gathered here to eat and drink in the company of the Lord. And when we do this we declare our desire to be gathered to the Lord with a place at the heavenly banquet. Let us reflect on what we are now doing, and ask the Lord to grant us forgiveness and a place in the kingdom.

Rite of Penance

Lord, grant us a place in your kingdom with Abraham, Isaac, Jacob and all the prophets. Lord have mercy.

Lord, grant us a place in your kingdom with people from east and west and north and south. Christ have mercy.

Lord, grant us a place in your kingdom with all who sit at table at your wonderful feast. Lord have mercy.

Headings for Readings
First Reading

The prophet reminds the people that God will gather the righteous to himself from every nation, and they will be made as welcome as if they had been priests in the temple in Jerusalem.

Second Reading

The writer wishes to encourage Christians who are suffering: they should see their suffering as the Lord training them.

Gospel

Jesus reminds the people that God will gather the righteous to himself from every nation, and Abraham, Isaac, Jacob, and all the prophets will welcome them.

Prayer of the Faithful
President

As children of the Father, let us put our needs before him.

Reader(s)

1. For the holy church, that we may be worthy of the fellowship of the saints. Lord hear us.

2. For this community, that we may not be complacent in our following of the Way of Christ. Lord hear us.

3. For all people of goodwill, that they may know the ways of truth. Lord hear us.

4. For all who serve in public office, that they may pursue justice and peace. Lord hear us.

5. *Specific local needs and topics of the day.*

6. For all who have died from every faith and none, that the Lord may show them mercy and gather them with Abraham, Isaac, and Jacob. Lord hear us.

President

Father, we pray as your children; hear us as sisters and brothers of Jesus, your Son. Amen.

Eucharistic Prayer

The Preface of Christian Unity [P75] fits with the gospel, and should be used with Eucharistic Prayer III which employs the prophetic image of the final in-gathering from east and west.

Invitation to the Our Father

The Lord Jesus announced the coming kingdom when people will be gathered from east and west and north and south; let us now pray for its coming:

Sign of Peace

People will gather from all parts of the earth to form the Kingdom of Peace; we here are expected to be a model of that final peace to all humanity. So let us offer one another a sign of peace.

Invitation to Communion
Behold we are the people who have been gathered from north and south and east and west to take our places at this feast. May we also have places at the feast in the kingdom of God.

Communion Reflection
Lord, you have called us to this feast;
May we be present at the feast in the kingdom of God.

Lord, you have gathered us from many places;
May we be gathered together again in the kingdom of God.

Lord, you have united us in your body and blood,
May we be united with you and Abraham and Isaac and Jacob and the prophets in the kingdom of God.

Lord, you have welcomed us as table companions;
May you recognise us as your people at the banquet of heaven.

Conclusion
Use the Solemn Blessing for the Dedication of a Church (Missal, p 376) in an adapted form:
The Lord of earth and heaven
has assembled you before him this day.
May he fill you with the blessings of heaven. Amen.

God the Father wills that all his children
scattered throughout the world
become one family in his Son.
May he make you the dwelling-place of the Holy Spirit. Amen.

May God free you from every bond of sin,
dwell within you and give you joy.
May you live with him for ever
in the company of all his saints. Amen.

COMMENTARY

First Reading: Isa 66:18-21

This comes from the final section of Third Isaiah, and of the whole book as it was transmitted. In the new world, when God's plan is fully revealed, all nations on earth will have a place. This completion is read in the church as coming about with the coming of the Christ who is not only the glory of Israel but the light for all nations (Lk 2:32).

Second Reading: Heb 12:5-7, 11-13

Heb 12:1-13 deals with God's treatment of his children in order to train them; and Jesus is the model of patient learning. However, this reading by omitting the middle three verses is virtually unintelligible as it omits the key reference to training children that makes sense of the remaining verses. As such, what we have is no more than some sentences that could be read as pious propositions – but the lection in no way represents the meaning of the author of Hebrews.

First Reading > Gospel Links

Continuity of a theme in teaching is the link. The continuity of the teaching is that at the eschaton the mercy of God will reach all humanity and people would be 'gathered in' as 'the chosen' irrespective of original bounds of the covenant community. The continuity of theme is that this is expressed using a geographical model of a centre and circular periphery. In the first reading the lands named are those surrounding the central lands of the eastern Mediterranean; in the gospel this periphery is referred to by indicating the extreme areas as those of the cardinal directions: 'the north', 'the east', and so on.

Gospel: Lk 13:22-30

This gospel reading, whose text is also found in Matthew, concerns exclusion from the kingdom, and the focus of its teaching is that there is no automatic link between being part of the people of Israel and a place in the presence of the Father. The Father can raise up children of Abraham from every place and people. When heard as part of Luke's preaching, this was the assurance that the Gentile converts could share fully in the promises made to Israel.

HOMILY NOTES

1. There is no automatic entry to the kingdom! Being part of the right 'party' or having filled in all the right forms or having ticked all the boxes is not what will lead us to be called to a place in the kingdom. God's love and mercy look to the heart, not to the outward appearance. This mystery that belonging to the church is not some sort of 'guarantee' has been expressed traditionally in a more extreme form: 'There are many with a place in the church who will not have a place in the kingdom, and there will be many in the kingdom who have not been part of the church.' We could express this far more positively: there are people in every age and culture and religion who will hear the voice of the Spirit and inherit everlasting life.

2. We could also note that this view of salvation, which has been the constant faith of the church, shows how wide of the mark is any exclusivist interpretation of salvation whether it be that as found in elect sects or in some narrow interpretation of 'outside the church is no salvation.' However, we should also note that most non-Christians either imagine that Christians have such a narrow interpretation of who will have a place in the kingdom, or else project such a narrow interpretation onto Christians so as to denigrate them. How often do we hear in an interview, 'But you Christians, or you Catholics, believe only those who believe in Jesus can be saved and the rest are damned!' The aim here is to show that any god who would be so mean to the vast majority of humanity over the history of world is so mean-spirited as to be unworthy of belief that proceeds out of loving freedom rather than servile fear. Then when the interviewee replies that 'Christians [or Catholics] do not hold such exclusivist

views,' they are accused of presenting a modern 'soft' option! An extremist misrepresentation is often preferred by questioners as it makes it easier to dismiss Christianity as foolish. Alas, there are many Christians who then accept this position and either adopt the extremist position thinking it the truth, or else reject it but then think they are not really at one with the tradition. Today is an ideal opportunity to lay out the standard Catholic position.

3. It can be done in three steps.

- The gospel expounds the position that membership of the club – Luke was thinking of the church – is not what grants salvation but seeking to do the will of God.

- Anyone who seeks out the voice of truth and justice in their hearts, this being a law knowable from within our human nature, and lives by it will be called to take her or his place at the feast in the kingdom.

- For those of us who have heard the word of God revealed in Christ Jesus there is the blessing of knowing the joy to which we are called by God, for example we seek to anticipate that feast each time we gather, but also the greater responsibility to build the kingdom of truth, life, holiness, grace, justice, love, and peace.

4. We have to always bear in mind that we must bear witness to the God who is love, rather than just willful force. Any action that if it were done by a human to another would be mean, is not an action with which we can imagine the activity of God. So for example, we cannot imagine giving two people life but then arbitrarily taking one life while rewarding another without imagining the actor as capricious. But capriciousness is not consistent with constant caring love and justice; therefore we cannot imagine God as capricious.

5. To state clearly that Christians are not exclusivist in their view of God's love towards them – which is a very different thing to stating some relativist notion that all religions are the same – can often lift a burden from members of a congregation who are troubled about the fate of their loved

ones. It can also put clear water between the great church and the many sectarian forms of Christianity that capture the headlines and the TV channels.

Twenty-second Sunday of Ordinary Time

Introduction to the Celebration

Today at our meal in this house we recall a Sabbath day meal when Jesus saw how people sought out places of honour at the table, and he reminded them that the values of the kingdom are the opposite of the earthly values of power and prestige: in the kingdom the humble shall be exalted. Now let us reflect on how we have gathered for this meal with Jesus: do we see each other as sisters and brothers; do we see ourselves as servants to each other; and do we see ourselves as the servants of all who are poor.

Rite of Penance

Option c vi (Missal, p 394) is appropriate.

Headings for Readings

First Reading

The way of gentleness and humility is the way of wisdom.

Second Reading

We Christians have gathered to form the church but this is not something that looks anything out of the ordinary; but to those who have faith it is the mystery of coming into the presence of God in Jesus, and so we use many images to try to communicate this reality.

Gospel

This is the story of a Sabbath-day meal, but it is also Luke preaching about the values and attitudes of those who gather for the Eucharist.

Prayer of the Faithful
President
We have gathered here for this Sunday meal of the Lord. With him let us place our needs before the Father.
Reader(s)
1. For all who are celebrating the Eucharist today, that we may all recognise each other as brothers and sisters in the Lord Jesus. Lord hear us.
2. For the whole human family, that they may know the Lord's goodness and share the riches of the creation justly. Lord hear us.
3. For all who have departed from our gathering, that they may rejoin the table fellowship of the church. Lord hear us.
4. For all those who are scandalised by the actions of Christians, that they may see through our failings to the Lord's truth. Lord hear us.
5. *Specific local needs and topics of the day.*
President
Father, we are unworthy of the hospitality of your Son, but rejoice in it, answer our prayers and grant that we may act with gentleness and humility in all we do. We ask this in the name of Jesus, your Son, our Lord. Amen.

Eucharistic Prayer
Eucharistic Prayer I for Masses with Children presents a very rounded, yet easily accessible, theology of the Eucharist. It is too good to be kept just for classroom celebrations or for when children form the majority. Its elegant simplicity makes it ideal for the average congregation on Sunday for whom the beauties of the four main prayers are often too intricate and require too much background knowledge to be fully appreciated.

Invitation to the Our Father
At this our Sunday meal, in the presence of Christ, let us now pray:

Sign of Peace

Our gatherings are to be models of love, caring for one another, and of peace, let us join with each other in praying that we will become the community Christ calls us to become.

Invitation to Communion

This indeed is the Lamb of God who takes away the sins of the world, and calls us to share in his banquet.

Communion Reflection

Lord Jesus, to your meal you invite the poor;
Having received your riches in this holy food may we be empowered to serve the poor.

Lord Jesus, to your meal you invite the crippled;
Having been healed by you in this banquet may we bring healing to all who are sick.

Lord Jesus, to your meal you invite the lame;
Having received strength from you may we learn to defend all who are weak.

Lord Jesus, to your meal you invite the blind;
Having been given the light of faith may we learn the way of humility and gentleness, and so radiate your light in our lives.

Conclusion

Solemn Blessing of Ordinary Time III (Missal, p 372) is suitable.

Notes

Preaching about the Eucharist at the Eucharist

Preaching about the Eucharist while actually participating in the Eucharist presents both special opportunities and special difficulties. The opportunities are obvious: you are drawing attention to what is actually going on, and as such there is no better way to explain anything than in the midst of practice. The difficulty is that if there is a chasm between what is preached about it and what is communicated by the actual celebration, then not only one's words but the reality is made to look a sham. Consider this introduction to the liturgy:

> You are all very welcome here today [while thumbing missal to find the right page] and this is the holy meal of all God's people. [Page found] Now! I would ask that mothers with crying children take them to the crying room over there on the right. Would the collectors of team B take up the collection this morning, and there is a special retiring collection this week on the way out which is to support the diocesan renewal scheme. And, by the way I notice that today we have a lot of visitors and I would just remind them that only Catholics, who are in a state of grace, can receive Holy Communion. Now let us call to mind our sins and ask God to pardon us: I confess … .

One could pick out any number of problems in this from sloppiness to a lack of understanding of the Rite of Penance in the rite of 1970, but the big problem is that the word of welcome is at odds with everything else, which belongs to the sort of instruction one might get on entering a bus or a train.

The problem is this: if this is the meal of the Lord to which we are joyfully welcome, how can we be given an introduction like this? If this sort of reception were given in a hotel, people would decide not to stay. What is happening is that there is a disjunction between the word's formal content, and the non-verbal communication. If one is going to refer to the Eucharist, then the whole communication (verbal and non-verbal, formal and informal) must have an element of consistency – it is this note of consistency that is the hallmark of the 'genuine' in liturgy.

COMMENTARY

First Reading: Sir 3:17-18, 20, 28-29
This is a collection of wisdom sayings that highlight a theme set by the gospel. As with much of the advice in the wisdom tradition it takes the form of a teacher addressing a student as a 'my son'.

Second Reading: Heb 12:18-19, 22-24

This is the famous description of the mystery of the church whereby the community of those linked to Jesus the mediator is constituted as 'Mount Zion', 'the city of the living God', 'the heavenly Jerusalem' … This language is far from most western approaches to ecclesiology, but we should note that it inspires much of the imagery of the liturgy. Indeed, the structure of this reading is shared with that of the prefaces where the community at the Eucharist joins with all the ranks (named more clearly in Latin than in translation) and then sings with them: 'Holy, Holy, Holy Lord …'

First Reading > Gospel Links

The link is continuity of teaching: in both readings wisdom is linked directly to humility.

Gospel: Lk 14:1, 7-14

This story is found only in Luke. The omission of vv 2-6 is a piece of careful editing as it removed a healing story which, if left with today's gospel, would have confused its message. Given that this text is being interpreted in the context of a Sunday Eucharist, it is an ideal text for exegesis in a homily.

HOMILY NOTES

1. One of the problems that beset the early generations of Christians was disputes at the Eucharistic meal over the rich looking after themselves and disputes over precedence in a highly stratified society. Indeed, these difficulties may have been responsible for the way the ritual community meal developed into the ritual formal meal that we know as 'The Eucharist' (a name that emerged in the second century for a specific religious ritual). Luke was fully aware of these difficulties as in Acts he presents an idealised 'original period' that he wants communities to take as their model for how they should behave at this meal. So when Luke presents Jesus at a Sabbath meal teaching on how people should be-

have at a meal if they are wise, he wants his audience to see this teaching as applying directly to them and their behaviour at the Sunday meal.

2. So hearing this gospel today at our Sunday Eucharist is a direct invitation to us to see if our community practice at our sacred meal measures up to Jesus's teaching.

3. The characteristics are:

- Everyone must act with humility. A practical consequence of this is that everyone must see themselves as the servants of the community rather than those whom the community might feel honoured to serve.

- There must be no pandering or favouritism for the rich and powerful. Around the Lord's table there is a state of equality for all are equally there by God's invitation, grace, and mercy. Practically this has implications when 'dignitaries' are present and given special treatment, but it also has implications for ordinary gatherings where there can be special groups that see themselves as being 'special' in some way within the community and who seek to have this recognised.

- There must be a welcome in the community for the needy – all those signified by the phrase 'the poor, crippled, lame, and blind'. This means that the community must be making special efforts to see that no individual or group are excluded from the Lord's meal or made feel that they are not 'our sort'.

- A tone of genuine welcome and a spirit of service to one another should be palpable qualities of the assembly.

- The community must be aware of the dangers of a small clique running the parish so that the community's assembly is only an excuse for their needs for self-importance to be fulfilled.

4. Asking these questions can be hard, but the more the questions are feared, the more they are needed – and the more there is a need for the community to hear this gospel.

Twenty-third Sunday of Ordinary Time

Introduction to the Celebration

We have gathered here because we are disciples of the Lord Jesus: we have chosen his way as our way. Today he reminds us that this is no easy choice for his way led to the cross. He reminds us: 'Whoever does not bear his own cross and come after me, cannot be my disciple.' Discipleship embraces every aspect of our lives. Discipleship means that we have to plan for the best way to live our lives in the light of his truth. Yet, we all fall short of that way, we follow other paths, we avoid the cross, we think of the immediate rather than the goal of life. So as we gather for this meal of discipleship, let us renew our commitment to the way of the Lord and ask pardon for our deviations from it.

Rite of Penance

Lord Jesus, for the times we have failed to carry our crosses and be your disciples. Lord have mercy.

Lord Jesus, for the times when we have not taken into account in our decisions the demands of being your followers. Christ have mercy.

Lord Jesus, for the times when we have placed possessions ahead of needs of the poor. Lord have mercy.

Headings for Readings

First Reading

We can only know the ways of the Lord though his gift of wisdom: wisdom enlightens our darkness and lets us see the plan of God for the creation and our lives. It is this wisdom that can enable us to see that the Lord's way of the Cross is the way of wisdom and the way to the fullness of life.

Second Reading

Paul here writes Philemon, who was the owner of the slave

Onesimus, telling him how helpful Onesimus has been in his mission. Now Onesimus is returning to Philemon: but he must now be seen as a brother Christian, not as a slave.

Gospel
This gospel tells us of the cost of discipleship in stark terms: following the Lord demands a decision about how we live and how we love.

Prayer of the Faithful
President
Friends, we have the joy of being the sisters and brothers of the Lord, but we have the challenge that we must courageously build his kingdom. Let us pray for the strength and wisdom we need to fulfill our ministries.
Reader(s)
1. For the whole church of God, that we may have the courage to take up Christ's cross. Lord hear us.
2. For our own local church, that we may have the wisdom to know how to witness to Christ in our lives. Lord hear us.
3. For all our sisters and brothers who are suffering for the faith, that their sufferings cease. Lord hear us.
4. For all who persecute us or speak ill of the gospel, that the Lord will give them light and new understanding. Lord hear us.
5. *Specific local needs and topics of the day.*
6. For all who have died in Christ, that they rise to new life through Christ's victory on the cross over death. Lord hear us.
President
Father, we have set out on the way of discipleship. Give us strength to keep walking, give us mercy and healing when we stumble, give us hope as we struggle, for we make our life's pilgrimage in union with Jesus Christ, your Son, our Lord. Amen.

Eucharistic Prayer
There is no Preface or Eucharistic Prayer that is especially attuned to today's gospel.

Invitation to the Our Father
Having gathered as disciples of the Lord Jesus, let us pray as he taught the first disciples:

Sign of Peace
We have chosen the way of the Lord, this is the way of peace and of forgiveness for those who have hurt us. Let us offer a sign of this peace to one another.

Invitation to Communion
We have chosen the way of the Lord, the Lord bids us to draw strength for our journey through sharing his table with us. Lord I am not worthy …

Communion Reflection
The first reading today is not a text that can be simply read and grasped by the mind in the way a story can be grasped in a series of mental pictures. It is sapiential in tone and requires slow chewing over by the mind. But it is such a key text in our history as Christians that it is a terrible loss that it is just read through quickly as the first reading. Taken at the pace at which one reads a reflection, and in a less proclamatory tone, it makes a very fitting Communion Reflection for this day.

Conclusion
Solemn Blessing for Ordinary Time V (Missal, p 373) picks up the theme of discipleship.

COMMENTARY

First Reading: Wis 9:13-18
This is one of the 'classic' passages in the whole of the Wisdom literature contrasting our understanding of created realities with our glimpses of heavenly realities. It stands behind a whole tradition in Christian theology which emphasises that 'God is always greater' (*Deus semper maior*). Moreover, its theme that wisdom is a gift from above, and that the 'holy spirit' – or as

Christian tradition would render it: 'Holy Spirit' – is wisdom sent from above, has played a central role in the development of Christian pneumatology and, indeed, is the source of the prayer 'Come Holy Spirit, fill the hearts of thy faithful … '

Throughout the Wisdom literature 'wisdom ' is personified as someone abiding in the presence of God, somehow distinct but also not distinct from the Godhead. In Christian tradition this has been read in a Trinitarian fashion – both as the Logos and as the Spirit – and in the liturgical assembly where we celebrate within the fullness of the wisdom given us in the Christ, this is the appropriate way to read the passage.

Second Reading: Philem 9-10, 12-17

This reading brings us face to face with one of those aspects of Christian history we would now like to forget: that the early church had no difficulty with the notion of slavery. Paul had used another's slave in the way one might today use another's car – a fact made very clear in v 11, which is why it has been omitted to make the text more palatable. Later on popes would own slaves; Patrick would see it as a crime that his cleric father's slaves were stolen, but has no notion that it was wrong to own them in the first place; while the first time that one will find general Catholic condemnations of slavery is after its abolition in Brazil in the 1880s. Paul wants slaves treated as brothers, but they are still slaves.

Texts like this one makes us confront some hard questions and assumptions: first, the notion that the early church was some perfect time; second, that the social arrangements of that time set some ideal paradigm for church organisation; and third, it reminds us that we are still developing our understanding of what it means to affirm that Jesus is the one who came to set us free. It is a pity it has been made more palatable, as that short omission obscures the challenge that this reading poses to us.

First Reading > Gospel Links

The link is very complex. The gospel speaks of a new way of living

demanding a new wisdom about 'the things of God' – indeed a
wisdom that can be at odds with human wisdom when it chooses
the way of the cross. The first reading is a commentary on the
nature of this divine wisdom and its origins in our minds and
hearts as a gift. As such, the first reading is a commentary on the
gospel; but since it is read before the gospel in the liturgy it can
be seen as preparing people for it.

Gospel: Lk 14:25-33
This section is found only in Luke (Mt 10:37-8 has a parallel only
of vv 26-7) and brings the cost of discipleship before us in a stark
way that seems at odds with the notion of 'the gentle Luke'.
However, this section repeats what Luke has already written at
9:23-27, 57-62.

That one can embark on discipleship and yet fail is brought
out by three images: the foolish builder, the unwise king, and
the salt that has lost its taste (these last two verses have been
omitted in the lectionary and this has given the text a well-fo-
cused and rhetorically more satisfying ending; these final verses
of ch 14 are, in any case, almost certainly an interpolation at that
point) all illustrate that it is easy to take up a life-demanding
task but it requires wisdom/fortitude/dedication to complete it.

HOMILY NOTES

1. We live in a world of 'communication': phones, faxes, emails,
   text-messages, the internet, the radio, the television … Never
   has there been so many ways to 'communicate' or so many
   messages travelling around. Everywhere there is someone
   trying to plant an idea in your eye or ear.
2. However, how many of these messages are actually direct
   and unmediated human speech? Information comes through
   media, an actual human voice communicating is rare: face to
   face seems to be for chatting. Indeed, apart form formal
   boardroom style meetings and classrooms, there is almost
   nothing that is communicated without first being either
   typed or committed to an electrically driven machine. Now

consider the homily: it is the only time in common experience when people are spoken to directly as a group. Just ask people when was the last time they went somewhere and actually listened to a speech? Politicians may speak of going on the stump or the hustings, but what they actually do is go before a specially chosen audience and then deliver sound-bites for the TV news and photo opportunities.

3. So when you actually get up and preach you are engaging in what is now a very rare form of activity in the developed world. It is personal, direct, and bare of defences, images, and games. From this two things flow:

   First, we should remind our congregations just how rare it is for something to be set out without the possibility for spin and razzmatazz that modern media allow. Yes, it may not be slick, but there are no hiding places when all you have is a voice and a message.

   Second, this direct human communication is a rare event today, so capitalise on it and do not block it. We block it when a homily becomes a written message delivered orally: it should be the well-thought out reflections given 'in living voice' (*viva voce*) with the anxiety and sharpness which only *ex tempore* speaking possesses. Equally, do not block it by standing behind a psychological security curtain made up of an ambo or lectern: there should be no physical object between you and those you address. Of course, many argue that this is beyond their abilities – if that is the case then preaching is probably not your vocation and you should ask why you are attempting it: there is probably someone in your community who does have this calling and you should be empowering them rather than seeking to do it yourself.

4. But few cannot preach without notes or lectern, it is simply a matter of practice. So here is a simple formula.

5. Point out to your audience that you are speaking directly to them without the benefits of all the gimmicks and training of those who try to get their money by selling them things or their support by persuading them of ideas with all the skills of the 'communications industry'.

Then ask them what they think about what has just been read: that loyalty to the Christ is supposed to be paramount in their lives and that they must work with deliberation at being disciples in the same way they set about other major tasks in life.

Give a moment – around 30 seconds – to let the question settle in.

Then ask: how many of us believe this is the truth?

Give another moment to let this question settle.

Then conclude by pointing out that if you believe it is true, then you have to draw conclusions for how you live your life.

Lectionary Unit V

Pardon and Reconciliation

This unit consists of just one Sunday: Sunday 24. Its focus is on the 'gospel within the gospel': Jesus's message of pardon and reconciliation. It is devoted to Lk 15 (all but three verses of which are only found in this gospel) and which consists of a string of three parables: (1) the lost coin; (2) the lost sheep; and (3) the prodigal son.

Twenty-fourth Sunday of Ordinary Time

Introduction to the Celebration

Each of us can stand here because the Lord has sought us out and forgiven us. We call Jesus is 'our saviour', but we could just as easily call him 'our pardon' or 'our reconciliation' or 'the One who reveals the Father's love to us'. Now we gather to join with Jesus in offering thanks to the Father for his love, and to grow in our awareness of how we are sought out and welcomed home by the Christ.

Rite of Penance

Option c iv (Missal, p 393) is appropriate.

Headings for Readings

First Reading

The Lord's nature as forgiving is shown in this reading through the little storyteller's device of someone remembering who he is. We imagine that God would be angry and act as we would when the people stray, but when he recalls who he is and his promises to his people, then he realises that he cannot do as we would expect, but rather he must act in a way that is true to his nature.

Second Reading

This reading is a prayer of thanksgiving to Christ Jesus for his mercy: he came into the world to save sinners.

Gospel

When the Lord Jesus had gathered people around him at table, many objected that he had 'the wrong sorts' at his table; so he told them these parables.

Prayer of the Faithful

President

As the successors of the sinners and tax collectors who sought to sit at table with Jesus, let us in union with him make our needs known to the Father

Reader(s)

1. For the whole church of God scattered across the globe, to whom the Lord has entrusted the ministry of reconciliation, that it may be the bringer of peace and understanding between nations, cultures, and individuals. Lord hear us.

2. For this church formed by being welcomed at the Lord's table, that we may become agents of reconciliation and understanding between each other, in our homes, in our work, and in our society. Lord hear us.

3. For all the various gatherings of Christians, that they may learn to love one another, and work for that reconciliation that would allow them to be models of peacemaking rather than division before humanity. Lord hear us.

4. For all who have responsibility for peace in our world, for those in public office, for those who advise on policy, for the armed forces, that they may be inspired by God to seek the ways of peace. Lord hear us.

5. For all those who are victims of the lack of welcome, understanding, and reconciliation, that their exclusion will not lead to bitterness or repaying like with like, but that they be given strength to forgive those who would not forgive them. Lord hear us.

5. *Specific local needs and topics of the day.*

6. For all who have died, that they may know the final reconciliation in Christ, and share in the eternal banquet of heaven. Lord hear us.

President

Father, all merciful, all kind, and all loving, hear us and answer us in Christ Jesus, our Lord. Amen.

Eucharistic Prayer
Eucharistic Prayer for Masses of Reconciliation II is most appropriate for today.

Invitation to the Our Father
Let us ask the Father to forgive our sins, and bring us to forgive those who sin against us:

Sign of Peace
We are here because the Father has offered us peace in Jesus Christ. We can only stay here if we are willing to forgive one another and make peace with one another. Let us offer each other a token of peace and reconciliation.

Invitation to Communion
This is the feast laid out to welcome us home, this is the feast that anticipates the Father's welcome at the heavenly banquet, happy are we who rejoice with the shepherd who has found his lost sheep: Lord I am not worthy …

Communion Reflection
Lord, you have gathered us at your table here.
Lord, you have provided us with heavenly food for our journey.
Lord, you have shared with us the cup of salvation.

Lord, you ate with the sinners who sought your company.
Lord, you sat at table with tax collectors.
Lord, you have welcomed us and sat with us.

Lord, you are the shepherd who calls his neighbours to a feast when a lost one is found.
Lord, you are the woman who calls her friends to rejoice when she recovers what is precious to her.
Lord, we are those whom you have found and reconciled to the Father.

Lord, may we welcome outcasts as you welcome us.
Lord, may we forgive others as your Father forgives us.

Lord, may we be temples of the Spirit and agents of the reconciliation you have achieved.

Conclusion
As the Father has granted us forgiveness, may we go forth forgiving all who have trespassed against us. Amen.

As the Son welcomed tax collectors and outcasts and ate with them, may we go forth bringing reconciliation into our world. Amen.

As the Spirit has come among us for the forgiveness of our sins, may we go forth in the power of the Spirit as peacemakers in our world. Amen.

Notes
1. Reading the gospel
The three parables are part of the basic memory of Christians about the content of the good news, so much so that we could go so far as to say that if someone did not have these stories in his/her store of memory, then they would be deprived of some of the keys to how Christians view God. So it is important that people hear these together as Luke preached them, but also hear their subtle differences: the first two stories are addressed to the cause of the welcome the Jesus offered sinners: more rejoicing in heaven over one repentant sinner than over the majority which have no need for repentance, while the third story is directed at the sense of indignation of those who feel that it is their constancy rather that the repentance of those who have strayed that deserves reward. Pausing for a second after the introductory verses, then after the first two parables, and then finally reading the verses, from 'He was angry', in a slower and more mournful tone, can help hearing these differences.

2. The shorter version of the today's gospel
Given the importance of all three stories, and because Luke intended them to be appreciated as a unit, it is regrettable that the compliers of the Lectionary offered this inappropriate shorter

version. If time is that pressing a feature of the assembly, then jettison in this order: 1 the second reading; 2 the psalm; 3 the homily; 4 ask why bother celebrating if people are confusing the Eucharistic Banquet with so-called 'Fast Food'.

COMMENTARY

First Reading: Ex 32:7-11, 13-14

The worship of 'alien gods' is a breach of the fundamental commandment – and so merits being cut off from Yahweh and, as a consequence, destroyed. However, the story exists to show that Yahweh is a merciful God and so one who when his anger has subsided, recalls his covenant history and relents. We often jib at these blatant anthropomorphisms that we find in the Pentateuch and see it as a symptom of a 'primitive' theology. I do not share this embarrassment and am often impressed by the depth of psychological insight, wedded to theological insight, of the writers; and here we have an example. How often have we ourselves being driven to an angry outburst at something that has happened or has been said to us, and we have reacted 'in the heat of the moment'. But with a moment's thought, when we 'have cooled down', we have regretted the outburst. This is the same insight that led an early medieval Christian theologian to suggest that a monk who hit another monk in the heat of a moment of anger was less culpable than one who hit in cold blood when there was malice aforethought. Here we have this human insight being used to show the deep nature of God that is beyond our immediate thoughts of how he would react: then as now many people think of God as just a super-sized dictator with a big stick. Moreover, this truth is then placed within a story context so as to get through the human filter which causes many people to ignore theological insights when they are not wrapped in well-formed narratives.

Two other points should be noted. First, Moses is presented not only as the servant of God – the one who does his will and brings his message to the people; but also as the genuine servant of the people: when they need someone to intercede for them to avert the Lord's rage, Moses does not fail in his task. It is in this two-fold role, servant of God and servant of the people, that we should view Christ as the new Moses. Second, v 12 has been omitted from the lection. It is perfectly in accord with the rest of the unit; one wonders why this bit of editing was undertaken, and to what purpose?

Second Reading: 1 Tim 1:12-17

This lection forms a unit within the letter and it begins and ends with a doxology, both of which may be derived from early Christian hymns. It is a prayer to Jesus, as the Son of God, sent to bring forgiveness and mercy, who is then addressed as the 'eternal king' and identified as 'the invisible and only God'. This whole prayer is christological, and it is a model of 'high christology.'

First Reading > Gospel Links

Continuity of message between the two covenants: God is merciful to his people, seen first in the story, then in the practice of Jesus.

Second Reading > Gospel Links

It is worth noting that this is one of the rare moments in the Ordinary Time when the gospel (chosen on the basis of continuous reading) and the second reading (also chosen on the basis of continuous reading) happen to share the same general 'theme' of mercy for sinners.

However, in the gospel we have the Father's forgiveness shown to us in the life of the Christ, while in the second reading we have the Christ as the one who brings mercy and forgiveness through the event of the incarnation. These are distinct christologies and distinct soteriologies so it is as well to avoid trying to boil them down to find some generalised 'common core'. Such 'common core' theologies usually betray the riches of the tradition for the simplicities of fundamentalism. Indeed, if one wanted to appreciate these readings what one should examine is how different are their approaches and theologies, and how little they have in common!

Gospel: Lk 15:1-32
The most important aspect of these stories when they are located in their context in Luke's gospel is that his theology of reconciliation is a subset of his theology of the Eucharist. The meal is the locus for the beginning of the new people which will find its fulfilment in the heavenly banquet. The reconciliation that is accorded to the sinners and the outcasts at the table is the this-worldly reality of the mystery of the Father's welcome for them. However, it is best not to preach on this theme as this Lukan theology of the Eucharist causes problems for many traditions of Christians today (e.g. most of the eastern Orthodox Churches, and for Roman Catholics). In these traditions the preferred preaching strategy is to focus on the content of the stories, reconciliation (as we see in what the Lectionary says about this Sunday), rather than the context (yet, the Lectionary reads the opening verses giving the context). The problem is this: if one preaches the Lukan theology of the Eucharist, then one would not be able to exclude people on the basic of canonical excommunication, or for serious sins which had not been submitted to the appropriate forum, or for those who were canonically irregular (e.g. divorced and remarried people) or those who were not canonically acceptable (e.g. Catholics or Protestants at an eastern Orthodox assembly or Protestants at a Catholic celebration). Yet, there are ancient roots for all such exclusions and they are an intrinsic part of the canonical tradition. The problem arises in that there was no single 'theology' of the Eucharist in the first century, but a wide variety of practices many of which were excluding of people for various reasons, and it is this actual practice that has passed on within the tradition which asks as a fundamental question: are you able to share in the Eucharist, and which has a fixed set of guidelines about who cannot do so. On the other hand, there is a tradition of theology, which is secondary to practice, that questions whether such practices are

appropriate and who stress inclusion, open commensality, or the notion that it is the ones who are not canonically regular who have greatest need for strengthening food. It is quite possible that Luke – who is consistent in his approach to the meals of Jesus throughout his gospel – was reacting to excluding tendencies in the practices he observed; and certainly the debate stills lives on as one can see in the varying approaches of Christian groups today to the topic of 'inter-communion'. So what is the preacher to do? Clearly, if one is in communion with Rome, one must recognise that Luke's open commensality is not part of the tradition of eucharistic theology and that it is the content of the stories upon which one should focus (as the Lectionary, p liii, makes clear). Equally, it is quite useless arguing about what is 'the' 'authentic' theology or practice of the Eucharist in the 'early church'. It is clear that there was no single dominant theology – in the early documents, most of which have been granted 'canonical' status, there is a wide range of theological approaches to the Eucharist, while practice with regard to exclusion seems to have varied with the cultural background of the various groups.

HOMILY NOTES

1. Given that these parables are only found in one gospel, it is a tribute to their immense power as stories that they have been central to Christian imagination down the centuries. When we remember that the only stories or incidents from the time of Jesus's public ministry that are equally well remembered are the Good Samaritan story (Lk 10) and the Zacchaeus incident (Lk 17) – and these too are only found in Luke – we get an insight into one of the key messages of Luke's preaching. God is mercy, God is forgiveness, God is reconciliation, God is peace, and God is love.

2. And when we gather as Christians, this is clearly something we want to hear: we desire mercy, forgiveness, a fresh start, and a welcome home. How we know that we want to hear it is the way we listen and react to this gospel.

3. That leaves us with a question: if this is a central message of Jesus – and it is – why is it not a message that people who are not Christians link with Christianity? This discrepancy between 'our core-message' and 'perceptions of us' reveals something very important to us. Jesus not only came to reveal the Father's love, but sent us his Spirit so that we would become agents of reconciliation. He came to bring us peace, but called us to become peacemakers. He came to seek out the lost, but calls us to welcome the outcasts and the poor. The message of the gospel is always two-sided: he reconciles us, we must reconcile others. Jesus is the centre of reconciliation in the universe; his followers must be little local centres of reconciliation throughout the universe. Alas, we are better at seeking reconciliation for ourselves than being reconcilers; better at wanting peace than being peacemakers; happier at being welcomed home than offering a welcome to the stranger.

4. Where can we see this two-sided message of reconciliation in a nut-shell? In the 'Our Father': we pray 'forgive us *as* we forgive those who trespass against us.' Yet we are very quick to think of how we need to ask God for his forgiveness; how often do we think of our need to reconcile others?

5. We have just read three stories about the nature of God; but they are also challenges to our nature.

Lectionary Unit VI

Towards Jerusalem, again

This unit is devoted to the second part of the 'travel narrative' and explores the obstacles facing those who follow Jesus.

It runs from Sunday 25 to Sunday 31; its sections/themes are:

Sunday 25	*The unjust steward*
Sunday 26	*The rich man and Lazarus*
Sunday 27	*A lesson on faith and dedication*
Sunday 28	*The ten lepers*
Sunday 29	*The unjust judge*
Sunday 30	*The Pharisee and the Tax-collector*
Sunday 31	*Meeting Zacchaeus*

In many ways this is the most characteristic section of Luke's gospel for none of these sections, stories, incidents are found elsewhere in the gospels.

Twenty-fifth Sunday of Ordinary Time

Introduction to the Celebration

In today's gospel we will hear a parable about a man who is the very opposite of everything we consider honest. Having been caught in his dishonesty, he proceeds to do a range of favours to people so that there will be plenty of IOUs to call in when he finally loses his job. He is the very model of the crooked accountant! This image is startling: in a matter of earthly survival that crook is a model of focusing on the distant goal and acting now so that he can get there. But this leaves us with a challenge: do we keep our eye fixed on our long term goal, the completion of our pilgrimage of faith, and let that goal determine the proper use we make now of the things of this world?

Rite of Penance

For the times when we have not used the things of this world wisely. Lord have mercy.

For the times when we have not been faithful to the tasks that have been entrusted to us. Christ have mercy.

For the times when we have not acted with the wisdom of the sons and daughters of light. Lord have mercy.

Headings for Readings

First Reading

The prophet warns us about hypocrisy: being careful to observe the laws of religion about the Sabbath, while at the same time cheating our neighbour in business.

Second Reading

Every Sunday when we gather we pray in the Prayers of the Faithful for those who have authority in the world. This reading reminds us that we do not pray for rulers out of patriotism or that they might be triumphant, but so that they might work to let people live in peace and security.

Gospel
The gospel asks us to choose where we are placing our trust, what is our true wealth, and then to consider how we can use material wealth with true wisdom.

Prayer of the Faithful
President
As fellow sons and daughters of the light we have been called to be wise and true stewards of God's gifts. Now let us ask the Father for the wisdom and insight we need to carry out the tasks he has entrusted to us.
Reader(s)
1. For all who have been baptised into Christ Jesus, all the sons and daughters of light, that we may act in every aspect of our lives with wisdom. Lord hear us.
2. For all the peoples of the world, our sisters and brothers, that we may all learn to act wisely as the stewards of the earth and its resources. Lord hear us.
3. For this gathering, we who are now the companions at the Lord's banquet, that hearing the gospel together may make us aware of our responsibilities within the creation. Lord hear us.
4. For all those people, our fellow creatures, who are suffering due to human foolishness and greed, that they may know the care of the Lord. Lord hear us.
5. For the world's leaders and others in authority, that we, and all humanity, may be able to live religious and reverent lives in peace and quiet. Lord hear us.
6. For the community of faith, whom we claim to be, that we may have the wisdom, courage and energy, to help all who suffer. Lord hear us.
7. *Specific local needs and topics of the day.*

President
Father of lights, from you comes all love, all wisdom, and all power; hear your children gathered here in your presence as they pray for their needs in Christ Jesus, your Son, our Lord. Amen.

Eucharistic Prayer
Preface of Sundays in Ordinary Time V [P33]; and either Eucharistic Prayer II or III.

Invitation to the Our Father
The wisdom that makes us daughters and sons of the light comes down to us from the Father of lights, so let us pray to him now:

Sign of Peace
Assembled as the daughters and sons of light, let us greet one another as brothers and sisters in Christ.

Invitation to Communion
There is no greater sign of welcome and acceptance than to be invited to share another's table. Happy are we who are accepted and loved by the Lord, and so are called to share in this heavenly banquet.

Communion Reflection
Blessed be the name of God forever and ever, to whom belong wisdom and might *(Dan 2:20)*.
All wisdom is from the Lord, and with him it remains forever *(Sir 1:1)*.
The Lord by wisdom founded the earth; by understanding he established the heavens *(Prov 3:19)*.
To get wisdom is better than gold; to get understanding is to be chosen rather than silver *(Prov 16:16)*.
The mouth of the righteous utters wisdom, and his tongue speaks justice *(Ps 37:30)*.

Wisdom is better than weapons of war, but one sinner destroys much good *(Qoh 9:18)*.

The crown of the wise is their wisdom, but folly is the garland of fools *(Prov 14:24)*.

I saw that wisdom excels folly as light excels darkness *(Qoh 2:13)*.

Wisdom is radiant and unfading, and she is easily discerned by those who love her, and is found by those who seek her *(Wis 6:12)*.

Wisdom teaches her children and gives help to those who seek her *(Sir 4:11)*.

The fear of the Lord is the beginning of knowledge; fools despise wisdom and instruction *(Prov 1:7)*.

The fear of the Lord is the beginning of wisdom, and the knowledge of the Holy One is insight *(Prov 9:10)*.

The fear of the Lord is instruction in wisdom, and humility goes before honour *(Prov 15:33)*.

The fear the Lord is the beginning of wisdom; she is created with the faithful in the womb *(Sir 1:14)*.

If any of you lacks wisdom, let him ask God, who gives to all generously and without reproaching, and it will be given you *(Jas 1:5)*.

The wisdom from above is first pure, then peaceable, gentle, open to reason, full of mercy and good fruits, without uncertainty or insincerity *(Jas 3:17)*.

Let the word of Christ dwell in you richly, teach and admonish one another in all wisdom *(Col 3:16)*.

Conclusion
Solemn Blessing for Ordinary Time II (Missal, p 372)

Notes
1. The environment
A church that is not concerned with the global environment is one that does not really accept that God is the creator of all, and that it is the created material environment that is the basis of all sacramentality. However, it is often hard to link such matters as

concern over global warming or the destruction of the rain forests – and with it both human societies and the habitat of living creatures that God has called into existence – with the readings we find in the Lectionary for Sundays. The simple fact is that ecology was not a major concern of writers more than two millennia ago, nor should it have been. However, it is a major concern for us today, and must be such a concern if we are to be true to a sacramental Christianity. This is one of the Sundays when our environmental concern can be intrinsically linked with the gospel we are hearing. This is precisely because that gospel concerns our acting with wisdom in our generation as the sons and, now we must add, daughters of light who are called to be good stewards of what has been entrusted to us. So this is a day when there can be displays or activities that show our concern for the environment or on development. And, in doing so it is important that such concern is not seen as 'an optional extra' to Christian faith and liturgy, or as something that is really distinct from liturgy; rather such concern must be seen as flowing out of our basic Christian calling and out of the very nature of the liturgy which is sacramental.

2. Sacramentality

Whenever we emphasise our stewardship of the gifts of God we are confronting the reality of creation as sacramental: God acts, and is known, within and through the cosmos. The *Logos* becomes a human being within the universe that is made through him, and comes to us now in the reality of a human meal. But if we are a sacramental people – every human reality comes from God, speaks of God, and returns to God – do we use the creation sacramentally in the liturgy or do we simply use objects as material 'tokens' as a convenient way to refer to invisible realities? We come from a background of confusing 'tokens' with 'symbols' and of making a rigid distinction between 'symbols' and 'realities'. If today we are recalling our human tasks of being wise stewards of the creation, then we should be seeing the creation as sacrament and sacred, and not simply as a source of objects which can be impressed with special religious meanings. Such a reduction would reduce the real presence of the Christ in the Eucharist to a virtual one which was dependent on our minds to make a jump: I see X, but I am not interested in that X in itself, but only because it reminds me of Y! This requires that we review the links between our liturgy and the gifts of creation: are little plastic-like wafers the best bread we can find, is a little jug of wine a sign of the goodness and generosity of God?

3. The Procession of Gifts

The theme of the sacramentality and stewardship can lead us to look again at the procession of gifts at the Preparation of the Gifts. Our task is to place within the context of the divine presence at our sacral meal the implements of our stewardship as an acknowledgement of thankful dependence, and as a petition for God's gift of wisdom, and for his continued care for us. Such a procession of gifts must relate to the actual people at the assembly and their various tasks, but it could include tools (everything from a spade to a mobile phone), fruits, foods, plants, and money – all the resources we have been given, and which we can use wisely. Sacramentality is difficult for most modern western adults used to working within a framework of separations, and so renewing that sense is of sacramentality is correspondingly difficult. However, we have to start somewhere and presenting the instruments of our stewardship as part of our act of thanks, and thereby asking God's blessing, is one place to start.

4. The shorter form of the gospel

What makes the four gospels special is that they locate the teaching of Jesus within a narrative – a story that links the life and teaching as a unity. However, there is always a danger that these narratives are reduced to snippets of wisdom or oracles. This has been the problem of reducing the scriptures to 'proof texts' or the notion that is at the heart of fundamentalism: one can extract verses which are simply 'true'. Today's shorter form comes very close to allowing the reduction of the gospels' narratives to such oracular utterances. As such it is to be avoided.

COMMENTARY

First Reading: Amos 8:4-7
This is part of the fourth vision of the prophet and in the vision he sees the danger of hypocrisy: care over the minutiae of the cult and its laws, while at the same time planning how to defraud others.

Psalm: 112
The response 'Praise the Lord, who raises the poor' is to be preferred.

Second Reading: 1 Tim 2:1-8
This short passage has three elements, but all connected with the intercessory prayer by the community in their liturgies:
1. Advice on interceding for world's powers
The background to this piece of advice on the conduct of the liturgy is the suspicion that the Christians were not loyal citizens because they did not offer incense to the emperor nor did they belong to a 'lawful religion'. The probable social context in which the letter was written in the first quarter of the second century is that which we see in Pliny the Younger's letter to the Emperor Trajan while he was governor of Bithynia and seeking guidance on how to deal with this group which did not seem to want to belong within the empire. The Christians, for their part, were both conscious that they were part of that social universe – and so the advice we are reading – but also aware that they were citizens of heaven and so it was also inappropriate for them to be fully 'at home' in the empire. This creative tension can be seen in the advice on prayer for 'kings and others in authority' that it is prayer so that we (just the Christians or all people?) can lead 'religious and reverent lives in peace and quiet'. This is a far cry from the style of most prayers for kings at the time which took the form of prayers for 'the king's intentions' and the suc-

cess of his armies. It is worth remembering that one of the recurring blind-spots of Christians down the centuries has been to assume that 'God is on our side in battles' and that when they pray for rulers that they pray for their success in warfare or their political intrigues (e.g. have a look at national anthems that invoke the name of God).

2. *A statement on God's universal salvific will*

The prayer of Christians is not limited to their own needs for God wills all to be saved.

3. *A christological confession*

Into his teaching on prayer the author – who in other places in this letter has interwoven items from the liturgy – here adopts an early credal statement, 'a saying that can be relied on' and this was no doubt one of those elements committed to memory, about who Jesus is: 'For there is one God, and there is one mediator between God and men, the man Christ Jesus, who gave himself as a ransom for all.'

First Reading > Gospel Links

Continuity of teaching between the covenants forms the connection. The Lord, says Amos, is the one who preserves justice – the desire for money cannot be at the expense of justice; in the gospel the message is that one who serves money cannot also claim to be a servant of God.

Gospel: Lk 16:1-13

This section of the gospel, often entitled 'The Unjust Steward', forms a unit in Luke's preaching, and it is a unit found only in Luke. It is made up of a story (16:1-9) and a piece of formal teaching (16:10-13 – and whose salient point has a parallel in Mt 6:24) which fit together but not without the seams showing. The two items had separate origins, and also separate uses in the tradition, and what we have here is the work of Luke the editor. So if you have a certain puzzlement as to how the jump was made from the parable – or more precisely 'example story' – to the teaching, it may be that what you are reacting to is Luke taking two items – one of which does not seem to be all that edify-ing – and hoping that by putting them together in his narrative he has made sense of both. Whatever was the original meaning of the parable – tuned by Luke into an example story – it is clear what Luke wants to draw out from the whole section: the disci-ple must decide where he is placing his trust. If you place your trust in wealth, then you will not serve God. However, where you place your trust now is relevant to what you will later de-pend upon. It is towards the final item of teaching ('You cannot serve God and wealth') that the rest of the text is directed.

HOMILY NOTES

1. We have all met the unjust steward or, at least, heard of him in the media. There is something attractive about the way he clearly sees the predicament he is in, his realistic grasp of his own personal make-up ('to dig I am unable and to beg I am ashamed'), and the speed and efficiency with which he puts his survival plan into action. It is a beautiful little story of a master storyteller, and we can see in an instant that 'the sons of this world are more shrewd in dealing with their own gen-eration than the sons of light'.

2. The challenge is, however, that we who are listening to the story have declared ourselves – by the very fact that we have gathered for the Eucharist – to be the daughters and the sons of light. So how are we to act swiftly, with clarity of foresight, and with wisdom?

3. When we wish to preach about God's gifts – the whole of reality is his gift – we need to have some convenient image and rhetoric so that what we say does not sound so all-embracing as to be sound vapid. Here is a possible way to approach it.

4. We are called to act wisely with the gifts the father has given us: he has stretched out his hand toward us and we can name five specific gifts he had given us. These are like the fingers of his hand.

    First, God has given us the gift of freedom and understand-ing. We are people who can appreciate the universe, can see beauty, can feel joy and sorrow and sympathy and elation. We can know the good and grow in our appreciation of the whole mystery of life and being. We are people who can make a difference – this is freedom – and build together a wonderful edifice or we can cause mayhem, destruction and chaos. Think of the genius of modern medicine and the genius of modern weapons. Both are a tribute to our inventiveness, understanding, skill, and creativity – all God-given virtues. But we have the choice of using skills for building or tearing down – the God-given ability to choose our path.

Second, God has given us the cosmos, the good earth that is our home, the context of our lives, and that sustains us. This is the same material creation that can reveal the presence and action of God to us. This is the creation for which we thank the Father at every Eucharist when we use its fruits to be the bearers of the gift of heavenly life. 'Blessed are you Lord God of all creation, through your goodness we have' this bread, this wine, fruits of the earth which become for us the bread of life and cup of eternal salvation. But do we use our understanding to appreciate it in its richness and use it wisely so that it can sustain generations to come as it sustains us? Or, do we use our brainpower to find out how to ransack it and 'use it up'? Wisdom is seeing it as our God-given home, a place of wonder, and treating it with respect.

Third, we have the gift of our human family. We can work together as brothers and sisters or we can try to live at the expense of those around us. The work of development which is the work of peace, and which tries to bring transformation to all who suffer or are in need, takes the same amount of resources, organisation, and skill, as does the work of war, aggression, and exploitation. Both are exercises of understanding and freedom. The wisdom of the children of light is to appreciate the choice and choose the way of peace.

Fourth, we have the gift of human love. We come to life in the context of human love, we are sustained by it, we discover who we are in it, and in human love we discover the God who is love. But here again we are creatures with freedom: we can act wisely and human love can become the gate of heaven or it can become another scene of exploitation and destruction.

And fifth, we have the gift of God's voice within our hearts. Do we hear it as the voice of wisdom or do we try to drown it out as something that gets in our way?

5. God has stretched forth his hand toward us and entrusted us with much. We are called to act with wisdom, to use our freedom well, and then in being just and wise stewards to discover the Giver of all.

Twenty-sixth Sunday of Ordinary Time

Introduction to the Celebration

Today the Liturgy of the Word presents us with God's call to us to remember the poor, to act with justice, to avoid sumptuous living when we know other humans are suffering and in want. To be the people of the Christ is to be a caring people whose love of neighbour reaches to everyone in need. This is not just a moral task that is laid upon us, for the tradition of the prophets was that God showed a preference for the poor, the needy, and sick, and in today's gospel we hear Jesus confirm that he stands in that prophetic tradition. The gospel presents us with a stark picture of a rich man and a poor man, Lazarus, and shows that the Lord has a preferential option for the poor, an option that should inform our style of living as his followers.

Rite of Penance

Lord Jesus, you come with your word of justice for the poor. Lord have mercy.

Lord Jesus, you call us to act with justice towards the poor. Christ have mercy.

Lord Jesus, you show us the Father's concern with justice for the poor. Lord have mercy.

Headings for Readings
First Reading

The prophet Amos now presents us with a picture of riches being abused: those who feast while others suffer are bringing woe upon themselves.

Second Reading

If used: This reading is an encouragement to persevere in living the Christian life until we finally come into the presence of Jesus Christ who is King of kings and Lord of lords.

Gospel

We are about to listen to one of the great stories told by Jesus about a rich man and a poor man, and the Father's preferential option for the poor.

Prayer of the Faithful
President

Friends, we shall now put our petitions before the Father not as a collection of individuals, but as a single people called into existence by Christ's love.

Reader(s)

1. For all Christians, that we will act with love and justice to the poor. Lord hear us.

2. For this church gathered here, that we will recognise our responsibilities to the poor. Lord hear us.

3. For people everywhere, that we will respect the gifts of God in the creation. Lord hear us.

4. For all who are poor, sick, and in need, that they may receive justice, comfort, and health. Lord hear us.

5. *Specific local needs and topics of the day.*

President

Father, lover of the poor, hear us and transform us that we may manifest your love and care to all humanity. We make this prayer through Christ our Lord. Amen.

Eucharistic Prayer

There is no Preface or Eucharistic Prayer that is particularly suited to today.

Invitation to the Our Father

We are called to manifest the Father's love for the poor, so now let us pray to him:

Sign of Peace

Peace is the fruit of justice; as we offer each other the sign of peace may it remind us of our calling to work for justice.

Invitation to Communion
The Lord does not leave us at his gate but welcomes us to his table filled with his blessings. Happy are we who are called to this feast.

Communion Reflection
Having had a time of reflection after the gospel, this is a time when those in the assembly who are concerned with the community's ministry to the poor (be it in the immediate area, or with the poor in the developing world, or both) can explain their particular ministry to the wider community. The link between such an explanation and the time after the Eucharistic sharing is intrinsic to the Eucharist and not simply gratuitous: if we have received the largesse of the Lord in partaking in his banquet, then on the basic theological principle that we act towards others as God acts towards us, so we must now be prepared to share the riches of our tables with those in need. We cannot share in the heavenly food of the Lord's table, if we are not willing to let the poor share in the earthly food of our own tables. So, having made this point, those who are charged with the care of the poor – what Luke sees in Acts 6:1-4 as the original work of service (*diakonia*) and of the first specially church-appointed ministers: the deacons – can explain what they do, and how their work could be advanced by additional support from the whole church that is gathered to receive the Lord's bounty.

Conclusion
There is no formula of blessing that is particularly suited to this day.

Notes
1. The Preferential Option for the Poor
When this phrase began to come into use as theological shorthand it was often taken to be primarily an attitude of the church that had its origins in some sort of social analysis. However, within the tradition, the church's concern for the poor is primarily

a reflection of the divine option for the poor. A useful corrective is to use the shorthand while noting that it is God's preference for the poor – as seen in the prophets and the Christ – that forms the pattern and mandate for the preferential option for the poor by Christians.

2. A man called 'Dives'

This gospel is often said by Catholics to be the gospel of 'Dives and Lazarus' and, especially with older congregations, it might be worth explaining why the rich man has lost his proper name.

COMMENTARY

First Reading: Amos 6:1, 4-7

A central theme running through Amos is that there must be justice in the land, and the poor must be free from oppression, if Israel is to be loyal to the covenant. Cult is false and luxury is oppression if the poor are not cared for.

Second Reading: 1 Tim 6:11-16

This is a concluding farewell of the letter, which presents a confession of faith that is formed using formal early Christian hymns/prayers. What is most interesting about this is the way that language that echoes phrases used within the earlier covenant with reference to Yahweh is here applied directly to Jesus as the returning Christ.

First Reading > Gospel Links

The link is based on the continuity of teaching within the prophetic tradition in Israel. Amos in his woes expresses the preferential option of God for the poor: God sees justice done to those who are oppressed. In the gospel reading, hearing the Lord's good news is to hear the call to care for the poor. The desire for the fullness of life and a life of oppression of the poor are mutually exclusive.

Gospel: Lk 16:19-31

This story is found only in Luke's gospel and it has a single focus: if one does not hear the basic laws of justice and mercy (contained in the law and prophets) then even the resurrection of the Christ will not bring conversion. Before anyone can be a witness to the resurrection and share in its life, they must already be followers of the ways of justice and care of the poor. This point is further emphasised in that the concern of the rich man for his brothers is a form of compassion, but this need to care for the poor is so basic that the story assumes that anyone so insensitive to the need of the poor whom they see would be wholly insensitive.

It is worth noting that in the history of exegesis the point of this story was usually lost in the pursuit of its details so as to provide geography of hell, the nature of its torments, and of the impossibility of a change from hell to heaven. This fascination is a distraction, albeit one that has sidetracked some of the most eminent minds in our history. It is impossible to avoid questions on these details, or even on the fact of the existence of hell, but this is not the focus of the story but justice.

HOMILY NOTES

1. Hearing our basic stories together is one of the key ways that we are formed within communities; and as a community of faith this is a key way through which we remain in union with the teaching of the Christ. These are the two basic reasons why we have them read to us at our Sunday gatherings. The telling and retelling of our sacred texts forms us into the body of Christ, and for this reason we say that one of the modes of Christ's real presence in the assembly is in the readings.

   However, this presence is all too easily obscured. This happens when, for example, a group all want to read the text as individuals from their own books rather than to listen to the text as a group. When this happens — and it is no longer confined to Reformation groups who explicitly adopt an individualist approach to the scriptures – the liturgical hearing of our inheritance of stories is more like many people sitting in a library all engaged in their own business, rather than an audience at a play where they react together in sadness, in sympathy or in joy.

Another way that the presence is obscured is when there are too many words or pieces of text that require assistance to make them clear or even comprehensible. A story that is too complex to its hearers is one that does not really create the common memories that make us one people. Therefore, actualising the presence of Christ in the Liturgy of the Word is one of the most difficult tasks than any president of the Eucharist faces today. But there are occasions when this challenge is far easier to meet; and this Sunday is one of those occasions.

2. The combination of the first reading and the gospel pick out for us that the message of these readings is the Lord's preferential option for the poor (and not, for example, the structure of judgement or the cosmology of hell – two themes for which this gospel has often been used in the past). And this theme is not only one that is central to the whole message of the Christ, but also one which is comprehensible because it touches some of our basic instincts. The proof that it is comprehensible can be found in the vehemence with which those with vested interests in making easy money at the expense of the poor turned their firepower on the proponents of Liberation Theology – how many other movements in theology can you think of that have generated such well-financed opposition?

Moreover, in the whole of the gospels (the infancy and passion narratives apart) there is probably no more memorable a story by Jesus: we can picture 'the rich man'; we can picture hungry Lazarus with his sores being licked by the dogs; we can imagine the flames and the cooling sip of water; and we can imagine 'being in torment'. To hear this story is to enrich one's imagination.

3. So today is a day to let these two readings seep into the imagination and contribute to the formation of a community of memory. How does one do this?

- Omit the second reading as a distracting interlude to the theme.
- Do not preach a homily, but call for a time of silent reflection: two minutes is usually enough.
- Ensure that people listen to the two readings: so remove the missalettes and 'Mass books'.
- Make sure that the reader of the first reading appreciates the plan for the liturgy today and reads each 'woe' distinctly as something that each of us can take on board as a basic idea.
- Read the gospel with special solemnity: procession with book, an escort of lights, and with incense.
- Read it out as if telling a story. Some translations are much better for this than others; but, on the whole, the suitability of any translation for capturing the storytelling tone of the original will depend on how it interacts with your own storytelling style. And our individual storytelling styles are as distinctive as our mannerisms, so you may have to experiment with several translations. Below you will see how I have adapted the RSV translation to suit my own style:

A reading from the Holy Gospel according to Luke.

As they travelled as a group along the road towards Jerusalem, Jesus told this story to his disciples:

Once upon a time there was a rich man. He wore the most expensive of clothes, the finest linen was used to make his shirts, and every day he feasted sumptuously on the best of food.

Outside his house, at his gate, lay a poor man named Lazarus, covered in sores. Lazarus was indeed so hungry that he would have been happy to be fed with whatever fell from the rich man's table. There Lazarus lay, day after day, and the dogs who came and licked his sores were his only comfort.

The poor man died and was carried by the angels to Abraham's bosom.

The rich man also died and was buried.

Then being held in the place of the dead, the rich man, now living in torment, lifted up his eyes, and saw Abraham far off and Lazarus in his bosom. He then called out:

Father Abraham, have mercy upon me, and send Lazarus to dip the end of his finger in water and cool my tongue; for I am in anguish in this flame.

But Abraham answered him saying:

Son, remember that you in your lifetime received your good things, and, at the same time, Lazarus only received suffering.

But now,

Lazarus is comforted here,

and you are in anguish.

And, in any case, between us and you a great gulf has been fixed, in order that no one might pass from here to where you are, and no one may cross from where you are to our side.

So the rich man then said to Abraham:

Then I beg you, father, to send Lazarus to my father's house, because I have five brothers and I want Lazarus to warn them, because I do not want my brothers also to come into this place of torment.

But Abraham answered this petition by saying:

Your brothers have Moses and the prophets; let them listen to them.

But the rich man then said:

No, father Abraham, that would not be enough for them to learn the truth that they must change the way they live their lives;

but if some one goes to them from the dead, they will repent.

Then Abraham said to the rich man:

If your brothers do not hear Moses and the prophets,

Then neither will they be convinced even if someone should rise from the dead.

This is the gospel of the Lord.

Twenty-seventh Sunday of Ordinary Time

Introduction to the Celebration

Life is a journey, and for us who follow Jesus Christ it is a journey to the fullness of life, but also a journey of faith. We live our lives and walk in the footsteps of the Christ knowing that there is a great mystery surrounding us, but knowing also that we walk by faith and not by sight. As we begin to celebrate these sacred mysteries, let us pray for an increase in faith and a new energy to follow in the path of the Son of God.

Rite of Penance

Son of the Father, increase our faith. Lord have mercy.
Son of the Father, increase our hope. Christ have mercy.
Son of the Father, increase our love. Lord have mercy.

Headings for Readings
First Reading

The prophet grows impatient that God is not caring for his people and not showing sufficient interest in their urgent needs, but the reply he receives is that part of faithfulness is waiting. This need to wait, if we are to see the mighty works of God is what we Christians call hope.

Second Reading

Timothy is encouraged to not be half-hearted in his following of Christ but to courageously witness to him.

Gospel

Disciples must be people who live by faith.

Prayer of the Faithful

Use the Sample Formula for General Intercessions for Ordinary Time II (Missal, pp 1002-3).

Eucharistic Prayer
Preface of Weekdays V [P41] is suitable as its central theme is the
interaction in Christian faith of the theological virtues. None of
the Eucharistic Prayers is particularly suitable.

Invitation to the Our Father
In the confidence of faith let us pray to the Father:

Sign of Peace
As the community of faith we believe that Christ's peace will triumph over human discord. Let us pray for that peace by exchanging a sign of peace with one another.

Invitation to Communion
We are gathered at the banquet of faith, and in faith we see that
this is the Lamb of God who takes away the sins of the world.
Happy are we who are called to his supper.

Communion Reflection
The first six stanzas of the Universal Prayer, Missal, pp 1021-2.

Conclusion
Solemn Blessing of Ordinary Time IV (Missal, p 373) is suitable.

COMMENTARY

First Reading: Hab 1:2-3; 2:2-4
We know nothing of the life or the dates of Habakkuk, although
internal evidence in the book suggests that he may have been a
prophet formally linked to the temple in Jerusalem. In today's
reading we have the beginning and end verses of the book's
opening section that is made up of complaints to God and re-
sponses to Israel. These complains, which echo many found in
the psalms, are concerned with God's justice towards his people:
'How long O Lord, will you forget us forever?' And the reply
comes in today's final verse (which is the high point and
conclusion of the first section): the righteous by his fidelity will

live. The reading today is designed to provide a context for this one line; a line which was to play such an important part in the early development of Christian theology as we see in Rom 1:17, Gal 3:11, and Heb 10:38-39.

Given the frequently noted echoes between the opening section of Habakkuk and many of the psalms (e.g. Ps 12) it is a little surprising that the Lectionary has opted for Ps 94 which is not linked to either the first reading or the gospel.

Second Reading: 2 Tim 1:6-8, 13-14

This reading presents part of the letter's opening call to Timothy to renew the spiritual gifts he has been given. However, as the reading is edited it lacks both a key message and a logical continuity. Given that in the second reading we have continuous reading of epistles over several Sundays one wonders why they did not opt for 1:6-12 (or even to 14) which would have given a clear focus on the need to rekindle the gifts of God.

First Reading > Gospel Links

The link is continuity of teaching between the covenants: in the first reading the key message is that the righteous man lives by faith/fidelity, and in the gospel there is a saying of Jesus on the importance of faith; there is also a common theme in that both readings praise steadfastness as a characteristic of doing God's will.

Gospel: Lk 17:5-10

The gospel today is made up of two distinct items handed down in the kerygma which have no inherent link; and in this the lection is no better than the gospel text that simply puts them together. The problem is that those who hear the gospel read assume unconsciously that this is a well-formed distinct item where all the ideas follow one another in a narrative or logical sequence. Since this is the assumption, they then either find the text perplexing and confusing, or create some rationale, however bizarre, to explain the sequence they imagine must be there.

What we have is a 'saying' by Jesus on faith (17:5-7) which is
also found in Mt 17:20, but which (as often happens in Luke) is
not given as a saying but as the reply to a question from the
apostles. Verse 6 has to be read as a single statement and remembered as such – the context is simply glue to hold it in a place
within the overall gospel narrative. The second element in
today's readings is a parable, found only in Luke, on the
Servant's Wages. The parable has one point: the disciples are to
do their work and expect no reward. The text has been a problem since the earliest exegesis of Luke and it is still wholly obscure what the original message of this parable was. Today's
gospel is a good case for shattering the fundamentalist assumption that the gospels are perfect documents.

HOMILY NOTES

1. The first saying in today's gospel gives an opening to preach
   on the topic of faith, although, in effect, this is really only
   using the gospel as a peg on which to hang a sermon rather
   than in any sense giving a homily on the readings. However,
   there is just not enough time in a homily to look at a question
   like 'what do we mean by "faith"?'; or, at least, to look on it in
   any satisfactory way. Indeed, given what we know about
   how adults learn, trying to address serious human questions
   in any format that is like that of a homily is at best of only
   marginal value because the homily does not permit any ex-
   change of ideas or questions. However, there are many for
   whom the homily is the only form of instruction to which
   they are exposed or to which they are prepared to expose
   themselves, so we have to try to formulate complex questions in snippets of five to ten minutes, and just hope that in
   such situations we do not betray our riches in order to deliver
   them in bite-sized chunks (and in a situation where we have
   no way of knowing how people are 'hearing' what we are
   saying).

2. 'Faith' is not a word that is widely used in everyday convers-
   ation. When it is used it tends to be a synonym for religion as

in 'She follows the Jewish faith'; or 'He kept the faith' meaning that he held onto those values of a time long past; or else
'She was acting in good faith' which is just a translation of the
technical legal phrase '*bona fides*'. What is interesting is that
in most uses it is something that another has, rather than a
quality of one's own life. When religious people use the word
it often means simply acceptance of the doctrines of their religion, and faith 'without doubts' is equivalent to full conviction. By contrast, when people say they have 'lost faith' they
mean they no longer 'buy into' the stories, doctrines, practices, or moral vision of the religion to which they once be-
longed. Faith is religion or a quality of adherence to religion.

3. But is this what faith means within Christianity? Faith is a
   quality of life, a way of living, and a way of seeing. To be able
   to see the world and all its bits and pieces from pebbles to
   galaxies is the faculty of normal sight. To be able to imagine it
   as beautiful and to see it as having order and goodness is to
   'see' in another way – this 'seeing' is faith. To see human
   lives with all their ups and downs is normal seeing, but when
   we commit ourselves that humans must be loved, cared for,
   and not treated as 'things' then we are seeing far beyond
   material structures, and this seeing, which imagines the
   whole human words of love and care, is part of faith. The
   gathering that we are presently taking part in may contain
   some siblings, but to see all of us as somehow related as sisters and brothers is to 'see' far beyond sibling groups and to
   be able to imagine bonds that are invisible and reach beyond
   the universe.

4. Faith is the ability to imagine life at its fullest. Faith is being
   able to imagine it as proceeding from God, proceeding under
   his care, and returning to God. In such a view of faith, doubts
   are not like faults in a motorcar – first indications that it is all
   going to break down – but part of normal life. Indeed, doubt
   is the growing edge of faith. Doubt forces me to ask questions
   of myself, others, the tradition, and of my own and others'
   ways of acting. Faith sees the big picture, but the big picture
   is never as clear as our view of the details.

5. But, when we form that big picture we are then confronted
   with the question: is this just a pretty picture or is it the truest
   grasp on the whole of life that I can find? If it is the truest
   grasp, if it has the ring of truth and solidity about it, then we
   must commit ourselves to it as The Truth, and then pattern
   our lives within that vision seen 'in a glass darkly'.

Twenty-eighth Sunday of Ordinary Time

Introduction to the Celebration

We have gathered here to encounter Jesus our Lord and give praise to God our Father. We meet Jesus in meeting one another, we meet him in the scriptures to which we will listen, and we meet him in sharing in his body and blood at his table, and in union with him we will offer prayer and praise to the Father. These thoughts of meeting Jesus and joining him in the praise of God are very central to our gathering today when we hear the story of the ten lepers who asked Jesus for healing, but of whom only one of the ten came back to thank him. Like those lepers seeking healing, our first thought when we gather is to cry: 'Jesus, Master, have mercy on us.'

Rite of Penance

Jesus, Master, we ask you to take pity on us. Lord have mercy.

Jesus, Master, we ask you to heal us. Christ have mercy.

Jesus, Master, we ask you to make us thankful. Lord have mercy.

Headings for Readings
First Reading

A foreigner suffering from leprosy comes to the prophet Elisha who asks the Lord to heal him. God's love and healing is not limited to any one group or tribe; and this foreigner is thankful to the prophet and praises God.

Second Reading

In the passage we are about to read we have two early sound bites about what is important for Christians to remember as they live their lives.

Gospel

God's blessing reaches out to all humanity: God loves Galileans and Samaritans, it reaches the healthy and the sick, it reaches the thankful and the ungrateful, it reaches you and it reaches me.

Prayer of the Faithful

President

Now, as the disciples of the Anointed One, let us offer our petitions to the Father.

Reader(s)

1. That the People of God may become attuned to the divine presence in the universe. Lord hear us.

2. That the People of God may become aware of the gifts we have been given. Lord hear us.

3. That the People of God may become attentive to the needs of the poor. Lord hear us.

4. That the People of God may grow in acknowledging our responsibilities to peoples around the globe. Lord hear us.

5. That the People of God may become appreciative of our need to care for the material creation. Lord hear us.

6. That the People of God may become alive to the healing forgiveness of God. Lord hear us.

President

Father, we are here to praise and thank you in union with your Son; but we are also conscious of our needs to grow in holiness, to be forgiven our offences, and to be healed of our diseases. Grant these gifts to us for we ask them through Jesus Christ our Lord. Amen.

Eucharistic Prayer

Preface of Weekdays IV [P40] highlights the theme of thanksgiving and praise to God ('Our prayer of thanksgiving adds nothing to your greatness …'), while Eucharistic Prayers II and III are each more explicitly prayers of thanksgiving than Eucharistic Prayer I.

Invitation to the Our Father
We are gathered in union with Jesus in offering thanks to the Father, so now let us pray as he taught us:

Sign of Peace
The Lord brings healing and peace to all. We too are charged to bring peace into our world; if we are ready to take on this work of the Christ let us begin by offering peace to those around us.

Invitation to Communion
We gather asking the Lord to have mercy on us, and the Lord rejoices in greeting us and offers us to share in his supper.

Communion Reflection
If we have died with him, we shall also live with him.

Lord, you have united us with your body,
You have shared you lifeblood with us,
Grant that we may live in you.

If we have died with him, we shall also live with him.

Lord, grant us the strength to endure as your disciples,
Grant us a place in your kingdom,
Grant that we may reign with you.

If we have died with him, we shall also live with him.

Lord give us the courage to profess you,
Help us to bear witness to your presence,
Let us never deny you.

If we have died with him, we shall also live with him.

Conclusion
Solemn Blessing 12 (Ordinary Time III), Missal, p 372.

Notes
The focus of the gospel in relation to the first reading
The combination of the first reading with the gospel highlights

the aspect of offering thanks and praise to God in response to his gift of healing as the focus of this day's readings, rather than the fact of the healing of the ten lepers. The subsidiary theme is that God's gifts are freely given to all humanity and not limited to a tribe or sect.

The hymn during communion

Today's second reading preserves a precious link with the earliest gatherings for the Lord's meal: an early Christian hymn used in the Pauline churches which the author expects his listeners to know by heart, presumably because it was used in the weekly gatherings for the Eucharist. We know directly from Pliny that at the eucharistic gatherings 'hymns were sung to Christ as if to a god' (*carnemque Christo quasi deo dicere*) and today we read a portion of one of those hymns which was probably incorporated into the letter not very long before Pliny wrote. Given the presence of this gem in today's liturgy it could be used either as a hymn/reflection after communion, or it could be used in the more ancient manner as a hymn that could be repeated (a *confractorium*) during the breaking of a loaf and then the slow process of drinking from a single cup.

COMMENTARY

First Reading: 2 Kgs 5:14-17

The Naaman story is a well-formed unit of text that runs from 5:1 to 5:19 (with the nice little subsidiary story of the crooked Gehazi being tacked on to make up the whole of ch 5). However, the nineteen verses of the story must have seemed too long to the creators of the Lectionary and so we are only given this chunk of text: we are thrown into the story in mid-stream, and we are deprived of its final end. In effect, we are not hearing the story that is part of the tradition, but getting an edited snippet that is meant to carry an independent meaning. The effect of this is that anyone hearing this lection who cannot from her/his memory fit these verses into the larger story – and I have serious doubts that in the average congregation there would be more

than one or two people who would know the story of Naaman
well enough to so locate the snippet – just hears an isolated set of
details that makes almost no sense.

It is impossible to offer any useful exegetical notes with reference to the lump of text in the Lectionary.

Psalm: 97:1-4
The goodness of God is not a reality that is only seen by Israel,
but is there for all humanity to acknowledge.

Second Reading: 2 Tim 2:8-13
The author is anxious that the communities – churches who
looked back to Paul as their apostle – to which he writes will be
steadfast to the gospel that they have received. This he does in
two ways. First, he seeks to emphasise by using a christological
slogan: 'Jesus is the Christ raised from the dead, sprung from the
seed of David.' So slogans were used in the early churches as
credal statements and they have the three key qualities of a
modern tagline: meaning, emotion, and information. Who is
Jesus? The Christ. What is our central belief and reason for hearing his gospel? He has risen from the dead. What is the background that enables us to approach Jesus? He is a man and the
fulfilment of the promises made by God through the generations reaching back to King David. Second, he quotes a hymn
in use in the Pauline churches as another snippet that can be
held in the memory and relied upon. This is the earliest explicit
example we possess of where a formula of the liturgy (the *lex
orandi*) is used to establish the content of the creed professed (the
lex credendi).

First Reading > Gospel Links
The relationship here is one of parallel narratives demonstrating
a continuity of message. First, God's mercy is not bounded by
geography or race or cult; second, the healing has a sacramental
dimension: in Elisha's case there is the immersion in the Jordan;
in Jesus's case the lepers must show themselves to the priests as
the cult's regulations require.

Gospel: Lk 17:11-19

This story is found only in Luke and is without any parallel in the writings extant from the first generations of Christians. Geographical locations in Luke are symbolical rather than historical: by placing this event on the border Luke is putting before us one of his key themes, in both the gospel and Acts, that Jesus is God's salvation for all people. The focus of the incident is not the fact that ten were healed, but that one could see what the fact of being healed meant. When the Samaritan saw that he was healed, he then understood that he had not only encountered healing but salvation. His return to Jesus, in the light of this seeing beyond the healing which is understanding, is then equivalent to conversion and a declaration of faith – hence the final words: 'Your faith has saved you.' Note that it was not faith that 'healed' him – that was the direct and generous act of God, but salvation demanded the response of faith which is his coming back to Jesus with understanding. This point is, however, obscured by sloppy translating in the JB version in the Lectionary: it reads 'finding himself cured', whereas the key verb is that of seeing and so the verse should be rendered as 'Then one of them, seeing that he was healed (*idón hoti iathé*), turned back ...'

The story also presents in a nugget Luke's comprehensive outlook on the work of Jesus: the story begins with bodily healing, it ends with the wholeness (healing for the whole person) that is the gift of the Saviour.

HOMILY NOTES

1. That only 10% of the lepers who were healed would show gratitude may seem to be unusual and indicative of a particularly ungracious group, but it is probably no better or no worse than normal. Do we appreciate the goodness of God to us, and thank him? Are we alert to the wonders of the creation, and then respectful of it? Do we see existence as a divine gift and then seek to live in such a way that all creatures are enhanced? Are we anxious to use our individual talents not for personal greed but to build-up a better life for all?

Can we see our riches as offering us the possibility of bringing development to the poor and needy? How often do we stop to count our blessings and then seek ways to share those blessings with those suffering under a variety of oppression? How often do we realise that assembling to offer worship to God is an acknowledgement of our predicament as the human family, rather than an activity that might meet some internal need or desire of me as an individual?

2. Ingratitude is not simply a failure to say 'thanks' by analogy with the way a child might forget to drop a note of thanks to a far-away aunt who has sent a birthday present. Ingratitude is a way of existing, a way of viewing the universe, a way of perceiving ourselves, and a way of acting in society and with society's blessing. Ingratitude does not see the larger picture of our place in the universe within the material creation, with other human beings, or beyond the universe to its source. Ingratitude is the attitude of those who think that they are self-sufficient, that the world and other people are there for my use or for general exploitation, and who think that my/our aggrandisement is the legitimate end of social and economic policy.

3. Developing awareness of our debt to God's goodness is, however, a complex matter. It needs us to become alive to the sacramental nature of the universe and other people: we discover God's love and activity in and through the creation of which we are a part. Gratitude results only from a new way of seeing those in need, human society, the world; and for that reason we as believers in the creating goodness and generosity of God can never separate such activities as (1) care of the poor in our society, (2) development in the Third World, (3) ecological concern about the exploitation of the planet, and (4) liturgy. Only someone who sees the goodness of God can understand why we offer thanks in Jesus Christ in the Eucharist. Only someone who knows how much our talents are God's gifts can see the logic of sharing our resources with the needy. Only someone who sees the creation as being

alight with the glory of God and pointing beyond itself to the mystery of its Creator will see that exploitation is inherently wrong.

4. The gospel places emphasis on seeing: the Samaritan experienced a moment of God's goodness – his healing – and this enabled him to see the larger picture and to become thankful. He discovered not only his healing but the source of wholeness. So this gospel is a call to us to see anew, to renew our imaginations, and to see the mystery of God in the people and world around us.

5. There is a series of 'A' words – all of them are variants of 'seeing' – that help us to focus on what the gospel calls us to do:

   To become *attuned* to the mystery of God's goodness hidden within people, situations, and the material world around us.

   To become *aware* of those in need of healing.

   To become *attentive* to the cries of the poor, the oppressed, the exploited.

   To *acknowledge* our obligations to others alive today, and to future generations who must live on this God-given earth.

   To become *appreciative* of the wonder around us.

   To become *alert* to how simply we can slip into a lifestyle of ingratitude.

   To *accept* the need to praise God if we are to fully understand our human situation.

   To become *awake* to the damage we can do to others and the earth by our carelessness.

   To become *alive* to the dimension of thanksgiving for God's goodness in the creation in our Sunday liturgy (e.g. the prayers over the gifts) and how that liturgy is linked to care for the poor.

Twenty-ninth Sunday of Ordinary Time

Introduction to the Celebration

Today we hear how Jesus told his disciples a parable about the need to pray continually and never lose heart. We are now gathered to pray for our needs and to thank the Father for his gifts; and the greatest of his gifts is his Son who is present among us. Now let us ask pardon for the times we have not prayed and for the times when we have lost our faith in God.

Rite of Penance

Lord Jesus, for the times when we have not prayed. Lord have mercy.

Lord Jesus, for the times when we have lost heart. Christ have mercy.

Lord Jesus, for the times when we have not trusted in you. Lord have mercy.

Headings for Readings

First Reading

Today we read an ancient story about Moses praying for the people of Israel, and the storyteller wants to make the point that prayer must be continuous and without interruption. So much so that the people could not even let Moses take a few moments off for a rest. Just how they achieved this gives one of the funniest images from the whole of the Old Testament.

Second Reading

This reading is a reminder that we are a people who are charged with remaining faithful to the teaching of the apostles.

Gospel

We all know about 'pester power'; in this passage Jesus reminds us that if pester power can gain the ear of an unjust human, how much more will prayer be heard by a just God.

Prayer of the Faithful
President

Sisters and brothers, we are charged to bring God's love and mercy into the world for we have declared that we are one with the Christ, the Sun of Justice, who wills all to have life in abundance. Mindful of our declared loyalty to the Christ, let us pray.

Reader(s)

1. For the strength to oppose poverty and work for justice. Lord hear us.

2. For the strength to avoid exploitation and treat everyone with dignity. Lord hear us.

3. For the strength to work against prejudice and promote human equality. Lord hear us.

4. For the strength to reject selfishness and use the planet's resources well. Lord hear us.

5. *Specific local needs and topics of the day.*

6. For the strength to carry on the work of the Christ and be found to have kept his faith. Lord hear us.

President

Father, you love every member of our human family and sent your Son to bring us life and life in its fullness. Hear us now and grant our petitions through that same Christ, our Lord. Amen.

Eucharistic Prayer

There is no Sunday preface that picks up the theme of continual prayer. However, there is a ancient and fruitful ambiguity in the term 'house of prayer' (based on the way Christians read Mk 11:17 in conjunction with Isa 56:7): the 'house' is primarily the whole church which is all nations in prayer to the Father, and then it is the ritual place (church, chapel, oratory) where a local church gathers to pray. We see the ambiguity of terms in that we can say 'the church gathers in the church on Sunday'. Given this fruitful ambiguity, then Preface of the Dedication of a Church II (P 53) (Missal, p 456) is suitable for today. Moreover, it is a rather beautiful preface that is rarely used. Eucharistic Prayer III uses the image of prayer from one end of the cosmos to the other rising up before the Father.

Invitation to the Our Father
The Lord Jesus reminded his disciples to pray continually. Now in union with all Christians let us do what he asked as we say:

Sign of Peace
If we are the people of faith, then we must be bringers of justice and peacemakers, so let us express our desire for peace with all around us.

Invitation to Communion
The Lord calls us to gather with him and to become a people continually praying to the Father; happy are we who have been called to this supper.

Communion Reflection
Given that prayer has come up repeatedly as a theme today, a structured silence for prayer is better than a reflection in words.

Conclusion
Prayer over the People 5 (Missal, p 380).

COMMENTARY

First Reading: Ex 17:8-13
This story was told as the account of a distinct phase in the war of conquest over the inhabitants of Canaan. The whole story runs from v 8 to v 16, and it has all the major foundation characters mentioned: Moses the prophet and lawgiver, Aaron the priest, and Joshua the warlord and divider of the land. When read with its final three verses ('Then the Lord said to Moses, "Write this as a reminder in a book and recite it in the hearing of Joshua: I will utterly blot out the remembrance of Amalek from under heaven." And Moses built an altar and called it, The Lord is my banner. He said, "A hand upon the banner of the Lord! The Lord will have war with Amalek from generation to generation".') the tale is a miraculous tale of God taking the side of one army over another, due to their possession of special spiritual

powers, and then making that victory part of a national epic of
conquest and land-rights. As edited in the Lectionary the focus
is shifted (at least in the minds of the editors of the Lectionary) to
Moses as the intercessor for Israel, who must not cease interceding, and so is the model for the notion of continuous prayer
which is mentioned in the gospels. In this Christian reading of
Moses as an intercessor, there is another text exercising a hidden
influence in today's choice: Jn 3:14. However, few hearers of this
reading will think of Moses as intercessor, and so it is doubtful if
it really helps throw another perspective on today's gospel.

However, the text does produce some real problems when
read to a congregation. First, the notion of the God of armies,
and of God showing his will in military victories is one that
many Christians find repulsive. Second, these 'God gave the
land' stories are used politically by conservative groups in the
United States and elsewhere to underpin foreign policy today,
and many people are concerned that this is a narrow theology
affecting the lives and material wellbeing of many people in the
Middle East today. Even reading these with the conclusion 'This
is the word of the Lord' is to invite mis-interpretation. We
should openly admit that there is little real chance that the average congregation will get sufficient catechesis to hear this story
at anything other than face value. Third, the story is part of an
historicising myth – parallel to Aeneid in Rome or Beowulf in
Anglo-Saxon England – and if someone asks 'Is it historically
true?' (i.e. 'Did this event happen?'), then we have to simply say
that there is no possibility of that, but that the story was com-
posed many centuries after its narrative moment to justify existing land boundaries, and then many will ask why is such 'stuff'
still read. Lastly, the success of the intercession is dependent on
the material performance of a ritual to affect the will of God, and
this is the classic definition of superstition. With all these problems – allowing that in an ideal situation an appropriate theological justification for the continued use of this text could be offered – one really has to question the appropriateness of having
this text in the Lectionary.

Given that the text is there but generates more heat than light, is there a way of sanitising its effect if you do not simply wish to omit it and use only the second reading today? One method I have found fruitful is to point out that it is a very funny story – just picture the old guy propped up with stones! So why would anyone have told a story like this about their hero? Possibly, to remind people that they had to keep on praying, and then still keep on praying. However, this is only a sanitising accommodation and not a genuine answer – and I do not use it with anyone who raises a serious question about this text's presence in the Sunday eucharistic Lectionary (it would, for example, pose far less problems in the Lectionary of the Office of Readings). So we must hope that in some future revision of the Lectionary, this text disappears.

Second Reading: 2 Tim 3:14-4:2

We tend to imagine the earliest Christian communities as models of unity, cohesion, unity of purpose, and fidelity to the mind of the Christ. And, indeed, this was a carefully fostered piece of preaching from at least the time of the Acts of the Apostles when Luke exhorts his hearers to be united precisely because in such unity they would be imitating the perfect ideal time of the first disciples in Jerusalem. However, the historical reality was almost the complete opposite of this romantic picture. The first disciples came from a wide variety of backgrounds, whether they were already adherents of the Law or gentile converts, socially, ethnically, and in terms of religion. So, as an example of the last type of diversity, there were those who came from apocalyptical groups within Judaism, those who were political revolutionaries, those from Galilee who imagined recreating an ancient ideal time under Joshua, those who brought the baggage of John the Baptist's preaching, those who came as trained scribes, some Pharisees, others from the sophisticated theological world of Greek-speaking Judaism, and still other varieties. This is not to mention the range of Greek and Roman ideas about religion, cultic organisation, and the legacy of their literatures in their imaginations that gentile converts brought with them. By the early second century these various strands were causing disruption in and between churches, and there were many groups that were tending to fragment from the broad central band of belief and practice that was widely recognised as 'Christian.' It is in such a situation of countering the related tendencies for churches to fragment in independent sects, or to continue evolving their practices and doctrines without recognising the distinctive thrust and dynamic of the Jesus-movement, that produced the search for order within the church that we see demonstrated in the reading from 2 Tim today.

The prescription is basically founded on the notion of being wary of novelty, for novelty is seen as characteristic of departure from the original deposit. The past is the guarantor of the present, and the maintenance of contact with the past – conservatism of its past – is the safe path to knowing what is true. The 'scriptures' – a phrase which by now had probably evolved from being just 'the scriptures' that were seen as pointing towards the Christ (i.e. our 'Old Testament') to include the four gospels – are seen as a basic source for guidance in this process. Moreover, the reference to 'all scripture' was probably made with those groups who wanted to abandon the Old Testament or else to only select a very restricted number of texts as 'their guide'. The other key direction finder is located in teaching. This is not only that which is adhered to, but itself must be regulated and care taken to 'refute falsehood' and 'correct error' because loyalty to the teaching and obedience (seen as being simultaneously obedience to the teaching, the church, and God) are already explicitly identified. In this text we have a snapshot of a moment in the complex process of the church evolving from being a scattering of local churches, *ekklésiai*, with an ecumenical vision (such as we see in the *Didache*) to being an ecumenical movement, the *ekklésia*, manifested in local groups scattered throughout the world.

First Reading > Gospel Links

The link here is found in the similarity of God's actions: Moses' prayer for divine help was heard; similarly, the prayers of people to God for justice will be answered. In both readings, God takes the side of his people when they pray to him. So the link is the continuity between Old and New Testaments.

Gospel: Lk 18:1-8

Today's reading forms a distinct section of Luke's gospel and is found nowhere else in the gospels. It is a difficult passage because it brings together the theme of prayer with that of the sufferings of the Christian community who must persevere in hope during the long wait to see God's justice, and also brings in, once again, the theme of the appearing of the Son of Man. This final theme has its most enigmatic exposure in Luke in 17:20-37 – a passage so difficult that it has been skipped in the Lectionary – where the moment of the appearing of the Son of Man is presented as sudden and wholly unexpected, but also as the day of the vindication of those who have remained faithful to God.

In preaching today we have to approach this text at two levels. The first is to concentrate on the core story: prayer and perseverance. On this we have a well-formed parable where the poorest of the poor, a widow (the very symbol of powerlessness in an agrarian patriarchal society) is shown as the contrast to the disciple who can stand before the righteous God. If you can accept that a mere widow can succeed before an unjust human power, then how can you doubt that God, who is goodness and righteousness, will not hear your prayers? This core, with its combination of teaching on prayer and concern for the poor, forms a more than adequate basis for catechesis today. However, there is also a second level of meaning within which Luke wraps the parable: not only have the Christians to wait for vindication, not only must they persevere in hope, but they must recall the coming of the Son of Man. So the final verse puts before the listeners this question: Yes, indeed, God is faithful and will in the end vindicate his chosen ones; but what of the disciples? Will they wait and persevere until that moment of vindication (which Luke describes here, and in 17:20-37, as the moment of 'the coming of the Son of Man')? This is a theme which is probably too complex to present in a homily at a Eucharist especially since the theme of the Son of Man is not part of our preaching tradition. However, it does add another dimension to how Luke sees discipleship.

HOMILY NOTES

1. 'Now will God not see justice done to his chosen who cry to him day and night even when he delays to help them?' When most Christians hear these words they immediately think of their own needs and wants, and their prayers, and their desire to have their prayers answered. This is an interesting move. We know that love is incompatible with selfishness or self-centredness, yet when we hear about prayer and the answer to prayer, we think first of our prayers, we think selfishly.

2. But if we are to be able to think about this gospel, then the first step is to move the focus out from our selfishness – only then will we have that purity of mind and heart that will allow us to glimpse the meaning of what the Christ is saying to us. The first question is not 'Why does God not answer my prayers?' but 'Who are the chosen ones of God for whom the Father will see justice done?' From the times of the prophets who spoke about God's defence of the *anawim*, to the Christ, and down through the life of the church, there has been but one answer: the poor. The Lord will vindicate the poor as the Lord vindicated Lazarus who sat, full of sores, at the door of the rich man's house (Lk 16).

3. The great Dominican theologian, Gustavo Gutiérrez, once said: 'Poverty is a multi-faceted, inhuman, and unjust reality; poverty is complex. Important though the economic dimension is, poverty is not simply an economic reality ... This point is reinforced when we see how complex the idea of 'the poor' is in the Old and New Testaments: it may refer to those who beg to survive; to the sheep without a shepherd; to those

ignorant of the Law; to those called in John's gospel 'the ac-
cursed' (Jn 7:49); to women, children, foreigners and notori-
ous sinners; to those afflicted with serious diseases ...
Poverty is not a matter of fate; but a condition brought about;
it is not a misfortune, but a matter of injustice ... It is the
work of human hands: of economic structures; of social
greed; of racial, cultural and religious prejudices that have
accumulated over history; of ever more overweening economic aspirations. It follows that its abolition lies within our
power.'

4. Of course, there will be many – included in the assembly
gathered to receive the gifts of the Lord's bounty at the
Eucharistic table – who will find such ideas subversive and
who would prefer an abstract homily on the 'problem of
unanswered prayers'. So is this something that should be addressed at the Eucharist? The answer lies in the fact that the
Eucharist is the celebration of love: God's love for us in
Christ, our attempt to pattern that love in our relationships,
and to return it as our sacrifice of thanksgiving and praise. To
quote Gutiérrez again: 'Christianity sees in the refusal to love
other people nothing less than sin: the ultimate root of poverty
and dehumanisation.'

5. Let us note the sad fact that poverty is becoming more widespread, not less, in the world. We live at a time when the
planet's population is clustering at the extremes of the economic spectrum: the gap between those with use of the resources, with scientific and technical know-how, and those
without, is widening. More and more the people of the planet
are falling into one or other group: the exploiting and the
exploited. And it happens variously in each society so, for example, even in poor societies women are more exploited than
men. Indeed, some economists talk of the 'feminisation of
poverty' because women are always more affected by poverty
in its various forms (economic, medical, educational) and,
then, in addition, women experience discrimination from
men, and may also suffer more if they belong to disadvan-

taged cultures or races. If one wants to know the facts one can just look them up in reports by the World Bank – all there on the internet.

6. This poverty in all its shapes insults human dignity and is contrary to the will of God. When we as Christians work to create a poverty-free world, we are not engaging in some sort of social crusade – although that is all it will appear to be to those who do not embrace of mystery of the Christ – but actualising the presence of the love of God for every human being that is seen in the coming of the Christ. It is because the Father has sent Jesus to all who are in need, that we can actualise this love in combating the inequalities and prejudices of our present situation.

7. But there is a sting in the tail of today's gospel: shall we be willing to take on this task of being the conveyors of God's love to those who cry for justice? It is the willingness to take on this task, the work of the Christ, that is faith. Faith is working with Jesus in his work, not an exercise in 'ticking boxes' about whether we accept some random religious ideas. So will the Son of Man find any faith on the earth? Or put another way, will we simply let injustice run rampant so that no one undoes the effects of that sin which enslaves so many of God's beloved?

Thirtieth Sunday of Ordinary Time

Introduction to the Celebration

Today we are going to reflect on self-knowledge and humility. By gathering here in public we are telling the world that we take the need to profess faith in God seriously; we are saying we are people with a definite way of life, that we have taken up the cross of discipleship. But without humble awareness of our faults and our need of God's mercy, we could be deceiving ourselves. Let us ask the Spirit to enlighten our minds that we might know our failings, and to give us the humility to ask for mercy.

Rite of Penance

O Lord, be merciful to me, a sinner. Lord have mercy.
O Lord, be merciful to me, a sinner. Christ have mercy.
O Lord, be merciful to me, a sinner. Lord have mercy.

Headings for Readings

First Reading

The opening phrase from this reading has passed into our laws as a basic principle: 'without respect to persons' – meaning that the highest and the lowest in a society should be treated alike before the law. Here we are reminded that ultimately it is the Lord who is no respecter of personages.

Second Reading

This is Paul's farewell to his collaborator Timothy: he has fought the good fight, he has finished the race, and he now looks forward to meeting the Lord.

Gospel

God's ways, thankfully, are not our ways. The Pharisee was the accepted icon of the God-fearing and devout person who took religion and its demands seriously: the 'Good Guy'. The tax collector, by contrast, was the very image of the outcast, the traitor, the sinner, and the 'Bad Guy'. But the Lord looks at the heart.

Prayer of the Faithful
President
Sisters and brothers, we gather as sinners made into a Holy People in Christ Jesus, and as needy people who have been made a Priestly People in Christ Jesus and so are able to stand before the Father and tell him of all our needs.
Reader(s)
1. For the whole church across the world, that we will be enabled to humbly bear witness to the truth. Lord hear us.
2. For all who have power and influence in the world, that they may act with honesty and integrity. Lord hear us.
3. For all who are publicly recognised as Christians, that they may have humility and self-knowledge. Lord hear us.
4. For this church, that we may seek mercy and forgiveness and be given the gift of humility. Lord hear us.
5. *Specific local needs and topics of the day.*
6. For all who have died, that they may receive mercy from the Lord who is no respecter of appearances. Lord hear us.
President
Father, we stand before you and ask you to be merciful to us sinners, and to all our brothers and sisters, for we pray to you through Jesus Christ, our Lord. Amen.

Eucharistic Prayer
This is a good day to use one of the Eucharistic Prayers for Reconciliation.

Invitation to the Our Father
Let us now ask the Father to show us his mercy as we show mercy to those who ask us for mercy:

Sign of Peace
We all are in need of mercy from God and forgiveness from one

another. Let us express that forgiveness now by sharing a sign of peace with each other.

Invitation to Communion
The Lord Jesus humbled himself for our sake by suffering on the Cross. Now he invites us to share in his holy banquet.

Communion Reflection
A structured silence: 'Let us spend one minute asking the Lord to help us to know ourselves better.' End the measured times of silence with 'Let us pray.'

Conclusion
Solemn Blessing 14 [Ordinary Time V], Missal, p 373.

COMMENTARY

First Reading: Sir 35:12-14, 16-18 [Note that in some printings of the Lectionary this lection is still introduced with the medieval Latin name 'Ecclesiasticus'; so change it to 'Sirach'.]
This reading as found in the 1982 printing of the Lectionary (volume 1, p 925) presents a problem. The reference is given as 35:12-14 and 16-18. But what is found there is, in fact, the text that runs from mid-way through v 15 to v 17, and then from v 20 to mid-way through v 22. Since there is no discrepancy in numeration between the Vulgate, the Neo-vulgate, nor any English translation with regard to these verses, this must be simply a blunder. However, it does have significance for if the reference is correct (and the official Lectionary of 1969 is only a set of references), then that reading places one slant on today's gospel; if the actual printed reading is correct, then a very different slant. Since what is printed in the book is what is read, it is that text (i.e. 35: 15-17, 20-22) that is commented upon here.

The key point in this reading is that God does not judge by outward appearances. This is the notion of making 'acceptance of persons' (*personarum acceptio*) that is found elsewhere in the Old Testament, and on six occasions in the New, and which has migrated from there to European law systems via Canon Law (e.g. the 1983 Code of the Latin Church, canons 626, 830 and 1181). The divine justice looks at each individual and her/his actions, not their status good or bad, and this forms the model for human justice.

To this standard of divine justice, Sirach adds the importance of prayer: the Lord hears those who are in need, those who have been wrongly judged, and those who have no one else to whom to turn. The characteristic of the prayer the Lord hears is, however, that which comes with humility, not with outward appearance. Even the poor – simply because they are poor – are not sure of a hearing. It is the inner attitude of humility that 'pierces the clouds' ('the clouds' is the classic image of that which separates the divine realm from the earthly world of our lives).

Psalm: 32
This is one of the great statements of faith in the Lord hearing the cries of his people. However, the response does not actually accord with what has just been read from Sirach. Sirach's point is that poor or not, the Lord acts justly and it is humility that gains access. This response makes a different point: that God is predisposed to the weak, the poor the down trodden. Both are precious parts of our inheritance, but neither is served by this jumbling.

Second Reading: 2 Tim 4:6-8, 16-18
This is a farewell address: all is over, now he praises God and waits his coming. The omitted verses tell of his helpers having left him or gone on to other tasks, he requests for items to be sent on to him, and also his anger over some of the things done against him. It is a pity this has been cropped to just those parts 'with a message' as the notes and greetings give the impression of a real man and saint. While it is usual to suppose that 'the pastorals' (i.e. 1 and 2 Tim and Tit) are not by Paul, a good case can be made that while 1 Tim and Tit are not from his hand, this letter is from him – and one of the key arguments for that is the list

of collaborators mentions in vv 9-15. So if you have time, it is worth reading the whole passage.

First Reading > Gospel Links
The first reading gives the 'theoretical' background to the parable of the gospel. The ways of God in dealing with his people, the divine message is consistent over the two covenants.

Gospel: Lk 18:9-14
This parable is only found in Luke, and is one of those few parables whose key point can still be readily grasped. We are all in need of mercy from God, and everyone needs to approach God with humility.

There are, however, two common blunders in interpreting this parable. First, it is because of this parable that the Pharisees get an undeserved and unintended 'bad press' in the tradition of preaching. It is often read it is as if a Pharisee is there because that group was intrinsically hypocritical – hence in common parlance the descriptions of hypocrite and Pharisee are interchangeable. The meaning is thereby obscured: a Pharisee is chosen precisely because they formed a group who took the demands of the Law seriously. What is wrong is not that the man is a Pharisee or that he did those good actions, but that all that goodness was set at naught by a wrong attitude. The same is true of the Tax Collector – it is his attitude that brings mercy, not that God is indifferent to the practices of the tax collectors in the ancient world. To see the effects of this shift in interpretation it is interesting to read the text replacing 'a nun' for the word 'Pharisee', and 'a drug pusher' for 'tax collector'.

Second, regular prayer, regular fasting, and definite alms giving – what the Pharisee boasts about – were seen as the three characteristic practices needed in the early church to train oneself as a disciple. It is against this church practice that we should view these activities. The message is not that these are simply externals of no consequence or simply 'add ons' or 'optional extras'. Rather, these form the basis for real, lived discipleship, but that must be animated by humility and sorrow for sin. Luke's audience already knew that they had to pray and fast and provide for the poor; this tale would have reminded them that the performance of the task was not enough, for the Lord also looked at the heart.

HOMILY NOTES

1. We live in an image-laden world. We talk about organisations getting a 'new image'. Political parties employ 'spin doctors.' Products and companies are 're-branded.' Advertising can change our buying habits, our perceptions of ourselves, our bodies, our politics, and even our religions. In a world of constant 'communications' there is a premium on being able to make things appear genuine, attractive, wholesome, and good. And for many that is the key demand: appearance. It might be good, but it must appear good; it might not be all its cracked up to be, but so long as it is branded properly and marketed well, then who cares? A newspaper owner once said that when legend replaces fact, then print legend. Another told his editor that selling papers was his business, not news. This is the world of the lie, where reality is in the background and perception is all that matters.

2. We as believers in a Creator have the task of challenging the lie: reality is our business because it comes from God and will return to God, and we shall be asked about our stewardship.

3. Getting behind appearance is, however, always difficult, and it always has been. We have to constantly pull ourselves up and have a reality check. We have to pinch ourselves to make sure that we see beneath the glittering images that strike our senses and which can deceive us. This is the wisdom captured in the proverb, 'Don't judge a book by its cover' – alas, most of us do just that more often than we like to admit and this is proven by the fact that giving a book 'hype' works time and again.

4. This task of not being taken in by illusions that we know is

important in our everyday lives: we do not want to be fooled, conned, or cheated. But it is also a Christian task for we proclaim the Christ to be the truth. Taking issue with hype and deception is part of our witness to the truth. Making sure that we are not engaged in deceptions is a basic of Christian discipleship.

5. This gospel challenges us at several levels.

First, there is the world of icons and brands. The very model of the devout follower of the Law is the Pharisee. The very model of the 'bad guy' is the tax collector. In the world of stereotypes and images we are to admire the first and condemn the second. But God acts at the level of truth, not the level of stereotypes and manufactured expectations.

Second, there is the contrast between external religiosity and a genuine desire to have a relationship with God. The two should go together, but just as a brand may have high appeal and not be the genuine article, so too with religion. But God does not dwell at the level of external and human display.

Third, there is the contrast between self-deception and self-knowledge. We can so easily con ourselves into believing our own propaganda without being aware of our faults and needs. We are all in need of greater integrity and of God's mercy.

6. We claim to be the people of 'The Way', we claim to follow 'the way, the truth, and the life'. This is a call to integrity, self-knowledge, and humility: these are not virtues that come naturally to us as beings who love our senses. But these are the virtues that will bring us life with God.

Thirty-first Sunday of Ordinary Time

Introduction to the Celebration

Is there a more memorable scene in the whole gospel than that of the little man Zacchaeus climbing a tree to catch a glimpse of Jesus? Then despite Zacchaeus being the outcast in the community, Jesus choosing to have supper with him. The Lord has come among us today, coming to seek and save, and calling us to share his supper now in this sacred banquet. Let us focus our minds on our need to be forgiven, our need to begin afresh, and that we are gathered around the Lord's table.

Rite of Penance

Son of Man, you call us to yourself even in our sinfulness. Lord have mercy.

Son of Man, you give peace and new life to those who share your table. Christ have mercy.

Son of Man, you have come to seek out and save what was lost. Lord have mercy.

Headings for Readings

First Reading

It is the Lord's love that brings the universe into existence and holds it in existence. And it is the Lord's will that every creature grow to perfection in harmony with the divine wisdom that permeates the creation. The Lord loves life, not corruption and death, and so offers us forgiveness and renewed life.

Second Reading

People are always predicting that God is about to bring an end of the world. Some people had been spreading this idea among the Christians of Thessalonica, but people should not get excited or alarmed.

Gospel

Zacchaeus is the sinner at whose table Jesus wishes to eat – despite the objections of those who were scandalised – and in being at table with Jesus, Zacchaeus received the strength to begin a new way of life.

Prayer of the Faithful

President

Friends, we have gathered to be around Jesus to learn from him and to be at his table, so with him let us pray to the Father for our needs and those of all humanity.

Reader(s)

1. Let us pray for the holy church of God, that we will have the strength to carry on the work of the Christ seeking out the lost. Lord hear us.

2. Let us pray for all of us, that we will have the strength to seek out reconciliation with God and with one another. Lord hear us.

3. Let us pray for all who are outcasts in our society, that we will have the strength to offer the hand of welcome and acceptance. Lord hear us.

4. Let us pray for all people of good will, that they will have the strength to work for a world of peace, of respect for human rights, and of justice. Lord hear us.

5. *Specific local needs and topics of the day.*

6. Let us pray for all who have died, that they may hear the Lord's call to rise in glory. Lord hear us.

President

Father, your Son sat at table with Zacchaeus bringing to that house the message of your abiding love. We too are gathered with him at table, so hear us and grant our needs in that same Christ Jesus, our Lord. Amen.

Eucharistic Prayer

Eucharistic Prayer for Masses of Reconciliation II.

Invitation to the Our Father

The Lord Jesus calls us to return to life in our Father's house, and so we pray:

Sign of Peace

The Lord Jesus crossed boundaries to bring peace to sinners as when he went in to stay with Zacchaeus. He calls on us to cross boundaries to create reconciliation. Let us begin with those around us.

Invitation to Communion

The Lord desired to dine at the table of Zacchaeus. Now he calls us to dine at his table.

Communion Reflection

As we thank the Lord for having fed us at his table, let us recall all the stories of the meals of Jesus we have been recalling over this Year of Luke.

You dined with your disciples at Simon's house in Capernaum;
You brought healing to Simon's mother-in-law. *(4:38-9)*

You dined with the tax collector Levi when you called him to follow you;
You sat at his table despite murmurs that you ate and drank with tax collectors and sinners. *(5:27-32)*

You ate and drank with your disciples even when it scandalised the Pharisees and the disciples of John the Baptist who fasted often, offering frequent prayers. *(5:33-39; 7:24-35)*

You accepted a Pharisee's hospitality and ate at his table when the woman from the city, the sinner, anointed your feet and wept;
You, sitting there amidst your followers, forgave her sins. *(7:36-41)*

You ate with the multitude in the wilderness;
You satisfied all with five loaves and two fish. *(9:10-17)*

You sat at table in Martha's house while her sister Mary listened to your words;

You taught all who sit with you the better path. *(10:38-42)*
You dined with another Pharisee who was shocked you did not
first wash;
You taught us there that what disqualifies us from the table of
the Lord is the neglect of justice and the love of God. *(11:37-12:1)*
You dined one Sabbath with a ruler who was a Pharisee;
You healed the man with dropsy at that meal and told us:
'Blessed is the one who shall eat bread in the Kingdom of God.'
(14:1-24)
You dined with Zacchaeus and changed his life;
You brought salvation to his whole household. *(19:1-10)*
You sat at table with your followers for the Passover meal,
You told them then to gather for this meal in your memory.
(22:15-20)
You revealed your risen life to the disciples at the table in
Emmaus;
You were recognised in the breaking of the loaf. *(24:13-53)*
You have dined with us here today;
Grant that when people come from north, south, east, and west
to sit at table in the kingdom of God, that we shall be with them.
Amen. *(13:29)*

Conclusion
Any of the Solemn Blessings for Ordinary Time are suitable for
today.

Notes
This is another Sunday on which time spent on breaking, eating,
and drinking – doing as Jesus did – is better than time talking
about what Jesus, as recalled by Luke, might have meant by this
or that action or saying. If you accept that one deed is worth a
thousand words, then doing the Lord's meal is better than talking about it.

First Reading: Wis 11:22-12:1

One of the themes running through this part of the Wisdom of
Solomon is God's fidelity to his people on their journey – a
theme that is picked up in the gospel. This loving care – God's
covenant fidelity – is seen in his concern with the creation, his
care for humanity even in the face of sin, and the forgiving welcome he offers all who come to him. God's presence is suffused
in the creation and it cries out to him, God hears and transforms
it for he is the 'lover of life'. It is this understanding of God's forgiveness as welcoming home into the family of the covenant,
that sets the scene for the gospel today.

Psalm: 144

The Lord is praised for his faithfulness. This means that no one
is abandoned, for God loves all his creatures.

Second Reading: 2 Thess 1:11-2:2

This letter was written by someone working with the churches
founded by Paul and appealing to Paul's authority in trying to
answer false views about the Second Coming. This need to rebut
those who take either (1) an apocalyptic view of the parousia, or
(2) those who simply think that it is about to happen in the immediate future, is the dominant theme running right through
the letter. Here we see this theme introduced and the author's
message spelled out in a nutshell: ignore those who say the end
is nigh.

First Reading > Gospel Links

Consistency between the two covenants: God's fidelity to his
people.

Gospel: Lk 19:1-10

This story, found only in Luke, brings together several of his
major themes in a most memorable incident. Zacchaeus is a marginal Jew, someone on the fringes of society, who is perceived as

abandoned by God because of his actions. He is typical of those to whom Jesus says that he is sent in his work of re-gathering the scattered flock and forming the New Israel.

Four themes come together in this reading. First, there is the theme of the hospitality of God and his acceptance of those who seek him. Jesus calls on the man to be hospitable and then accepts him. Both Zacchaeus and Jesus behave in a God-like way – so distinct from the expectations of those around that they voice their horror – and by so doing they mirror the Father's love and forgiveness. Second, Zacchaeus becomes part of the new table fellowship that is centred on Jesus. This new belonging and eating together forms the New Israel where the boundaries are those of welcome for all who seek the Lord and care for all who are in need. Third, there is the theme of a proper attitude to wealth, which must be seen in the context of care for the poor, and of acting with justice. Lastly, it is a Son of Abraham who is converted. He is not converted back to what he was or should have been, but is converted to be part of the new people who have accepted the Son of Man.

How this story was understood in the late first century is revealed to us in a little detail that is certainly the voice of Luke: 'Today salvation has come to this house' – note it is not to this man. This shows that it belongs to the time of the household churches – found in Acts where baptism is often of households – and these households (which cannot be identified with what we call 'a family') were the location for the gatherings of the Christians for the eucharistic meal. Therefore, the meal of Jesus and Zacchaeus would have been seen as one in a series of meals of the new people, of which their own Sunday assembly at a eucharistic meal would have been another.

HOMILY NOTES

1. There is a tendency with the story of Zacchaeus to reduce it to such a simple message that we lose sight of what it might show us about God's love for us. The reduction works like this: Zacchaeus is a sinner, Jesus seeks him out, Zacchaeus re-

pents and has a 'firm purpose of amendment,' Jesus forgives him and now one who was lost is saved. This then leads to a practical point: this forgiveness through meeting Jesus is available in the Sacrament of Reconciliation. So what is wrong with this presentation? After all it has been used in this way in umpteen catechetical programmes. What is wrong with this approach is, firstly, that when the divine-human encounter is presented in this way it becomes a simple transaction ('he has what I want and I can do something to get it from him' – the encounter with a dentist or buying the paper are functionally similar). Secondly, that message can be taken out of any number of gospel scenes or parables which reduces the richness of the gospels to a series of oft-repeated slogans. Thirdly, it is driven by its sacramental conclusion. If one starts from the position that the Sacrament of Penance is of great importance, then any gospel story that seems to promote its frequent reception is then seen to be understood if it serves that purpose. However, the task of the preacher of a homily at the Eucharist is to present the good news as it is found in the church's stories, and preaching on the importance of a particular practice is another matter.

2. There is a central theme of reconciliation in this story, but the key to it lies in its particular context of welcome and acceptance. Moreover, there is no hint that Zacchaeus considered himself a sinner or that he was penitent or contrite. He merely states that he will now be someone who will care for the poor and that if he has cheated anyone, he will repay fourfold.

3. The starting point is a society that is riven with divisions, riven with injustice, where some are wholly excluded, while others are claiming holiness. It is a scene that is further complicated by people having a sense of being occupied by foreigners, of racial questions as to who have the right bloodlines, and that their religious purity has been compromised. This is the familiar scene of fractured societies where prejudice and bigotry have become substitutes for commitment and faith. What is particularly wrong in this case is that the

society is intended to be a community: they are all children of a single father – Abraham – and they are supposed to be the community of the covenant which bears witness to God's working in human history.

4. The first act of Jesus is to cut through all the divisions and offer welcome and acceptance to this son of Abraham.

5. Jesus then welcomes Zacchaeus back, not to an abstract notion descriptive of an ideal covenant community (the *qahal/ ekklesia* of the Lord) but to an actual table fellowship. He is welcomed back into the community and the community can accept his hospitality: a new society is formed around the table of the meal. This new table fellowship is, for Jesus, the coming kingdom of God: in the new mutual acceptance of his table, the transgressions of Israel become past events, a new way of living is begun, and the Father's home – salvation – is foreshadowed.

6. Zacchaeus can rejoice that the new life of the kingdom had begun and he has been given a place in its banquet, so he too can begin to live life in the new way that is appropriate in the age of the Christ.

7. Jesus's welcome and acceptance is both the good news and the new life. It is sacramental – but not in terms of the Sacrament of Reconciliation – because sharing in his table both establishes the new covenant and anticipates the life to come; and it is in terms of that sacramentality of the Lord's table fellowship that we gather for the Eucharist.

8. If there is to be a practical challenge at the end of the homily it might go like this:

- Is our table fellowship today, here, one which breaks down the barriers and divisions that prevent us acting as the New People?
- Is our gathering one which can be seen as modeling the welcome of the kingdom?
- Is our community one with the right attitude to wealth and the care of the poor?

Lectionary Unit VII

In Jerusalem

This unit is devoted to Jesus's ministry in Jerusalem. It consists of just Sunday 32 and Sunday 33; and it has an eschatological theme running through it.

On Sunday 32 we have the debate about the nature of the resurrection; and then on Sunday 33 we have 'the signs' announcing the End.

Thirty-second Sunday of Ordinary Time

Introduction to the Celebration

We gather here on Sundays because this is the 'day of the resurrection'. We call ourselves the people of the resurrection and of new life. We proclaim the mystery of faith: 'Christ has died, Christ is risen.' But we often do not stop and think about what we mean by 'resurrection' and 'rising from the dead'. These questions will echo through our celebration today.

Rite of Penance

Son of God, share with us the new life that flows from your cross and resurrection. Lord have mercy.

Son of God, gather us to live with Abraham, Isaac, Jacob, and all the saints. Christ have mercy.

Son of God, judge us worthy of a place in the resurrection as sons and daughters of God. Lord have mercy.

Headings for Readings
First Reading

In the face of death, the holy Maccabees placed their trust in God who would give them the gift of new life and of victory over human wickedness.

Second Reading

Paul concludes one of his letters with a blessing, a request for prayers, and some final words of encouragement. When we read this now we are invoking this blessing on ourselves as another local church gathered to hear his words.

Gospel

Do not use the shortened version, as it is simply an answer without its question, and cannot be appreciated without its context.

We can call ourselves 'the people of the resurrection' for we believe that God will share his life with us. Here we see Jesus confronted by a group who thought that a belief in the resurrection was some sort of miraculous stunt which could form the butt of curious questions.

Prayer of the Faithful
President
We are the people of the resurrection. We believe that Jesus has stood again among us, and because of this we now are able to stand in the presence of God, ask him for our needs, and intercede for all humanity
Reader(s)
1. For the holy church of God, that we may bear witness to the new life given to humanity in Christ Jesus. Lord hear us.
2. For this holy church, that we may have a share in the joy and peace that flow from Christ's resurrection. Lord hear us.
3. For all who are lonely, despairing, fearful, or without hope, that the Spirit who raised Jesus may give them light and comfort. Lord hear us.
4. For all those people who cannot believe in the resurrection of the Lord, that they may receive the gift of faith. Lord hear us.
5. *Specific local needs and topics of the day.*
6. For all who have died in Christ, that they may rise with him in glory. Lord hear us.
President
Father, we gather here in the presence of your Son who has conquered death and given us new life, hear the prayer we make to you in union him, who lives and reigns with you and the Holy Spirit, now and forever. Amen.

Eucharistic Prayer
Preface of Sundays in Ordinary Time VI (P 34), which uses the theme of the pledge of an eternal Easter, is ideal for today. Then use either Eucharistic Prayer II or III as in each of these the theme of sharing in resurrection is formally voiced.

Invitation to the Our Father
Jesus Christ stands among us. Through him, with him, and in
him we pray to the Father:

Sign of Peace
The risen Christ's greeting to his followers was to wish them
peace; as the people of the resurrection, let us offer each other
the greeting.

Invitation to Communion
Behold the risen Christ is among us and bids us to share this
banquet as a foretaste of the banquet of heaven. Lord I am not
worthy …

Communion Reflection
The central section of Preface of Christian Death I (P 77), (Missal,
p 480), can make an appropriate reflection for today, especially
given the eschatological note that runs through these Sundays.
Begin at: 'In him who rose from the dead …'
End at: 'we gain an everlasting dwelling place in heaven.'

Conclusion
Solemn Blessing 7 for the Easter Season (Missal, p 370) is ideal
for today.

COMMENTARY

First Reading: 2 Macc 7:1-2, 9-14
It is only on rare occasions that 2 Macc is used in the liturgy, and
in that entire book no story has had more use than the story of
the mother and the seven sons who preferred death at the hands
of King Antiochus than to deny the Law. However, this long
well-told story, the whole of ch 7, has been reduced to two snippets here which do little more than show that the belief in resurrection was already present in Second Temple Judaism, and as
such this reading provides a context for today's gospel.

This reading has a long history of use among Christians as a text on the nature of martyrdom, and the Mother and the Seven Brothers had a feast day as martyrs ('The Holy Maccabees') on 1 August until the reform of the calendar in 1969. Given that this is a well-told tale that has a very long history of use among Christians, there is a strong case to be made for dropping the Second Reading today and reading the whole of 2 Macc 7 – all 42 verses of it – as it is a story that will leave its imprint on the memories of those who hear it. The text has the careful repetition with progressive difference of the well-formed tale, and is its own exegesis as one-by-one the brothers have to face the crucial question of whom they will serve, strengthened by their faith in the Lord. If you do read the whole story, rather than the two somewhat free-floating snippets given in the lectionary, then the NRSV preserves the art of the storyteller far more effectively than the JB.

Second Reading: 2 Thess 2:16-3:5
This is a final blessing and a request for prayers. As it is used in today's liturgy it can only be made sense of as a source of staccato slogans such as 'the Lord is faithful.' This piece of text, as it stands, is not successful as a liturgical lection, and this is one day when dropping the epistle reading is probably the best option. Better to have no reading than one which is read simply because it is 'in the book' and which has no focus on to which an audience can latch.

First Reading > Gospel Links
1. Continuity of belief/faith between the times of the two covenants is the basis of the link. Jesus's preaching of the new life offered by the God of Abraham, Isaac and Jacob is the same faith professed by the Maccabees.
2. Moreover, it provides a context explaining how Jesus could be involved in a debate on the nature of resurrection.

Gospel: Lk 20:27-38

This gospel section is found in all three synoptics, but the version in Luke is by far the most rounded and coherent. The situation is a dispute with those for whom the notion of 'resurrection' was ludicrous, and as such the object of curious questions. But Jesus refuses to get involved in such a materialistic imagining of God's plan as their questions suggest, and rather asserts that God is the God of the living for all have life in him. This controversy, in turn, became for the church a commentary on its own faith in the resurrection as that which Jesus shares with his disciples.

Since this section of Luke's gospel has a natural termination at 20:40, it is a pity that the last two verses have been omitted in the lection for today.

HOMILY NOTES

1. We bandy the word 'resurrection' about with gusto. No celebration of the Eucharist is complete without some use of the word, while we cheerfully say that 'we shall rise with Christ,' or use similar expressions with the ease that we use a phrase like 'I'm popping out to the shops for some milk.' The assumption is that the meaning of 'resurrection' is immediately obvious. Yet this is the exact opposite of the case.

2. First, the notion of resurrection is, in popular contexts, very often thought of as little more that some sort of resuscitation (a corpse being brought back to life), or that it is no more than a verbal variant on the quite widespread belief in the immortality of the soul as a natural quality of human (or indeed animal) existence, or indeed some even think it is just another term for some vague *post mortem* existence (e.g. 'There is something beyond the grave') or otherworldly place (e.g. the media expert who says 'What the Vikings called *Valhalla* was called *Heaven* by the Christians who converted them'). These confusions are 'where people are at' and today's gospel provides an opportunity to address them.

3. Second, the term 'resurrection' (literally 'standing up again')

is itself but a label for a mystery that is beyond us but which we glimpse in our experience of the presence of the Christ still with us, but also in the glory of the Father. The 'resurrection' is not some miracle to be either proved or disproved as 'having happened' in the historical order, rather it is the attempt in our human, earth bound language to give expression to our conviction, shared with the very first disciples, that Jesus's presence did not end on the cross, but continued in a new way within the creation, and that he showed this new way of being, this new existence at the 'right hand of the Father,' was also the destiny of all who became one with him. Resurrection is about both now and the future, and it is about transformation both now and in the future. But this transformation in Christ is only glimpsed in this life in shadows and images; perhaps the greatest of these shadows that expresses this transformation is the ritual of baptism, while one of the simplest is the word 'resurrection'.

4. But because resurrection is a mystery, it is, of its very nature, very difficult to preach or communicate verbally. By far the best positive preaching of resurrection takes the form of our great actions of faith: baptism, the movement from darkness to light at vigil services, or in the presentation of the Eucharist as the encounter with the risen One now in his meal. Yet we cannot remain silent for we are also creatures of language and words, and words can clarify and refine our understandings and open up the mind to the realities beyond words. So what can we say in a few moments about resurrection?

5. One method is to use a series of simple statements in the form of 'not that, but this'. Here are four such statements that may clarify key aspects of Christian belief from some of the counterfeits found in contemporary popular culture:

1. Resurrection is communal, not individual.

We become the new People of God, the emphasis is not on *my* escape from the grave.

2. Resurrection is transformation, not resuscitation.

We can so easily get lost in materialist questions about empty tombs and miracles, but this is to see resurrection as one more event in the historical order, rather than the beginning of a new possibility of existence in God whose nature and form are beyond our imaginings.

3. Resurrection is life in God, not 'spiritual' endurance.

Our focus of interest is not on some 'soul' that might survive death, or some 'place of the dead' in an 'otherworld' or 'after-life' – all of which are very commonly held religious beliefs – but that we become part of the Body of Christ sharing in the life of God.

4. Resurrection is God's gift, not some quality of the immort-ality of the soul.

In any average congregation there will be some people who are interested in the 'paranormal', in so-called 'near death ex-periences,' or in practices that claim to speak to the dead. Such people often simply assume that the abilities they claim are justified by the Christian belief in resurrection. But such claims for an existence after death – while not contradictory of the belief in resurrection – are wholly distinct from it. The new life is God's gift in Jesus Christ – we share in his resur-rection – not simply an individual human life force having its own continued existence.

Thirty-third Sunday of Ordinary Time

Introduction to the Celebration

Over the past months we have, each Sunday, being reading from St Luke's telling of the good news of Jesus. We have heard him talk of how we are to live our lives, how we are to celebrate this meal, how we are to treat each other as baptised sisters and brothers. Today our thoughts move to the future: our future as individuals, as the community that is one body in Christ, and the ultimate destiny of the creation. As we come to the end of the year, it is a case that we now start thinking of 'ends' rather than 'means'. We have been called by Jesus to move along our pilgrimage of life toward our final destination; so now let us fix our thoughts on that destination and ask the Father to forgive us our wanderings in other directions.

Rite of Penance

Option c ii (Missal, p 392) is appropriate.

Headings for Readings

First Reading

The Lord will judge the universe, but this judge is the God of righteousness and healing.

Second Reading

In our community as the People of God everyone of us must pull his or her weight to the best of their abilities.

Gospel

In the midst of trials and sufferings the God of mercy is with his people giving them wisdom, strength, and eventually the new life for which they have endured.

Prayer of the Faithful

President

In our readings today we have heard of the coming judgement and of the abiding mercy of the Father. Now conscious that we have to be responsible for how we live our lives, and conscious of God's generous love for all creation, let us place our concerns before him.

Reader(s)

1. For the People of God, both the church gathered here and the whole church scattered across the world, let us ask the Father for the gift of perseverance that we may endure the trials that come our way. Lord hear us.

2. For all people of good will, wherever they may be, that God may give them the strength to continue working for peace among peoples, the relief of suffering, and the removal of all forms of injustice, and that they do not succumb to discouragement. Lord hear us.

3. For those who work in the governments of this world, that they may have a share in God's wisdom so that they can learn to respect the creation as a gift, protect the environment, and have a genuine sense of human values. Lord hear us.

4. For each member of this community of faith, that we may have the wisdom to bear witness to the Lord in the face of trials and opposition. Lord hear us.

5. *Specific local needs and topics of the day.*

6. For those sisters and brothers who have died that they may know the mercy of God's judgement and the new life he offers all of us. Lord hear us.

President

Father, we are the people who seek to follow your Son to the end. Hear our prayer today for we make it through your Son, Jesus Christ, our Lord. Amen.

Eucharistic Prayer
Preface of Sundays in Ordinary Time V [P 33] is suitable as it
stresses the plan within the creation and the place of humanity
within it; and Eucharistic Prayer III picks up the theme of God's
faithfulness found in the first reading.

Invitation to the Our Father
The Father's kingdom will come to its perfection at the end of
time. Let us pray now for the coming of that kingdom:

Sign of Peace
We seek to stand together witnessing to the Lord in the face of
contradiction and opposition, and, therefore, between us there
should be no strife or discord. Let us now express our desire to
live as one community of love in the sign of peace.

Invitation to Communion
Behold the One who has come and will come again in glory.
Happy are we to be present now at his supper.

Communion Reflection
Because next week is Christ the King, this is the last 'ordinary'
Sunday of Ordinary Time and this is worth mentioning as a
moment that marks for us the passing of time. A moment of
thanksgiving thus:

> For the past six months each week when we gathered to be
> fed at the table of the Lord we have been listening to St
> Luke's preaching of the good news of Jesus. Now the year of
> Luke is coming to an end: next week we will celebrate the
> feast of Christ the King, and then we move on to Advent and
> begin the yearly cycle over anew. So let us reflect for a mo-
> ment how each week in our gathering the Lord feeds us with
> his word when we listen to the readings and then shares his
> life with us in our eating of the bread of life and our drinking
> of the cup of salvation.

Then have a moment of silence ended by: Let us pray.

Conclusion

The eschatological tone that runs through this day makes Solemn Blessing 20, for the dead (Missal, p 377), very suitable for today.

COMMENTARY

First Reading: Mal 3:19-20

Note: This reading is given this reference in the 1981 English Lectionary, p 934, following the Hebrew numeration, but the passage has a different reference, following the Septuagint/Vulgate numeration, in the Latin lectionary where it is cited as 4:1-2. This is confusing as usually, as with the psalms, the Lectionary slavishly follows the Vulgate.

This passage is not a piece of apocalyptic, though it might appear to be such when read in conjunction with today's gospel. Its actual focus is the problem that faces every preacher: how come that those people who are most prosperous in this life are often the biggest rogues and the least concerned with the law of the Lord? In other words, why don't bad things happen to bad people? The prophet's answer is that the reckoning will not take place till the end and at that moment the Lord will not be fooled. It will be those who have feared the Lord – even though they may have suffered much in the meantime – that will come out ahead. It is rare that a question that was posed to a prophet more than two thousand years ago is one that still comes up for preachers today, but this is one of those occasions. You can test how useful an answer it is to this problem (i.e. the soft end of the problem of innocent suffering) by seeing if it satisfied your questioners.

Second Reading: 2 Thess 3:7-12

One of the features of the earliest churches was the way (1) they accommodated Christians who were moving from one part of the empire to another, and (2) they had real meal gatherings as their occasion for offering thanksgiving (what would be formalised under the name 'The Eucharist'). Under both these head-

ings there was concern over disorderly conduct. It is these disorderly brothers and sisters – they are more than simply the
'idlers' that the Jerusalem Bible imagines – that is the concern of
this passage. The problem is that some people realised that they
could 'free load' on the hospitality of the church without con-
tributing to the work and life of the community. The best commentary on this passage is the set of regulations laid down in the
Didache (roughly contemporary with the letter) to deal with
these problems:

> All who come in the Lord's name are to be made welcome.
> But they are then to be examined and you can then find out
> what is true and what is false – and you will have the insight
> to do this. If someone is simply passing through, then help as
> best you can, but only let the visitor stay for two days or three
> if really necessary. However, if he wants to stay there, and is
> in a trade, then he must work for his living. If he is not in a
> trade, then come to a decision as to how he can be a Christian
> among you, yet without him being without work. If he does
> not accept this then he is trading on Christ, and you must be
> very careful about such people. But if a genuine prophet
> wishes to settle among you, he deserves his food. Likewise
> with genuine teachers: they are workers worthy of their food.
> (12:1-13:2)

First Reading > Gospel Links
Between the readings there is continuity of theme: the prophet
looks to a time of trial, but also to a God of righteousness and
healing; Luke looks forward to a time of catastrophe and trial
but the Father – for the speech is placed in the mouth of the
Christ – will care for, and preserve, his people.

Gospel: Lk 21:5-19
This is the opening of the Lukan version of 'the synoptic apocalypse' which is found in all three synoptic gospels. In both
Matthew and Luke it follows the pattern found in Mark closely,
and so it is an item which clearly had resonance in the early

church in that both Matthew and Luke believed it had to be incorporated into their preaching. We have to read it as part of that strand of early Christianity that took over an apocalyptical outlook from their existing religious milieu in Second Temple. Given how diverse is the evidence for this outlook – not only this passage but the Book of Revelation, and a steady stream of such material which never became canonical but left its imprint on the church's memory – we can conclude that this outlook was quite widespread among the first churches. However, this leaves a major question: was this future which was part of the message of John the Baptist, also part of the original message of Jesus? There is much in the gospels to suggest that this was a major point of difference between them: for John, the future was the great crunch from which the elect would escape; for Jesus, the future was the new creation of the Lord's forgiveness. If this is the case what we have in the synoptic apocalypse is the position of a group who have moved from John to Jesus without realising that their apocalyptical outlook was something they had to leave behind. It is only by using such an hypothesis that we can account for the dissonance about the future which we find in the gospels: for the most part Jesus is preaching the coming of the Father's kingdom of forgiving love, yet here we have the great crunch for all who are not part of the elect.

This dissonance produces a problem for our preaching. On the one hand, few mainstream Christians are prepared to take the apocalyptical approach that is found among fundamentalist TV evangelists; yet, this gospel does lend itself to that approach. On the other hand, if one ignores this gospel then it can appear that one is only 'taking a partial view' (even if such a partial view is probably closer to the preaching of Jesus. It is this confusion in message that has caused the tensions over 'the end of the world' that has afflicted Christianity down the centuries: do we look forward to a loving Father of mercy, or the stern patriarchal figure of impending wrath? So how can we preach this text, yet not contribute to the apocalyptic outlook which had always been firmly rejected by the church's formal teaching?

One way is to concentrate comment on just the final verses of today's lection: come what may, no matter how bad it might get, the universe is still loved by God and 'not a hair of your head will be lost'. As such it is a story about hope in the face of adversity, rather than a piece of apocalyptic cosmology. This solution is, incidentally, not a new one; we see the same approach in use in the final sermon in the *Didache* (c 16), which was in use before Luke wrote his gospel, and which stressed the joy of the return of the Lord in conjunction with acknowledging the fears of those of an apocalyptic bent.

HOMILY NOTES

1. Karl Marx famously described religion as the opium of the people: a comforting message that distracted people from the horrors of life – and, as such, like most analgesics it could be said to be no bad thing. But the message of the gospel is radically at odds with any idea of a religion that it is there to quieten people down, act as a social glue to keep the show on the road, support the *status quo*, and help people to whistle past the graveyard. Just read the list of what will come whether we follow the way of the Lord or not: wars, revolutions, more wars, earthquakes, plagues, famines, and fearful sights. And you do not even have the consolation of thinking that these indicate the world is going to end; it seems as if there is just going to be more of the same. Then there are the sufferings that will be there only for believers: persecutions, imprisonment, treachery, family disarray, being reviled and even killed. This is not a very comforting religion and it does not preach comfort. Far from being dulling opium that might help one cope with the pain and stress of life, it is a call to open your eyes and view the suffering around us without any false hopes or illusions.

2. Yet it was not just Karl Marx that had not taken account of this aspect of Christianity: a failure to hear this part of the message of Jesus is all about us, both among those who reject

his gospel, and among those who are loud in claiming to believe in his message.

3. On one side we have people who every time they hear about a disaster (natural or manmade) immediately say that 'that shows there cannot be a god' or 'I cannot believe in a god as if there is a god such-and-such could not happen.' They know the mind of God so well that they can know what God can and cannot do.

4. Then there are Christians who go round predicting the end of the world and giving timetables and sequences for predictions that show 'the end is coming'. Again, these people know the mind and plans of God so well that they can tie God down to days and dates. The fact they get all these predictions wrong and have to start over afresh in each generations with their so-called 'study of the bible' does not seem to deter them. In fact, they think the scriptures are some sort of secret code that only they can crack, rather than the church's records of its early faith.

5. In the face of all such people, there are those of us who have to tread the path of endurance. We do not know the future; we do not claim to know the mind of God or to fathom his mystery; rather in the midst of suffering to look to the Christ whose own path ended on the cross. But in following this path, seeking to love neighbour and God, walking humbly and acting for justice, we see through that suffering to the new life. We are people with eyes wide open, called to have moved beyond optimism and pessimism. But we are people of hope.

6. For us who fear his name, the sun of righteousness will shine out with healing in is rays.

Lectionary Unit VIII

The Christ is King

This unit consists of just one Sunday: Sunday 34, the Last Sunday of the Year.

The focus is upon reconciliation and this is expressed through reading the account of the repentant thief from the passion narrative. This story is only found in Luke's gospel.

The Last Sunday of Ordinary Time
The Feast of Christ the King

Introduction to the Celebration

Way back in January we began the year by celebrating the Baptism of Jesus when a voice was heard calling him 'the beloved Son'. During the year we have greeted Jesus under all the views of him we find in the gospels. Now today, at the end of the year, we greet him with the all-embracing title: Jesus Christ, Universal King.

The Christ is the one who will gather us all together at the end of time, the one who will judge the living and the dead, and then present his kingdom to the Father. In our pilgrimage of faith that kingdom of justice, truth, and peace is to be our beacon, and Christ our guide. But before we join Christ in his banquet, we must ask pardon for the times when we followed other paths and other ways, when we listened to false prophets of greed and materialism, and for when we have failed to work for the coming of the kingdom.

Rite of Penance

Lord Jesus, you are our leader and our prophet. Lord have mercy.
Lord Jesus, you are our light and our peace. Christ have mercy.
Lord Jesus, you are our beacon on our journey and our king. Lord have mercy.

Headings for Readings
First Reading

When David was anointed as the one chosen by the Lord to lead Israel, his task was not described in terms of ruling or conquering, but of shepherding.

Second Reading

Today we read a Christian hymn older than the gospels. It praises
Jesus who is the image of the unseen Father, and declares that all
creatures, visible (namely us humans) and invisible (namely the
angels) look to him, for in him is found all perfection.

Gospel

On the cross, the Christ is silent before the insults of those who
persecute him, but to those who turn to him he offers the gift of
heavenly life.

Prayer of the Faithful
President

Friends, our thoughts are on 'endings' this week: the end of the
cycle of celebrations we began a year ago with Advent, the end
of the cycle of reading when we have focused on St Luke's
gospel, and today on Christ as our Lord who will present a kingdom to the Father at the end of time. Conscious of this time of
'endings,' let us put our needs before the Father.

Reader(s)

1. We have gathered here as a priestly people, so let us intercede
for the whole church on earth, that it may be worthy of the kingdom. Lord hear us.

2. We have gathered here as a priestly people, so let us intercede
for all peoples, that they may receive the gift of peace, and discover a kingdom beyond the powers of this world. Lord hear us.

3. We have gathered here as a priestly people, so let us intercede
for who have positions of power in this world, that they recognise that there is an order in the creation, and respect it. Lord
hear us.

4. We have gathered here as a priestly people, so let us intercede
for those who have lost hope, lost faith, or lost courage. Lord
hear us.

5. We have gathered here as a priestly people, so let us intercede
for all in this community, that we may be found in the kingdom
of Christ at the end. Lord hear us.

President
Father, you sent us your Son as our prophet, our priest and our king, and so made us your holy people. Hear our prayers and grant our needs through that same Christ, our Lord. Amen.

Eucharistic Prayer
Today has a proper preface (P51), Missal, p 454.

Invitation to the Our Father
Christ our King stands at the end of history gathering us together as the kingdom he presents to the Father; now, in union with Christ, let us pray to the Father:

Sign of Peace
We look forward to the time when Christ will be the universal king and bring the age of peace; until then we must be peace-makers and remind each other of this calling. So now we wish peace and forgiveness to our brothers and sisters.

Invitation to Communion
The Lord has prepared a banquet for his people; he bids us look towards the banquet of heaven; behold he now bids us to share in his life at this table. Lord I am not worthy …

Communion Reflection
As we sit around your table O Lord,
We recall that the Father anointed you,
With the oil of gladness,
As the universal King,
You claim dominion over all creation,
Yours is a kingdom of truth and life,
Yours is a kingdom of holiness and peace,
Yours is a kingdom of justice, love, and peace.
(Adapted from today's Preface)

Conclusion

May Christ the universal King guide your steps in ways of justice, guide your words with his wisdom, and guide your hearts towards his holiness. Amen.

May Christ the universal King be your leader, your light, and your peace both now and always. Amen.

May Christ the universal King grant this church a place in the kingdom he presents to the Father.

Notes

Today's feast is a celebration of a central aspect of our faith in Jesus as the *Logos*: that he is the One through whom all came to be from the Father, and the One who draws all the creation together bringing it to perfection in handing it back to the Father. As such the feast touches the very mystery of the creation and incarnation, and ends the liturgical year on a high point. When we say that Christ is 'the Alpha and Omega' – as for example on the Paschal Candle using a title for him that can be found since the first century as it is witnessed in Apoc 1:8, 21:6 and 22:13 – we are focusing on today's celebration: we are in the gathering because he is the Alpha – he has brought us into existence and has called us to be his people – and we are looking forward to the Omega. The task posed to us today is to rejoice that we are travelling in and with the *Logos* to the consummation of the creation when he presents it to the Father having been brought to perfection in himself.

Today we preach about the mystery of Christ and about the end-times, but this is for orthodox Christians the full realisation of the divine plan; it is the joy of a harvest, the quiet moment when a great work of art is completed, the advent of the rest and fullness of the life implanted in all human hearts. Alas, 'the end' has always provoked another strand of thinking by Christians: the end is the great reckoning, the great crunch, the vengeance of God. This is a legacy of apocalyptic groups who became followers of Jesus and whose thought has always been mixed in with the kerygma – so we have to be aware that there are two contradictory strands in our inheritance. The question that we have to ask is this: which sort of end – 'the great crunch' or 'the completed divine artwork' – is more compatible with the good news of the *Logos* made flesh? The answer of the liturgy is clear: we celebrate the end as this joyful feast; looking forward to when the Anointed *Logos* is all in all having reconciled all realities in heaven and earth, and established peace by the blood of his cross (cf Col 1:20). However, in a culture that is primed by the media to fear the future and be watchful for the next disaster threat 'to our way of life', this good news gets drowned out. We must remember two things: first, apocalypticism is media friendly as it creates good stories that sell; second, there are far more preachers of an apocalyptic brand of Christianity than of the liturgy's: just count the number of such religion channels your congregation can receive through digital television.

However, this day also presents us with a serious case of linguistic dissonance. For a start, many today do not take naturally to the language of the kingship. Kings and queens are, for many, stuffy symbols at best, the equivalents to dictators at worst. Kings, dictators, emperors are the opposite of the 'democratic', 'representative', 'transparent' ways of doing things that are the desired hallmarks of our culture. The crime that then is associated with 'kings' is that 'they don't listen' – and this must not be a message our liturgy sends out about God. Another aspect of the linguistic problems posed by this feast is the use of cosmological language. In the East this aspect of the *Logos* is celebrated under the title of Christ the Pantocrator (ruler of all) and can be seen in great icons in the domes of churches as well as on small portable icons; in the West it became the image of Christ wearing a crown holding images of powers (e.g. a scepter) and the title 'king of the universe'. Both images in their different ways take the notion of an earthy ruler, express it in terms of the cosmos, and declare it to be true in a super eminent way. At the heart of this way of speaking about God is a form of irony: that which is apparently not a force in the cosmos is seen with the eyes of faith to be *the* force in the cosmos. Alas, this currency has been devalued by the language of sci-fi films: 'great ruler of the cosmos' sounds to many more like the name of a character from a cult movie than a way of speaking of the mystery of the Christ.

COMMENTARY

First Reading: 2 Sam 5:1-3

This is part of the royal propaganda found in the books of Samuel-Kings: the actual ruler is there as the representative of God. However, as such there are special demands made on him: he is to be the one whose authority comes from being the anointed of the Lord – that is literally 'the Christ' – then he must lead the people in justice as he exists in the Lord's presence.

In today's liturgy this passage about a christ, an anointed king, is read as the antetype and foreshadowing of the appearance of the final christ, and final king: Jesus. Jesus is the one who dwells in the intimacy of the Father, but also is among humanity. He is the final king, leading humanity into the divine presence.

Psalm: 121:1-5

The choice of this Psalm is based on Jerusalem being the image of the final city (Gal 4), the image of the eschatological kingdom which is flooded with Christ's light (Apoc 21-22).

Second Reading: Col 1:12-20

This early Christian hymn is the earliest witness we possess to the aspect of the mystery of the Christ we are celebrating today. The Christ is the Beginning and the End: the one who brings all to perfection and brings about the final peace. See the Notes section above.

First Reading > Gospel Links

There is no link between the readings, rather both are tuned to the theme of kingship in today's feast. The Old Testament passage is not, however, linked to the notion of the eschatological king, but to the notion of God's on-going care for his people. While the gospel gives a very precise turn to the meaning of

Christ as king, the passage from 2 Sam merely asks what is a godly king: one provided by God who sees his power in terms of being a pastor.

Gospel: Lk 23:35-43
This is Luke's crucifixion scene immediately before his account of the death on the cross, and to appreciate it we need to break it into two parts: first, vv 35-39; and second, vv 39-43 (v 39 forms the link between the two parts). The first section is made up of the various groups that mock and revile Jesus as he hangs on the cross and its content is found in all three of the synoptics. However, while Matthew follows Mark in both content and sequence, Luke re-arranges the material. Why he does this is not clear, but the second part of this scene suggests that he wants to create a deliberate contrast between the expectations of those who mock Jesus as a fraud and the genuine way that the Royal Son of God, the Christ – when he is actually with humanity – behaves in history.

The key transition moment is v 39: 'One of the criminals who were hanged railed at him, saying, "Are you not the Christ? Save yourself and us!"' What is remarkable here is that in Mark and Matthew it is both of the robbers on either side of him that revile him. Luke takes the scene of the three crosses (23:33 // Mk 15:27; Mt 27:38, Jn 19:18) and makes it a scene for the fundamental human decision. In Mark and Matthew there are no words given to those crucified with Jesus, so the whole section vv 39-43 is found only in Luke. One behaves exactly like the chief priests, elders and soldiers and mocks Jesus using their very words – we have to note the irony here that he sides with the persecutors of Jesus who are also his own persecutors, rather than with a fellow sufferer. *In extremis*, he can still only think of himself and his own perceptions of what God should be. The world of his selfishness and his demands is the only universe that exists. Then there is the contrast of the other criminal who can see both himself, his predicament, and the predicament of all three of them, and can ask for mercy.

This petition from the 'good thief', as he has become known in the tradition, then brings out Luke's even deeper irony: the false perceptions of the Christ and of the Royal One elicit nothing; but the call in need elicits the divine words of mercy: 'Today you will be with me in paradise.' The irony points to the paradox at the heart of the mystery of the incarnation in Luke that can be seen from his crib scene (2:7) right through to this moment: there are the expectations of power, might, and noise from the Christ of God, yet there is silence, suffering and powerlessness. When there is a divine judgement, a word of divine power ('truly, I say to you'), and a display of divine knowing, it comes in response to a cry of need from a suffering criminal.

HOMILY NOTES

1. A good starting point today is to try to get the assembly to see what images – not their theological theories or sound-bites from a catechism – the words 'the End of the World' bring to their minds. First, it is not something that people like to dwell on; second, there is a natural fearfulness about the future in most people; third, there is legacy of apocalypticism in western culture; and fourth, disasters that are looming is big business in our society.

2. It depends on the size of the gathering and on how used they are to homily-experiences other than the talking head as to how people access these images. If they can talk about it, or if even a few people can give their images, it will be a much richer learning experience than if one just says: 'Now think about this for a moment.'

3. The likelihood is that many will have images that portray the universe as a dangerous, unfriendly place, indeed, a place where God is either just an impersonal force or else the Juggernaut of vengeance. It is part of our complexity as human beings that we can say 'God loves each of us' – and mean and believe it – while at the same time having images deep within our consciousness of the cosmos that imply that God does not care or is cruel judge. Having that mind of

Christ is not something that just happens when we accept a creed; it is a slow process of love and conversion.

4. It is worth dwelling on the sources of fear and giving them names.

5. We tend not to like to think far into the future – it brings up the thoughts of times of loss and death. This is something that seems common to all of us: we want to put the future beyond tomorrow or after the next few years 'on the long finger'. Many do not like thinking about retirement, pensions or making a will.

6. We have another natural, and seemingly universal, fear of the future: if the future is open, then things can go right or they can go wrong. This is the fear that makes us prudent and it is also the frisson of excitement when we make a bet. The future is a challenge to us and we are fearful lest we fail. We have all felt this whether it is before a test, or before doing something in public, or even trying to figure out the way to fill in a form we have just been sent.

7. There is a long tradition of using the images of disaster as part of the Christian message: God will come with fire and brimstone, and punish the wicked. We have to simply acknowledge this and ask is it the only Christian image?

8. A looming disaster is big business. We are all offered far more insurance than we need on every conceivable bit of kit we have. Movies and newspapers all need to hear about the latest disaster that is about to befall us. Governments use fear of 'the threat' from some vague other group or disease as a way of forming and justifying policy. It is much easier to lead by seeming to react to threat than to have a positive vision.

9. Now contrast the image of Christ as the one who hands back a kingdom brought to perfection in him through his love and forgiveness, to the Father. Christ is the omega point of our existence in his love and forgiveness.

10. Just such a contrast of expectations is at the heart of today's gospel: the accusers think they know how the Christ will or should behave; but the reality is radically different. Today's

doom mongers are just as certain about the end, but we celebrate the end as Christ being all in all, ruling over all in love,
and establishing peace. At this point it might be word reading the central section of today's preface.

11. Where do we see a foretaste of that omega point: in today's
gospel. The end of the Christ in our bodily existence is not a
moment of vengeance, but of love towards one suffering
with him: Today you will be with me in paradise.

12. Lastly, we need to acknowledge that many religious people
do not like this vision of the End as it seems to make 'God'
too soft and too soppy. A God of power and stern justice
seems a more robust being than one of love and forgiveness.
And these people seem to be in the majority among the
shareholders of religion TV stations. But does this 'robust-
ness' belong to the very group that Luke sees being rejected
for their images of the Christ in today's gospel?